MORE FILMS OF THE

Greta Garbo and Henry Daniell in "Camille."

MORE FILMS OF THE

JERRY VERMILYE

A CITADEL PRESS BOOK
PUBLISHED BY CAROL PUBLISHING GROUP

ACKNOWLEDGMENTS

The author would like to express his gratitude to the following individuals and organizations who helped arrange screenings, make possible the viewing of videocassettes, locate rare stills and give generously of their time to offer editorial assistance:

Laurie Britton, Danny Burk, Judy and Paul Caputo, Robert Finn, Dolores and Al Kilgore, Franklyn Lenthall and the Boothbay Theatre Museum, Robin Little, Mark Ricci and The Memory Shop, Michael Scheinfeld and Allan Turner.

And a salute of gratitude to the companies which distributed these movies and employed the anonymous still photographers whose artistry illustrates these pages: Columbia, Fox, Metro-Goldwyn-Mayer, Paramount, RKO Radio, 20th Century-Fox, United Artists, Universal and Warner Bros.

To
ROBIN AND ALLAN AND BOB
For
All Their Help

and
Their Friendship

A Citadel Press Book
Published by Carol Publishing Group

Editorial Offices
600 Madison Avenue
New York, NY 10022

Sales & Distribution Offices
120 Enterprise Avenue
Secaucus, NJ 07094

In Canada: Musson Book Company
A division of General Publishing Co. Limited
Don Mills, Ontario

Queries regarding rights and permissions should be addressed to: Carol Publishing Group, 600 Madison Avenue, New York, NY 10022

Designed by A. Christopher Simon

Manufactured in the United States of America

Library of Congress Cataloging-in-Publication Data

Vermilye, Jerry.
  More films of the thirties / by Jerry Vermilye.
     p.   cm.
  "A Citadel Press Book."
  ISBN 0-8065-1146-6 : $16.95
  1. Motion pictures--United States--Plots, themes, etc. 2. Motion pictures--United States--History. I. Title.
PN1997.8.V456   1989
791.43'75'0973--dc20   89-39008
                                                              CIP

10 9 8 7 6 5 4 3 2 1

CONTENTS

7

A PORTRAIT GALLERY

Nancy Carroll

Mae Clarke

George Arliss

9

Joan Crawford

Gary Cooper

Dorothy Lamour

James Cagney

Johnny Downs

Carole Lombard

Douglas Fairbanks Jr.

Merle Oberon

W.C. Fields

Walter Huston

Joel McCrea

Lilyan Tashman

Barbara Stanwyck

Shirley Temple

Paul Muni

13

Helen Hayes and Marie Prevost in
"The Sin of Madelon Claudet"

Gary Cooper, Charles Laughton and Tallulah
Bankhead in "Devil and the Deep"

Will Rogers and Tom Brown in
"Judge Priest"

INTRODUCTION

Seven years ago, in an effort to pay tribute to a moviemaking decade that remains unparalleled in the abundance of its riches, we brought forth *The Films of the Thirties*. At that time, it was explained that our intent was not only to cover acknowledged classics, but also to discuss motion pictures that had been neglected, as well as including a handful that, while perhaps understandably forgotten, nevertheless typified their era. In short, by selecting one hundred movies to discuss, the approach was to encompass a wide selection of types and genres that would well represent that decade bordered by the stock market crash and World War II.

One critic, who may have misunderstood that book's intent, speculated upon the notable omission of such landmark films as *It Happened One Night*, *The Public Enemy*, *The Great Ziegfeld*, *The Hunchback of Notre Dame*, *A Star Is Born*, *Cavalcade*, *Little Women* and *Ninotchka*. Within the following pages, all of those titles have been included, as well as a host of other prestigious movies that belong in any fair assessment of the decade. But, as we pointed out in our preface to the previous volume, nearly 5,000 American feature films were turned out during the Thirties, for it was a period in which the motion picture was America's most popular and inexpensive form of entertainment. And with the prevalence of double-bill cinema palaces throughout the land, the studios were virtual celluloid sausage factories, constantly grinding out product to meet a never-ending demand. That so much of what was thus churned out in Hollywood achieved such a high degree of artistry is what continues to amaze the film scholar. The discipline and dedication of the studio artists and artisans, both before and behind the camera, is what seems astounding today, when the major movie companies distribute only a fraction of the number of annual releases they once did—and at incredibly inflated production costs.

In selecting the films to include in a book like this, it was decided not to encompass foreign films; American-made pictures are more than sufficient to supply material for a whole *series* of volumes on the Thirties alone. Hundreds of titles were considered, evaluated and discarded, before the eventual one hundred were selected. Some readers may deplore the exclusion of one or another of their favorite stars or favorite movies. In some cases that might be because those performers were saluted in our earlier volume: i.e., Hedy Lamarr, Charles Boyer, Eleanor Powell, Robert Donat, Tallulah Bankhead, John Boles, Evelyn Brent, Victor McLaglen, Herbert Marshall, Eddie Cantor, Anna Sten, Robert Young, Claude Rains, Bob Hope and Warner Baxter. Others were left out perhaps because their careers belonged more to an earlier decade, like John Gilbert, Lillian Gish, Corinne Griffith, Norma Talmadge, Thomas Meighan, Mary Pickford and Louise Brooks. Still others were eliminated since their careers, while begun in the Thirties, would not peak until the Forties, among them: Rita Hayworth, John Payne, Joan Fontaine, Dennis Morgan, Ann Sheridan, Walter Pidgeon, Lana Turner, Ronald Reagan, Gene Tierney, Alan Ladd, Ingrid Bergman, Jane Wyman, Victor Mature and Linda Darnell.

As with *The Films of the Thirties*, the thrust of this book is to present a cross-section of the decade, blending a few little-known titles with an admitted majority of the more famous movies. And so, while a number of the inclusions will be among those most frequently revived on TV or available on videocassette, there will be others—like *The Big House*, *Counsellor at Law*, *The Young in Heart* and *Night Must Fall*—little seen in recent years, yet eminently

Stan Laurel, Oliver Hardy and Charley Chase in "Sons of the Desert"

Josephine Hutchinson and Paul Muni in "The Story of Louis Pasteur"

deserving of reevaluation. Nearly every genre is represented by at least one entry, with the emphasis on the major Hollywood studios. If the smaller, independent releasing organizations have been overlooked, it's simply that the decision was made to focus on the more Establishment studios. Some films have been included chiefly to represent their stars—i.e., Dolores Del Rio in *The Bad One*; Dorothy Mackaill in *The Office Wife*; Elissa Landi and Laurence Olivier in *The Yellow Ticket*; Nancy Carroll in *Hot Saturday*; Clara Bow in *Call Her Savage*; Ruth Chatterton in *Frisco Jenny*; Marion Davies in *Going Hollywood*; Margaret Sullavan in *Little Man, What Now?*; Maurice Chevalier in *Folies Bergere*; and Henry Fonda and Joan Bennett in *I Met My Love Again*. Not that the above titles are otherwise worthless (each still retains a certain entertainment value), but quite often the degree of enjoyment sustained by these star vehicles depends on one's appreciation of the name featured with the movie's title.

Today, of course, many a vintage film is only as important to many a viewer as the name of its *director*—which means that, in this book, the obscure *A House Divided* and *Counsellor at Law* will be of most interest to followers of William Wyler, *Girls About Town* to fans of George Cukor, and so on. Others may have more interest in those movies that have won Academy Awards, and for them the

Rita Hayworth and Cary Grant in "Only Angels Have Wings"

inclusion of *Cimarron*, the 1930 version of *The Dawn Patrol*, *Cavalcade*, *Dangerous*, *Come and Get It* and *The Life of Emile Zola* will be among the more important inclusions. On the other hand, lack of space has, regrettably, necessitated leaving out such Academy statuette holders as Helen Hayes in *The Sin of Madelon Claudet*, Wallace Beery in *The Champ*, Katharine Hepburn in *Morning Glory*, Paul Muni in *The Story of Louis Pasteur*, Spencer Tracy in *Boys Town* and Robert Donat in the Anglo-American *Goodbye, Mr. Chips*.

The Films of the Thirties was also criticized for neglecting the illustrious careers of such stars as Clark Gable, Cary Grant and Gary Cooper; this volume attempts to rectify that oversight with four movies each for Gable and Grant, and three for Cooper. And this time there is likely to be disappointment expressed by some reader over the absence of Sonja Henie, Will Rogers, Laurel and Hardy, Grace Moore, Bela Lugosi, Deanna Durbin and Lily Pons. For those, the author can only offer apologies and suggest that interested parties write the publisher of this book suggesting a third volume of Thirties films.

Edward Norris and Lana Turner in "They Won't Forget"

Lily Pons, Gene Raymond and Lucille Ball in "That Girl From Paris"

Ilissa Landi and Lionel Barrymore in "The Yellow Ticket."

THE FILMS

"There are no rules in filmmaking, only sins. And the cardinal sin is Dullness."

— FRANK CAPRA (1971)

LADIES OF LEISURE: Barbara Stanwyck and George Fawcett.

LADIES OF LEISURE: Ralph Graves and Barbara Stanwyck.

LADIES OF LEISURE: Ralph Graves, Barbara Stanwyck and Lowell Sherman.

LADIES OF LEISURE

1930

CREDITS

A Columbia Picture. A Frank R. Capra Production. Director: Frank Capra. Producer: Harry Cohn. Screenwriter: Jo Swerling. Based on the play *Ladies of the Evening* by Milton Herbert Gropper. Cinematographer: Joseph Walker. Editor: Maurice Wright. Art Direction: Harrison Wiley. Sound: John P. Livadary. Costumes: Edward Stevenson. Running Time: 98 minutes.

CAST

Barbara Stanwyck (*Kay Arnold*); Ralph Graves (*Jerry Strange*); Lowell Sherman (*Bill Standish*); Marie Prevost (*Dot Lamar*); Nance O'Neil (*Mrs. Strange*); George Fawcett (*Mr. Strange*); Johnnie Walker (*Charlie*); Juliette Compton (*Claire Collins*); Charles Butterworth (*Party Guest*).

After starring in two melodramatic flops, *The Locked Door* and *Mexicali Rose*, stage-trained Barbara Stanwyck was contracted to the unprestigious Columbia Pictures at a time when that studio's busiest young director, Frank Capra, was casting *Ladies of Leisure*, a romantic melodrama he was preparing to film from a 1924 play called *Ladies of the Evening*.

Stanwyck was not Capra's idea of Kay Arnold, the slightly tarnished heroine of his upcoming movie, although he agreed to interview her for the role. Their initial meeting went badly. Discouraged and withdrawn, the actress arrived without makeup and plainly attired, and appeared sullen and uncooperative. When, eventually, Capra asked her to make a test for him, the director reports that Stanwyck jumped up, snapped, "Oh, hell! You don't want any *part* of me!" and ended the interview. When he learned of the ill-fated audition, Stanwyck's husband, actor Frank Fay, persuaded Capra to view a three-minute test (performing a scene from her Broadway hit *The Noose*) she had made for Warner Bros. Fay explained that his wife's negative interview was the result of her natural shyness, coupled with professional doldrums.

Capra viewed the test, and he claims that it put a lump in his throat the size of an egg. He insisted that Columbia honcho Harry Cohn sign her at once for *Ladies of Leisure*. It was the beginning of a fortunate working partnership that would encompass five films, two of which would be among the milestones of her career.

Released in the spring of 1930, *Ladies of Leisure* became Columbia's greatest box-office success to date, and attracted critical praise. "Miss Stanwyck triumphs," read the review headline in *The New York Times*, and in his notice, Mordaunt Hall lauded the film as "a searching portrayal of a type of metropolitan girl known as a 'gold-digger.'" He cited the "restrained performances of nearly all the players" and "the general lightness of handling that commends the direction of Frank Capra." Stanwyck, he added, "shows a most gratifying ability for comprehending the requirements of her role."

Ladies of Leisure, blending touches of *Pygmalion* and *Camille*, relates how Jerry (Ralph Graves), a wealthy young aspiring artist, picks up a tough waterfront girl named Kay (Stanwyck), because he sees in her face a quality he wants to capture on canvas. Making her his model, he also works at grooming her, in the process of which they fall in love. Their romance collapses when Jerry's parents object to having a daughter-in-law with a dubious background, and his mother pleads with Kay to give him

LADIES OF LEISURE: Nance O'Neil and Barbara Stanwyck.

up. They are reconciled, but only after Kay has attempted suicide.

Novice screenwriter Jo Swerling, who had been churning out "poverty-row" productions for Columbia, brashly convinced Capra that he could take the director's sow-eared script and turn it into the proverbial silk purse. This Swerling proceeded to do, giving Capra a screenplay that the director considered "human, witty and poignant."

In Barbara Stanwyck, Capra discovered an actress of rare honesty and sensitivity. He later said: "Stanwyck doesn't act a scene; she *lives* it. Her best work is the result—not of timing and rehearsing and study but of pure feminine reaction." Capra also discovered that his new actress had a peculiar problem: her natural approach to a scene resulted in her giving everything on the first take, after which both her energy and honesty flagged. To combat this, he took to rehearsing the other actors without her, taking Stanwyck aside for a brief coaching conference before she went on camera, and then capturing her performance at its most natural and spontaneous. "She remembered every word I said," he recalls, "and she never blew a line."

As a result of Frank Capra's insight, care and sensitivity, Stanwyck turned in a performance in *Ladies of Leisure* that still holds up well. The film is now seldom shown, but it's amazingly truthful in depicting human relationships, despite the passage of time and the changes in acting styles. Yet it won no awards, or even any nominations, and Frank Capra credits this with Columbia's very minor position at that time among the Hollywood studios.

Ladies of Leisure made an important star of Barbara Stanwyck at a time when her husband's strength as a movie name was rapidly diminishing.

THE BAD ONE

1930

CREDITS

A United Artists Picture. Director: George Fitzmaurice. Producer: Joseph M. Schenck. Supervisor: John W. Considine, Jr. Screenwriters: Carey Wilson and Howard Emmett Rogers; Based on a story by John Farrow. Photographer: Karl Struss. Editor: Donn Hayes. Art Directors: William Cameron Menzies and Park French. Costumes: Alice O'Neill. Music Arranger: Hugo Riesenfeld. Running Time: 70 minutes.

THE BAD ONE: Dolores Del Rio and Edmund Lowe.

CAST

Dolores Del Rio (*Lita*); Edmund Lowe (*Jerry Flanagan*); Don Alvarado (*The Spaniard*); Blanche Frederici (*Madame Durand*); Adrienne D'Ambricourt (*Madame Pompier*); Ullrich Haupt (*Pierre Ferrande*); Mitchell Lewis (*Borloff*); Ralph Lewis (*Blochet*); Charles McNaughton (*Petey*); Yola D'Avril (*Gida*); John St. Polis (*Judge*); Henry Kolker (*Prosecutor*); George Fawcett (*Warden*); Boris Karloff (*Monsieur Gaston*); Victor Potel, Harry Stubbs and Tom Dugan (*Sailors*).

The breathtakingly beautiful, Mexican-born Dolores Del Rio first made her impact in silent films like *What Price Glory*, *The Loves of Carmen* and *The Red Dance*. And despite the sensation caused when Al Jolson first spoke in 1927's *The Jazz Singer*, she publicly announced, "Never will I make a talkie. I think they are teerrible." But, by the time she appeared in 1929's basically silent *Evangeline*, Del Rio agreed to sing the film's title tune and deliver a few lines of dialogue. The following year, in *The Bad One*, she took the inevitable plunge and, influenced by a lucrative new United Artists contract, assumed the responsibility of her first full-fledged talking-singing-dancing role.

In this unlikely romantic melodrama, Del Rio portrays Lita, a Spanish dancer who performs in a Marseilles cafe and dwells in what can only be a bordello, where she passes out keys to other rooms while saving herself for the right man. All this while, the ever-lively, ever-vivacious young miss constantly reminds all and sundry, in her carefully enunciated, Mexican-accented English, "I'm a very *smart* little girl." She's also never quiet, always singing or humming to herself the infectious Spanish-flavored melody she dances to in the movie's early cafe sequence, Irving Berlin's "To a Tango Melody."

Apparently, the right man for Lita is American sailor Jerry Flanagan (Edmund Lowe), and perhaps that's because he, too, is given to bursting into periodic song—trumpeting his love for Lita. But, just when you think *The Bad One* will blossom into a full-fledged operetta, things get very serious. On the day the pair plan to marry, a former suitor tries to claim Lita, and in the ensuing fight Jerry accidentally kills him. At his subsequent murder trial, our sailor is sentenced to prison, innocently implicated by Lita. Now certain she has betrayed him, Jerry refuses to see her before he is sent to prison on what looks like Devil's Island. To be near her man, the ever-resourceful Lita befriends a vicious prison guard named Pierre (Ullrich Haupt), whom she agrees to marry, since only the wives of guards are

permitted on the island. Further plot complications ensue, a prison riot breaks out and Jerry takes command. The other prisoners surrender, and Jerry wins a pardon, to be reunited with Lita.

THE BAD ONE: Edmund Lowe and Dolores Del Rio.

THE BAD ONE: Ullrich Haupt *(left)*, Dolores Del Rio, Boris Karloff *(right)* and players.

23

Director George Fitzmaurice (1885–1941) was a seasoned hand at romantic melodramas like this, and although he'd had better scripts in the past (*The Son Of The Sheik, Lilac Time*), he managed to carry off *The Bad One*'s various excesses with unembarrassed flair and dispatch, delivering all this nonsense in a tight, 70-minute package. And his stars respond in kind, with Edmund Lowe clearly enjoying himself throughout, and Dolores Del Rio undeterred by the exaggerated acting style that harked back to her silent screen origins.

As an interesting footnote to the film, those who don't blink will catch brief glimpses of Boris Karloff in the bit role of a prison guard called "Monsieur Gaston," who speaks but two lines of the Carey Wilson-Howard Emmett Rogers dialogue. In 1930, who could predict that Karloff would soon become a household name with the following year's *Frankenstein*?

THE BIG HOUSE

1 9 3 0

CREDITS

A Metro-Goldwyn-Mayer Picture. Producer: Irving Thalberg. Director: George Hill. Screenwriters: Frances Marion, Joe Farnham and Martin Flavin. Cinematographer: Harold Wenstrom. Editor: Blanche Sewell. Art Director: Cedric Gibbons. Sound: Robert Shirley and Douglas Shearer. Running Time: 84 minutes.

CAST

Chester Morris (*John Morgan*); Wallace Beery (*Butch Schmidt*); Lewis Stone (*Warden James Adams*); Robert Montgomery (*Kent Marlowe*); Leila Hyams (*Anne Marlowe*); George F. Marion (*Pop Riker*); J.C. Nugent (*Mr. Marlowe*); Karl Dane (*Olsen*); DeWitt Jennings (*Captain Wallace*); Matthew Betz (*Gopher*); Claire McDowell (*Mrs. Marlowe*); Robert Emmett O'Connor (*Donlin*); Tom Wilson (*Sandy, the Guard*); Eddie Foyer (*Dopey*); Roscoe Ates (*Putnam*); Fletcher Norton (*Oliver*); Adolph Seidel (*Prison Barber*).

Director George Hill (not to be confused with the much later George *Roy* Hill) was a highly respected filmmaker who began his career in motion pictures working as a 13-year-old stagehand for D.W. Griffith. Later he wrote scripts and worked as a cameraman, before becoming a director during the silent era, starting in 1921. In the early Thirties, at the top of

THE BIG HOUSE: Chester Morris and Wallace Beery.

his form, Hill turned out his three best films for MGM: *The Big House, Min and Bill* and *The Secret Six*. Married to screenwriter (and frequent collaborator) Frances Marion, Hill was working on preparations for filming Pearl Buck's novel *The Good Earth* when he was found dead, an apparent suicide, in 1934.

The Big House is generally considered to be Hill's best work. Later in the Thirties, it would be Warner Bros., the Hollywood studio most closely allied to pictures of social consciousness, that would make prison films a part of their regular output. But it was MGM which started the trend with this hard-hitting early talkie. *The Big House* now seems familiar and predictable, not surprising in the light of all the behind-bars melodramas that have emerged from the movie capital in the intervening years. Many of what are thought of today as standard prison-movie conventions were established in *The Big House*.

As the story begins, we are shown the routine processing of a naive young playboy named Kent Marlowe (Robert Montgomery), who's been found guilty of manslaughter, the result of a drunk-driving accident. Beginning a ten-year prison term, Marlowe is forced to share a cell with two hardened criminals, holdup man John Morgan (Chester Morris) and vicious killer Butch Schmidt (Wallace Beery). The pair make incarceration tough for the cowardly Marlowe, particularly when he pulls a stunt that puts Morgan in solitary confinement. The latter vows revenge and, after making a successful prison break, he meets Marlowe's sister Anne (Leila Hyams), with whom he falls in love. But Morgan's recaptured and returned behind bars just as Schmidt is plotting a Thanksgiving Day break with his gang.

Morgan informs on Schmidt and the guards are ready for him and his cohorts, with the result that one wing of the prison becomes the scene of a desperate shoot-out. A guard is murdered, but not even that will pressure the warden (Lewis Stone) to give in to Schmidt's demands. Although Morgan has stayed clear of the riot scene (to maintain good behavior in order to get out and marry Anne), Schmidt accuses him of ratting on his old chums, and he shoots him. But Morgan manages to kill Schmidt before the prison officials regain order. Eventually, Morgan wins his parole.

Originally, *The Big House* was designed as a vehicle for Metro's master character actor of the silent screen, Lon Chaney. But after only one talkie (the 1930 remake of his silent classic *The Unholy Three*), Chaney died of bronchial cancer. He was replaced in the prison melodrama by an unemployed actor who had recently been dropped by Paramount—Wallace Beery. Of heavy physique, coarse personality and gravel voice—but with a twinkle in his eye—Beery

possessed the canny ability to be simultaneously appealing and repulsive. At MGM, he found the basis for a revitalized career, beginning with *The Big*

THE BIG HOUSE: Charles Boyer in the French version.

THE BIG HOUSE: Chester Morris, Robert Montgomery and Wallace Berry.

House, in which he leaves a vivid impression as the intimidating Butch Schmidt. And, under Hill's inspired direction, his professional prison-mates aren't far behind him, with both Chester Morris and Robert Montgomery delivering solid, professional work.

In search of an international movie market, Hollywood was then shooting alternate-language versions of their potentially more popular pictures, and in the French edition of *The Big House*, shot on the same sets but retitled for export *Revolte dans la Prison*, Charles Boyer assumed the Chester Morris role.

The Big House won Academy Awards for Frances Marion's screenplay and Douglas Shearer's sound recording. But it was also nominated for Best Picture (*All Quiet on the Western Front* won the statuette) and Best Actor Wallace Beery (he lost out to George Arliss for *Disraeli*).

THE DAWN PATROL

(FLIGHT COMMANDER)

1930

CREDITS

A Warner Bros./First National Picture. Producer: Robert North. Director: Howard Hawks. Screenwriters: Howard Hawks, Dón Totheroh and Seton I. Miller. Based on the story *The Flight Commander* by John Monk Saunders. Cinematographer: Ernest Haller. Editor: Ray Curtiss. Music: Leo F. Forbstein. Special Effects: Fred Jackman. Running Time: 95 minutes.

CAST

Richard Barthelmess (*Dick Courtney*); Douglas Fairbanks, Jr. (*Douglas Scott*); Neil Hamilton (*Major Brand*); William Janney (*Gordon Scott*); James Finlayson (*Field Sergeant*); Clyde Cook (*Bott*); Gardner James (*Ralph Hollister*); Edmond Breon (*Phipps*); Frank McHugh (*Flaherty*); Jack Ackroyd and Harry Allen (*Mechanics*).

Director Howard Hawks had always found compatibility with male-oriented stories of action and adventure. In this World War I drama, he made his first foray into talking pictures, with a war tale that *Variety* likened to an aviation version of that same year's trench-based *Journey's End*. Indeed, R.C. Sheriff, author of that play and film, went so far as to sue Warner Bros. for "lifting substantial portions" of

his work for their *The Dawn Patrol*. At the same time, Howard Hughes made the claim that airplane footage from his *Hell's Angels* was used in the Warner picture. But both parties lost their cases, and the resultant publicity only benefited *The Dawn Patrol*.

Somewhat stilted and dialogue-bound at the time, because of the primitive sound techniques of the early talkie screen, *The Dawn Patrol* is at its best when the cameras take to the skies. Despite some awesome strides in aerial photography made by William Wellman's 1927 Academy Award winner *Wings* and Hughes' 1930 *Hell's Angels*, the critics had high praise for *The Dawn Patrol*'s bravura flying scenes and the inevitable cloud-bound dogfights, for which Ernest Haller took photographic credit. As Howard Hawks later explained, the flying sequences were "all for real, even the forced landings." He further revealed, "There were a number of scenes where I piloted the airplane with the camera up front." Much of that footage was later recycled in 1931's *The Last Flight*, as well as *The Dawn Patrol*'s excellent 1938 remake of the same title, which starred Errol Flynn, David Niven and Basil Rathbone.

This is more a director's than an actor's film, and although its nominal stars (Richard Barthelmess, Douglas Fairbanks, Jr. and Neil Hamilton) are all good, the viewer is more likely to come away from *The Dawn Patrol* impressed with the movie itself, rather than with any individual performances.

Today, this World War I tale seems terribly familiar (even a bit clichéd), predictable and overly long for its content. The story concerns members of the Royal Flying Corps, despite a notable dearth of British accents among its cast (not even Fairbanks had yet then assumed the toney diction that later made audiences mistake him for English). They're stationed at an airfield whose frequent and perilous bombing missions against the Germans continually decimate the ranks of these mostly English-gentlemen types. *The Dawn Patrol*'s major social commentary apparently appears to be directed against the wasting of youth: so many of the enthusiastic, gung-ho types are shown here as being barely of age, and more likely than not to be killed their first time out. It's Neil Hamilton, the base's no-nonsense flight commander, who's responsible for the decisions that send so many young men to an early end, and many a survivor to drink. Taunted by the enemy for their lack of prowess, flying pals Barthelmess and Fairbanks take off on their own, deliberately strafing a defenseless German squadron and

THE DAWN PATROL: Richard Barthelmess, Clyde Cook and Neil Hamilton.

THE DAWN PATROL: Clyde Cook, Douglas Fairbanks, Jr. and Richard Barthelmess.

killing many of the enemy before they can leave the ground. The outraged Hamilton is subsequently reassigned to another post, with Barthelmess replacing him as commanding officer. Finally, with Fairbanks set to go on an especially perilous mission, Barthelmess gets him too drunk to function, and takes his plane, heroically blowing up a strategic enemy supply depot before crashing in flames.

The Dawn Patrol's original story won an Academy Award for aviation specialist John Monk Saunders, although later reports have actually credited the work to Howard Hawks.

THE DAWN PATROL: Gardner James, Richard Barthelmess and Douglas Fairbanks, Jr.

ANIMAL CRACKERS: Zeppo Marx *(left)*, Louis Sorin *(in cutaway coat)*, Groucho Marx and Margaret Dumont.

ANIMAL CRACKERS

1930

CREDITS

A Paramount Picture. Director: Victor Heerman. Screenwriter: Morrie Ryskind. Based on the Marx Brothers musical by George S. Kaufman, Bert Kalmar, Morrie Ryskind and Harry Ruby. Cinematographer: George Folsey. Sound: Ernest F. Zatorsky. Music and Lyrics: Bert Kalmar and Harry Ruby. Songs: "Why Am I So Romantic?" and "Hooray for Captain Spalding" by Bert Kalmar and Harry Ruby, "Collegiate" by Moe Jaffe and Nat Bonx, and "Some of These Days" by Shelton Brooks. Running Time: 98 minutes.

CAST

Groucho Marx (*Capt. Jeffrey Spalding*); Harpo Marx (*The Professor*); Chico Marx (*Signor Emanuel Ravelli*); Zeppo Marx (*Horatio Jamison*); Lillian Roth (*Arabella Rittenhouse*); Margaret Dumont (*Mrs. Rittenhouse*); Louis Sorin (*Roscoe Chandler*); Hal Thompson (*John Parker*); Margaret Irving (*Mrs. Whitehead*); Kathryn Reece (*Grace Carpenter*); Robert Greig (*Hives, the Butler*); Edward Metcalf (*Hennessey*); The Music Masters (*Six Footmen*).

After their successful feature-film debut in 1929's zany *The Cocoanuts*, the four Marx Brothers (Groucho, Harpo, Chico and Zeppo) turned to their 1928 Broadway musical hit *Animal Crackers*, which had played around the nation for three years, for their next film vehicle. Morrie Ryskind adapted the screen version from the stage show he and George S. Kaufman had originally devised for the Brothers, with music and lyrics by Bert Kalmar and Harry Ruby.

The simple plot—concerned vaguely with the theft of a valuable painting and its replacement with a fake—served mainly as a framework for the comedy team's expected sight gags and nonsense patter. Filmed during the day at Paramount's New York studios in Astoria (while the Marxes continued in the Broadway original at night), *Animal Crackers* resembles little more than a photographed play, scarcely abetted by Victor Heerman's direction, and with the dialogue sounding more like inspired ad-libbing. This is especially evident, for example, when Groucho turns to grimace and joke directly into the camera with quips like "Well, *all* the jokes can't be good! You've got to expect that once in a while." Or, "Pardon me while I have a *Strange Interlude*: How happy I could be with either of these two if both of them just went away."

The setting is the posh Long Island estate of Mrs. Rittenhouse (played by that perfect Marxian foil, statuesque Margaret Dumont), where a house party is invaded by the dubious "African explorer" Capt. Jeffrey Spalding (Groucho) and his secretary, Horatio Jamison (Zeppo, the sanest of the Brothers, who was present strictly for stand-by good humor). Close behind them come another pair of zanies, "The Professor" (the mute, blond-wigged, girl-chasing Harpo) and Signor Emanuel Ravelli (Chico, with his whacky, Italian-accented malaprops), who

ANIMAL CRACKERS: Margaret Dumont, Margaret Irving, Harpo Marx and Chico Marx.

ANIMAL CRACKERS: Louis Sorin, Groucho Marx and Margaret Dumont.

ANIMAL CRACKERS: Chico Marx, Groucho Marx, Harpo Marx and Margaret Dumont.

get to provide their respective harp and piano musical interludes. What remains of the "plot" need hardly be described. Sufficient to report that the pace is frantic and the puns are thick and awful as the Marxes thoroughly disrupt Mrs. Rittenhouse's lavish home, pursuing the female guests and spreading absolute, hilarious chaos as they deliver exchanges as outrageous as—"Shall we get married?" "That's bigamy!" "Of *course* it's big of me!" Or— "You're the most beautiful woman I've ever seen— which doesn't say much for you." And so on.

The Marx Brothers' later vehicles, *Horse Feathers*, *Duck Soup* and *A Night at the Opera*, would be better motion pictures, from every point of view. But for all its technical faults (microphones in clear view, crude sound effects on the soundtrack), *Animal Crackers* remains an early sound classic, to be appreciated for what it is: a visual record of one of the best comedy acts of all time, practicing their artistry in a manner once considered the height of popular low humor.

THE OFFICE WIFE

1930

CREDITS

A Warner Bros. Picture. Director: Lloyd Bacon. Screenwriter: Charles Kenyon. Based on the novel by Faith Baldwin. Cinematographer: William Rees. Editor: George Marsh. Running Time: 59 minutes.

CAST

Dorothy Mackaill (*Anne Murdock*); Lewis Stone (*Lawrence Fellows*); Hobart Bosworth (*Mr. McGowan*); Blanche Frederici (*Kate Halsey*); Joan Blondell (*Catherine Murdock*); Natalie Moorhead (*Linda Fellows*); Brooks Benedict (*Mr. Jameson*); Dale Fuller (*Miss Andrews*); Walter Merrill (*Ted O'Hara*).

Some readers may be surprised that a Thirties romantic drama might run just under an hour in length. However, at Warner Bros., speed and economy were of the essence. If any studio could be

30

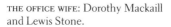

THE OFFICE WIFE: Joan Blondell and Dorothy Mackaill.

termed a "factory," surely it was Warners. And a worth-his-salt "house director" like Lloyd Bacon, the man behind *The Office Wife*, obviously knew how to satisfy his bosses, since he was used to churning out an average of five motion pictures a year. Prior to this, his claim to fame had been Al Jolson's greatest hit, *The Singing Fool* (1928). In Bacon's future would be the major (non-Busby Berkeley) portions of *42nd Street*, *Footlight Parade* and *Wonder Bar*, among a succession of James Cagney, Joan Blondell and Joe E. Brown comedies.

The Office Wife is no landmark of the early talking screen. It is, however, an entirely competent program picture that pleased general audiences in its day, no doubt in the company of another Warners movie of similar (or longer) length. Its success brought its female star, Dorothy Mackaill, a contract with that studio which, unfortunately, did little to prolong a screen career that had spanned the Twenties. A skilled and attractive actress, Mackaill is among the many silent stars who moved successfully into early talkies, producing voices that were entirely compatible with the microphone. Those who have seen her strong performance in William Wellman's 1931 melodrama *Safe in Hell* will realize that she could—and should—have gone on to greater fame and fortune in the Thirties. For some reason, she failed to conquer the new medium. But while Mackaill's career was on the wane, that of another blonde, Joan Blondell, was just beginning.

THE OFFICE WIFE: Dorothy Mackaill and Lewis Stone.

Following their success in Broadway's *Penny Arcade*, she and fellow "legiter," James Cagney had already made the show's film version, *Sinners' Holiday*. But, typical of the strange patterns in which Hollywood then operated, *The Office Wife*, her second film, was the first to be released. In it, she provided comedy relief as the pal of leading lady Mackaill, getting most of the script's laughs and generally making a strong impression.

The Office Wife differed from the many similar romantic yarns in that it allowed the young heroine to wind up with an older man. In fact, at the outset the movie has Anne Murdock (Mackaill) involved with a young reporter named Ted (Walter Merrill). She moves up from office temp to secretary when her predecessor (Dale Fuller), the middle-aged secret admirer of advertising agency head Lawrence Fellows (Lewis Stone), takes a leave of absence. As business brings boss and secretary closer for professional purposes, Fellows' wife Linda (Natalie Moorhead) feels sufficiently neglected to seek the company of other men. Eventually, on a trip to Paris, she gets a divorce, leaving hubby free to wed his secretary—once Anne has freed herself of Ted.

Novelist Faith Baldwin was a practiced hand at this sort of storytelling, but it took the combined forces of screenwriter Charles Kenyon, director Lloyd Bacon and his engaging cast to convince Thirties audiences that 27-year-old Dorothy Mackaill could be happy facing a future with fatherly, 51-year-old Lewis Stone.

MOROCCO

1930

CREDITS

A Paramount Picture. Producer: Hector Turnbull. Director: Josef von Sternberg. Screenwriter: Jules Furthman. Based on the novel and play *Amy Jolly* by Benno Vigny. Cinematographers: Lee Garmes and Lucien Ballard. Editor: Sam Winston. Songs: "Give Me the Man" and "What Am I Bid for My Apples?" by Karl Hajos and Leo Robin; and "Quand l'Amour Meurt" by Millandy and Cremieux. Art Director: Hans Dreier. Costumes: Travis Banton. Sound: Harry D. Mills. Running Time: 92 minutes.

CAST

Gary Cooper (*Legionnaire Tom Brown*); Marlene Dietrich (*Mademoiselle Amy Jolly*); Adolphe Menjou (*Monsieur La Bessiere*); Ullrich Haupt (*Adjutant Caesar*); Eve Southern (*Madame Caesar*): Francis McDonald (*A Sergeant*); Paul Porcasi (*Lo Tinto*); Juliette Compton (*Anna Dolores*); Albert Conti (*Colonel Quinnevieres*); Michael Visaroff (*Barratire*); Theresa Harris (*Camp Follower*).

Morocco was the sensational movie that officially introduced Marlene Dietrich to American audiences. Although she had already made *The Blue Angel* in Germany for the director of both films, Josef von Sternberg, her foreign vehicle was deliberately held back, and then shown—in its English-language version—after U.S. audiences had become acquainted with this extraordinary star in the manner in which Sternberg *wanted* them to meet her. For Dietrich is far more alluring, and less *zaftig* and *fraulein*-like in *Morocco* than in *The Blue Angel*. This was no accident; her director/mentor took great pains to see that his protégée would make the impression that he visualized, and one must credit his intuitive genius that the gorgeous, world-weary creature that early Thirties moviegoers knew as Marlene Dietrich was everything Sternberg had intended she should become—a great international star.

With Josef von Sternberg directing her every move and utterance (she had pronunciation problems that her director feared might draw laughter and break the spell he was working to create) and the skilled cinematographer Lee Garmes lighting her with the greatest care, Marlene Dietrich emerged from *Morocco* an immediate star of awesome proportions. It's not difficult, some 60-odd years later, to understand the reason. In her sexual magnetism and her radiant, woman-of-the-world beauty, Dietrich is absolutely unique. And it's obviously much more than an exquisite doll being moved and dressed and photographed to perfection by masters; instead, this woman brings her own inner magic to the cameras, and the collaborative art that is filmmaking takes it from there.

Morocco's storyline is what its star, in her reclusive, twilight years, has summarily dismissed as *kitsch*. A cabaret entertainer named Amy Jolly (pronounced "AH-mee Zhahl-LEE") arrives in Morocco by steamer, after rebuffing the gentlemanly attentions of another passenger, the wealthy and debonair Monsieur La Bessiere (Adolphe Menjou). At the nightclub where she's engaged to perform, Amy is advised by her employer (Paul Porcasi) to find herself a "protector," as the vicinity isn't safe for a European woman of her beauty, and it's further suggested that she seek out one of the Foreign Legion officers. That night, she daringly performs her opening number, brazenly attired in male white tie and tails, in which she ends up taking a flower from a woman patron, whom she kisses full on the mouth, then flings it to the handsomest legionnaire in the room. This is Tom Brown (Gary Cooper), a deceptively shy womanizer who's been having an affair with the wife (Eve Southern) of his senior commanding officer, Caesar (Ullrich Haupt).

Slowly but inevitably, Tom and Amy are drawn closer together, while La Bessiere continues to admire her from a distance. Following a night incident that nearly reveals Tom's liaison with Madame Caesar, her suspicious husband has him arrested, then released to be sent off on a mission into the Sahara. Before his departure, Tom and Amy talk about running off to Europe together, but he changes his mind and leaves. In retaliation, she accepts the eager protection of La Bessiere, but, at the dinner party planned to announce their engagement, she hears the sound of drums and bugles that signal the legionnaires' return, and Amy becomes transfixed by her obsession with Tom. Rising from the dinner table, she looks wildly about her like a frightened animal before bolting with such suddenness that she breaks her pearl necklace. And, as the pearls fall noisily to the floor, she dashes off to find Tom, leaving the unflappable La Bessiere explaining to his embarrassed guests that he'll willingly accept her as she is.

MOROCCO: Marlene Dietrich and Adolphe Menjou.

MOROCCO: Marlene Dietrich and Gary Cooper.

MOROCCO: Gary Cooper and Marlene Dietrich.

Amy finds Tom in a local bar, and their meeting is as wary as it is ambiguous. We never find out just how much her love for Tom is reciprocated. As the legion gets ready to move out again, Amy and La Bessiere bid him farewell. Tom marches off and, as the column disappears into the desert, the traditional band of camp followers brings up the rear. Impulsively, Amy kisses her protector goodbye and runs after them, her dress adding an incongruous touch to the peasant garb of her sisters-of-the-desert. In a final touch of "camp," Amy removes her high heeled shoes and leaves them behind in the sand. One wonders how long this luxurious creature will survive in such rugged surroundings.

The New York Times was not swept away by the exotic new star. After allowing that she was a "German film favorite" who had "won favor abroad in a picture called *The Blue Angel*," it begrudgingly noted, "Miss Dietrich bears a resemblance to Greta Garbo, but her acting hardly rivals that of the Swedish star." However, the Academy of Motion Picture Arts and Sciences disagreed sufficiently to nominate Dietrich for the Best Actress award that ultimately went to Marie Dressler for *Min and Bill. Morocco* also garnered nominations for Josef von Sternberg, Lee Garmes and the properly exotic sets of Hans Dreier.

MOROCCO: Gary Cooper, Adolphe Menjou and Marlene Dietrich.

In his autobiography, *Fun in a Chinese Laundry*, Sternberg later wrote, "In passing, it should be mentioned that less than a year later Adolph Zukor confided to me that the company had been saved from bankruptcy by the success of this film."

MIN AND BILL

1930

CREDITS

A Metro-Goldwyn-Mayer Picture. Director: George Hill. Screenwriters: Frances Marion and Marion Jackson. Based on the novel *Dark Star* by Lorna Moon. Cinematographer: Harold Wenstrom. Editor: Basil Wrangell. Art Director: Cedric Gibbons. Costumes: Rene Hubert. Running Time: 66 minutes.

CAST

Marie Dressler (*Min Divot*); Wallace Beery (*Bill*); Dorothy Jordan (*Nancy Smith*); Marjorie Rambeau (*Bella Pringle*); Donald Dillaway (*Dick Cameron*); DeWitt Jennings (*Groot*); Russell Hopton (*Alec Johnson*); Frank McGlynn (*Mr. Southard*); Gretta Gould (*Mrs. Southard*); Jack Pennick (*Merchant Seaman*); Henry Rocquemore (*Bella's Stateroom Lover*); Hank Bell (*Sailor*).

Min and Bill starred a pair of homely character actors in an unusual serio-comic story with a downbeat ending—and became 1930's biggest box-office hit. Marie Dressler and Wallace Berry in the movie's title roles appeared well matched as, respectively, the tough proprietor of a rundown dockside hotel and her fisherman-beau. In reality, Beery was then some 17 years Dressler's junior. At 61, that bulky, bulldog-faced actress was then riding the crest of a highly successful motion picture comeback. A veteran of vaudeville and stage plays, she had teamed with Charlie Chaplin and Mabel Normand in the 1914 silent comedy classic, *Tillie's Punctured Romance*. But her career had suffered an eclipse with the end of World War I, and she owed the fruits of her great success in talking pictures to the intercession of her good friend, screenwriter Frances Marion, who was responsible for Dressler's being cast as Marthy, the scene-stealing old waterfront floozie of Greta Garbo's *Anna Christie*.

The equally heavy-set Beery had enjoyed a long succession of roles, both as comedian and villain, in silent films, chiefly at Paramount. At MGM, early that year he had already won acclaim in a pair of

MIN AND BILL: Dorothy Jordan, Marie Dressler and Wallace Beery.

MIN AND BILL: Wallace Beery, Marjorie Rambeau and Marie Dressler.

important films; George Hill's previous picture, *The Big House*, and as Pat Garrett, the lawman nemesis of *Billy the Kid* in that King Vidor Western. But it was Beery's teaming with Dressler that gave his ca-

MIN AND BILL: Marie Dressler and Wallace Beery.

MIN AND BILL: Wallace Beery and Marie Dressler.

girl who was abandoned as a child by her trampish mother Bella (Marjorie Rambeau). In the midst of her battles with school authorities over Nancy's education, Min also has to contend with the return of blackmailing Bella, who raises Min's ire by flirting with Min's boyfriend Bill (Beery). The intruder also threatens to ruin Nancy's chance for a better future with Dick (Donald Dillaway), the well-to-do youth she's planning to wed. In a confrontation scene, Min is driven to shoot Bella for Nancy's sake. At the story's close, Min's led off by the police as Nancy sails away on her honeymoon. Somehow, we know that Min will survive and that Bill will be waiting for her when she gets out again.

In *The New York Times*, Mordaunt Hall called this offbeat blend of slapstick and melodrama "a far from pleasant film"—which was scarcely the picture's intent. *Variety* was better tuned to the public taste, terming *Min and Bill* an "excellent balance of pathos and comedy all the way through," and expressing certainty that "no other woman anywhere could have played Miss Dressler's role convincingly at all."

This is more Dressler's film than Beery's, for she has far more footage, sharing scenes alone with ingenue Dorothy Jordan and the excellent scene-stealer Rambeau (whose vocal patterns here seem a bit influenced by Broadway's Mae West—then yet to

reer the big boost that made him one of the Thirties' most popular stars.

Waterfront innkeeper Min (Dressler) has found time to raise Nancy (Dorothy Jordan), an attractive

36

make her film bow). But it was rough-talking, boozy Dressler who made the film's biggest impression with members of the Academy of Motion Picture Arts and Sciences. Over nominees Marlene Dietrich (*Morocco*), Irene Dunne (*Cimarron*), Ann Harding (*Holiday*) and Norma Shearer (*A Free Soul*), she walked away with the Best Actress statuette for the 1930–31 season.

Min and Bill's popularity resulted in a reunion of the Beery-Dressler team in 1933's even more popular *Tugboat Annie*. But illness began to afflict Marie Dressler, and after making *Christopher Bean*, she died of cancer in the summer of 1934.

FAST AND LOOSE

1930

CREDITS

A Paramount Picture. Director: Fred Newmeyer and (uncredited) Bertram Harrison. Screenwriters: Doris Anderson, Jack Kirkland and Preston Sturges. Based on the play *The Best People* by David Gray and Avery Hopwood. Cinematographer: William Steiner. Sound: C.A. Tuthill. Running Time: 70 minutes.

CAST

Miriam Hopkins (*Marion Lenox*); Carole Lombard (*Alice O'Neil*); Frank Morgan (*Bronson Lenox*); Charles Starrett (*Henry Morgan*); Henry Wadsworth (*Bertie Lenox*); Winifred Harris (*Carrie Lenox*); Herbert Yost (*George Grafton*); David Hutcheson (*Lord Rockingham*); Ilka Chase (*Millie Montgomery*); Herschel Mayall (*Judge Summers*).

This film had its origins in a 1924 Broadway success entitled *The Best People*; whereupon Paramount was moved to bring it to the screen the following year as a silent with Warner Baxter, Margaret Morris and Esther Ralston. In 1930, they added sound and renamed it *Fast and Loose*. Like many of Paramount's late-silent/early-talkie productions, this was filmed at their East Coast studios in Astoria, New York, a ploy that often enabled them to film on Long Island during the day New York actors and stars who played on Broadway at night.

Miriam Hopkins, a Broadway fixture throughout most of the Twenties, was acting on the New York stage in *Lysistrata* when she agreed to make her

FAST AND LOOSE: Miriam Hopkins.

FAST AND LOOSE: Miriam Hopkins and Charles Starrett.

motion picture debut as Marion Lenox, the willful and capricious debutante heroine of this slight comedy. Marion is engaged to Lord Rockingham (David Hutcheson), who is what used to be known as a "silly-ass Englishman." Obviously, there's no love attached to this match-of-convenience which has, of

FAST AND LOOSE: Charles Starrett, Carole Lombard, Frank Morgan, Herbert Yost, Henry Wadsworth and Miriam Hopkins.

course, earned the full approval of her snobbish, high-society parents. Marion's brother Bertie (Henry Wadsworth) sides with her. He in turn is the family's black-sheep son, spending most of his time partying and, when not downright drunk, romancing a quite respectable chorine named Alice (Carole Lombard), whom he fully intends to marry, with the knowledge that his parents will be outraged.

Bored with her socialite crowd, Marion walks out on her own engagement party, parks her car in a sandy area by the Long Island Sound, and encounters an oafish young hunk named Henry (Charles Starrett), whose job as a mechanic allows him time for swimming only at night. It's an immediately sour beginning to what of course develops into true love as the couple trade sarcasms, and Henry helps Marion extricate her car wheels from the wet sand into which they've sunk. The following night, they meet again under similar circumstances, only this time she's brought along her bathing suit. Their swim leads to a steamy clinch. Eventually Marion breaks off her engagement, while at the same time Bertie's relationship with Alice has become known. All this leads to an arranged meeting between Marion's father Bronson (Frank Morgan) and Uncle George (Herbert Yost), who pose as theatrical producers in

order to get to know Alice, who arrives at the meeting with her roommate Millie (Ilka Chase). Suffice it to say, by the film's close, Alice has reformed Bertie and won over her future in-laws, and Marion has convinced them that her upstanding mechanic (Henry) is worth their coming down from their high horses to accept into the family. In short, social reform has been complete, and this fluffy comedy of manners concludes on a note of unbelievable happiness for one and all.

Fred Newmeyer, who directed in collaboration with dialogue director Bertram Harrison, had enjoyed more prominence during the silent era, when he had been responsible for such Harold Lloyd classics as *Grandma's Boy*, *Safety Last* and *The Freshman*, as well as W. C. Fields' *The Potters*. But his career declined with the talkies, although he manages well enough with the superficial social comedy of *Fast and Loose*. For Miriam Hopkins, this marked the quiet beginning of a fairly noteworthy movie career, although she frequently returned to the theatre at the same time she starred in pictures. In reviewing Hopkins' debut, *Variety* remarked, "This stage artiste plays tick-tack-toe with the camera, sometimes winning, sometimes losing, but the merit of her performance will be universally obvious."

With her carefully enunciated stage speech (and occasional lapses into her native Georgia twang), frizzy hair and pretty though unglamorous face, Hopkins offered a different sort of movie leading lady: one who would obviously need to rely more on ability than looks. Fortunately, she had the talent. On the other hand, second-lead Carole Lombard, who had already been acting in films for a number of years, displayed the talent *and* the beauty. The role doesn't allow her much footage to make an impression, but everything Lombard does works. Of the movie's male cast, Frank Morgan is solid as her father. And a legit-theatrical background enabled tall, dark and handsome Charles Starrett to provide everything needed in a young leading man during those early years of his career before he took permanently to the saddle, and discovered his greatest success with the Westerns he starred in from 1935 to 1952.

PAID: Joan Crawford.

PAID

1930

CREDITS

A Metro-Goldwyn-Mayer Picture. Director: Sam Wood. Screenwriters: Lucien Hubbard and Charles MacArthur. Based on the play *Within the Law* by Bayard Veiller. Cinematographer: Charles Rosher. Editor: Hugh Wynn. Art Director: Cedric Gibbons. Sound: Douglas Shearer. Costumes: Adrian. Running Time: 83 minutes.

CAST

Joan Crawford (*Mary Turner*); Robert Armstrong (*Joe Garson*); Marie Prevost (*Agnes Lynch*); Kent Douglass/ Douglass Montgomery (*Bob Gilder*); John Miljan (*Inspector Burke*); Purnell Pratt (*Edward Gilder*); Hale Hamilton (*District Attorney Demarest*); Polly Moran (*Polly*); Robert Emmett O'Connor (*Cassidy*); Tyrrell Davis (*Eddie Griggs*); William Bakewell (*Carney*); George Cooper (*Red*); Gwen Lee (*Bertha*); Isabel Withers (*Helen Morris*).

Prior to this motion picture, her 27th, Joan Crawford had spent five years turning out a succession of increasingly popular comedies, light dramas and melodramas for MGM. But she had yet to tackle a heavy dramatic role that would prove she could really *act*. The opportunity came when Metro began preparations for a Norma Shearer vehicle that Shearer was unable to do because she was pregnant with the son and heir of that studio's production

PAID: Joan Crawford and Robert Armstrong.

chief, Irving Thalberg. That vehicle, Bayard Veiller's *Within the Law*, had proven a great theatrical success for young Jane Cowl in 1912. On the screen, it had twice been filmed during the silent years, first in 1917 with Alice Joyce, then remade with Norma Talmadge in 1923.

PAID: John Miljan, Joan Crawford and Kent Douglass (Douglass Montgomery)

Crawford begged Thalberg to let her do the updated Charles MacArthur adaptation planned for Shearer, and he reluctantly agreed. With all the considerable ambition and determination at her command, Crawford worked hard on the picture, now called *Paid*. No dummy, she realized that this excellent dramatic script was the role she needed to convince Metro bosses that she was deserving of better than her two most recent movies, the lightweight *Montana Moon* and *Our Blushing Brides*. In his biography *Joan Crawford*, Bob Thomas writes: "She started the film in a state of terror, fearful that she would fail in her first real challenge. She found no support from Sam Wood, who directed in a perfunctory manner and made no comment on her performance." Be that as it may, Crawford herself is quoted in Roy Newquist's *Conversations With Joan*, "*Paid* was my first really heavy dramatic role, and I did a good job, a damned good job, thanks to Sam Wood and a script by Charlie MacArthur." So who does one believe? Whatever the motivation for her performance, *Paid* offered a great opportunity for an actress, and Joan Crawford made it her personal triumph, transforming herself from soft to hard, and then finally back to soft and sweet before the story's completion. *Paid* also afforded her the opportunity to appear both drab and devoid of make-up, as well as furred and gowned to the hilt, courtesy of MGM designer Adrian.

Mary Turner (Crawford) is a shopgirl who's sentenced to three years in prison for a crime she didn't commit. Before she leaves the courtroom, Mary speaks words that presage the Joan Crawford screen image of the future: "You're going to pay for everything I'm losing in life!"

Mary serves her term, after which she falls in with three crooks: Joe Garson (Robert Armstrong), her prison sidekick Agnes Lynch (Marie Prevost) and a fellow named Red (George Cooper). In their dubious company, Mary dabbles in larceny, blackmail and embezzlement—but so cleverly that she always remains within the law. To get even with her former employer, the department store owner Gilder (Purnell Pratt), who sent her to prison, Mary charms and marries his son Bob (Kent Douglass, before he changed his professional name to "Douglass Montgomery"). Gilder tries unsuccessfully to have the marriage annulled. Finally, he engages Griggs (Tyrrell Davis) to play informer, abetting Red and Joe in a robbery at Bob's house. However, Mary discovers the plot in time to expose Griggs, who's killed by Joe. The police are quick to arrest Mary, but after Joe is forced to confess everything, she's freed to return to the arms of Bob, with whom she's now genuinely in love.

Not only did Joan Crawford make this role work for her, but she was by then sufficiently experienced in camera technique and the mechanics of film acting to know just how to make that low, well-modulated voice and those big, expressive eyes reveal what she was thinking. *Paid* exemplifies genuine star quality in action. From this point on, the Crawford career would rise to rival that of Norma Shearer, although Joan would later complain that she got only second best at MGM, after Shearer got *her* way.

Paid proved one of 1930's biggest hits for Metro. It was far less successful nine years later, when the studio remade it under its original title of *Within the Law*, as a non-starmaking vehicle for ingenue Ruth Hussey.

CIMARRON

1931

CREDITS

An RKO Radio Picture. Producer: William LeBaron. Director: Wesley Ruggles. Screenwriter: Howard Estabrook. Based on the novel by Edna Ferber. Cinematographer:

CIMARRON: poster art.

CIMARRON: Irene Dunne and Richard Dix.

CIMARRON: Richard Dix, Douglas Scott and Irene Dunne.

Edward Cronjager. Editor: William Hamilton. Art Director and Costumes: Max Ree. Running Time: 124 minutes.

CAST

Richard Dix (*Yancey Cravat*); Irene Dunne (*Sabra Cravat*); Estelle Taylor (*Dixie Lee*); Nance O'Neil (*Felice Venable*); William Collier, Jr. (*The Kid*); Roscoe Ates (*Jess Rickey*); George E. Stone (*Sol Levy*); Robert McWade (*Louie Heffner*); Edna May Oliver (*Mrs. Tracy Wyatt*); Frank Darien (*Mr. Bixby*); Eugene Jackson (*Isaiah*); Dolores Brown (*Ruby Big Elk, eldest*); Gloria Vonic (*Ruby Big Elk, younger*); Otto Hoffman (*Murch Rankin*); William Orlamond (*Grat Gotch*); Frank Beal (*Louis Venable*); Nancy Dover (*Donna Cravat, eldest*); Junior Johnson (*Cim, younger*); Douglas Scott (*Cim, youngest*); Reginald Streeter (*Yancey Jr.*); Lois Jane Campbell (*Felice Jr.*); Ann Lee (*Aunt Cassandra*); Tyrone Brereton (*Dabney Venable*); Lillian Lane (*Cousin Bella*); Henry Rocquemore (*Jonett Goforth*); Nell Craig (*Arminta Greenwood*); Robert McKenzie (*Pat Leary*); Bob Kortman (*Killer*); Clara Hunt (*Indian Girl*); William Janney (*Worker*).

Released in 1931, this time-spanning saga of Oklahoma homesteaders by Edna Ferber remains the only Western ever to lay claim to a Best Picture Academy Award. In its day, *Cimarron* typified the kind of big, expensive (almost $1½-million) production that impressed critics, attracted moviegoers and won accolades, including Academy statuettes for Howard Estabrook's screenplay and Best Set Decoration. The nearly 60 intervening years have witnessed so many large-scale family epics—including an unremarkable Metro-colored *Cimarron* remake in 1960—that this film now looks quite dated, of interest primarily to buffs.

The movie gets off to a rousing start with its most exciting sequence, the Oklahoma Land Rush of 1889, with thousands of extras seen racing in wagons, on horseback and on foot, as would-be settlers anxious to stake their claims. But the episodic narrative elects to focus on the family of Yancey Cravat (Richard Dix) and his young bride Sabra (Irene Dunne in her first important film role), as they manage to stake their marker on a prize piece of land. However, it's removed by the ruthless Dixie Lee (Estelle Taylor), who takes it for herself. Yancey and Sabra must settle for less desirable property.

As time passes, the quick-triggered Yancey establishes a crusading frontier newspaper. Delivering the sermon at a local revival meeting, he's challenged to a showdown by Lon Yountis (Stanley Fields), whom he's forced to kill in self-defense. Dixie, who's become the town madam, reenters his life when she's arrested and tried for prostitution and, against Sabra's wishes, her husband defends his old nemesis in court. But wanderlust takes Yancey away to other parts, leaving Sabra to carry on with the paper and raise their children. And the storyline now shifts its emphasis to her. Yancey returns to his home periodically, but never for long. As he seeks adventure elsewhere, Sabra enters local politics. By 1911, she's a distinguished U.S. Congresswoman. Before the story's end in 1929, 40 years have taken their toll on Yancey Cravat; he dies broke, having ended his itinerant adventures as an oil rigger.

Wesley Ruggles would later win notice as an excellent comedy director. But in 1931, he won deserved credit for guiding this massive production—the biggest and costliest RKO Radio Pictures had ever attempted. *Cimarron* brought an Academy Award nomination to Ruggles, as well as others for Best Actor Richard Dix, Best Actress Irene Dunne and cinematographer Edward Cronjager. Although the Academy's "Best Supporting" categories had yet to be established, had they then existed, there would have been strong competition for Supporting Actress between Estelle Taylor's colorful Dixie Lee and the amusing Edna May Oliver's performance as a salty frontier widow. Watching Oliver's comedy technique here, one can see the genesis of a future master-comedienne named Rosalind Russell.

CIMARRON: Irene Dunne, Nance O'Neil, Richard Dix and Frank Beal.

CITY LIGHTS

1931

CREDITS

A United Artists Picture. Producer-Director-Screenwriter: Charles Chaplin. Cinematographers: Rollie Totheroh, Gordon Pollock and Mark Marlatt. Art Director: Charles D. Hall. Assistant Directors: Harry Crocker, Henry Bergman and Albert Austin. Music: Charles Chaplin. Musical Arranger: Arthur Johnston. Music Director: Alfred Newman. Running Time: 86 minutes.

CAST

Charles Chaplin (*A Tramp*); Virginia Cherrill (*A Blind Girl*); Florence Lee (*Her Grandmother*); Harry Myers (*An Eccentric Millionaire*); Allan Garcia (*His Butler*); Hank Mann (*A Prize Fighter*); Henry Bergman (*Janitor/Mayor*); Albert Austin (*Cook/Streetcleaner*); Stanhope Wheatcroft (*Man in Cafe*); John Rand (*Old Tramp*); James Donnelly (*Foreman*); Eddie Baker (*Referee*); Robert Parrish (*Newsboy*); Jean Harlow (*Blonde in Night Club*).

Charlie Chaplin was nearly 40, with an enviable pantomimic career in silent movies behind him when, in 1928, he began work on *City Lights*. He hadn't realized the extent to which the advent of sound would revolutionize the motion picture industry, and he was about to put his life's work to the test. Chaplin agonized, but ultimately decided to go

through with *City Lights* as originally intended—without dialogue. His only concessions: sound effects and a score which he himself wrote (with the exception of the popular Spanish song "La Violetera," which serves as the recurring theme of the film's female lead, a blind flower girl).

Chaplin resented the intrusion of sound in his magic world of silent film. According to the perfectionist filmmaker, *City Lights* was two years in the making and at cost to him of $2-million. Before its release, he told his friend Sam Goldwyn: "I've spent every penny I possess on *City Lights*. If it's a failure, I believe it will strike a deeper blow than anything else that has ever happened to me in this life." Shortly before its eventual 1931 release, Chaplin contributed an article to *The New York Times* in defense of pantomime in which he stated: "Pantomime, I have always believed and still believe, is the prime qualification of a successful screen player."

Chaplin's big gamble paid off. The press enthusiastically received *City Lights*, and the public followed their long-established comedy favorite, despite his maverick attitude toward talkies. *City Lights* continues to appear on many all-time Ten Best lists of movies, and is usually included in most publications centering on "great film."

City Lights' storyline is simple, but, true to Chaplin, weaves a number of episodic threads into its structure. Basically, it's the familiar Little Tramp, this time taken with the plight of a blind flower girl (Virginia Cherrill), for whom he attempts to raise

CITY LIGHTS: Virginia Cherrill, Charles Chaplin and Harry Myers.

CITY LIGHTS: Charles Chaplin and Virginia Cherrill.

money so that she can afford the operation that might restore her sight. Charlie saves the life of an alcoholic and suicidal millionaire (Harry Myers), someone who only recognizes Charlie as his friend when he's drunk. The Little Tramp attempts to get his wealthy friend to part with the money for the girl, but the unpredictable millionaire's mood swings when sober present insurmountable obstacles. Charlie becomes a street cleaner, then enters a boxing match, but neither job brings in the required cash.

During a subsequent visit to his friend the millionaire, whom he once again finds drunk, Charlie almost gets the money—until the house is invaded by burglars. The thieves knock out the would-be benefactor, and when he regains consciousness (and sobriety) in the presence of investigating policemen, he again fails to recognize the Little Tramp, who grabs the money and runs. He leaves it with the blind girl, but the police arrest him, and he's sent to prison. When he's finally released, he goes looking for the girl, only to find her not only with her sight restored, but the owner of her own busy little flower shop. Noticing the Little Tramp at the window and

thinking him in need, she puts money in his hand, only to recognize his touch as that of the man who helped her in the past. "You?" she inquires (in a title frame). Nodding, he asks, "You can see now?" Pressing his hand, she says, "Yes, I can see now," as *City Lights* comes to its sweet and poignant end.

Perhaps this film classic might have been even more moving had Chaplin found a more experienced actress for his leading lady. Beautiful though she undoubtedly is, socialite Virginia Cherrill was making her film debut for an exacting taskmaster who had only cast her because he had been taken with her appearance at a boxing match and decided to play Pygmalion. Cherrill went on to appear in a number of other films over the next few years, but this is the only one for which she is remembered—and perhaps for the fact that she briefly numbered Cary Grant among her five husbands.

As for *City Lights*, not only was it well supported by Charlie Chaplin's faithful public, but it went on to make a reported $5-million profit on its initial release alone. No wonder that the comedian's next picture, *Modern Times*, also refrained from using dialogue.

CITY LIGHTS: Charles Chaplin and Harry Myers.

45

THE PUBLIC ENEMY: James Cagney and Jean Harlow.

THE PUBLIC ENEMY

1931

CREDITS

A Warner Bros.-Vitaphone Picture. Producer: Darryl F. Zanuck. Director: William A. Wellman. Screenwriters: Kubec Glasmon, John Bright and Harvey Thew. Based on the story *Beer and Blood* by John Bright. Cinematographer: Dev Jennings. Editor: Ed McCormick. Art Director: Max Parker. Music Director: David Mendoza. Costumes: Earl Luick and Edward Stevenson. Running Time: 84 minutes.

CAST

James Cagney (*Tom Powers*); Jean Harlow (*Gwen Allen*); Edward Woods (*Matt Doyle*); Joan Blondell (*Mamie*); Beryl Mercer (*Ma Powers*); Donald Cook (*Mike Powers*); Mae Clarke (*Kitty*); Mia Marvin (*Jane*); Leslie Fenton (*Nails Nathan*); Robert Emmett O'Connor (*Paddy Ryan*); Rita Flynn (*Molly Doyle*); Murray Kinnell (*Putty Nose*); Ben Hendricks, Jr. (*Bugs Moran*); Adele Watson (*Mrs. Doyle*); Frank Coghlan, Jr. (*Tommy as a Boy*); Frankie Darro (*Matt as a Boy*); Robert E. Homans (*Pat Burke*); Dorothy Gee (*Nails' Girl*); Purnell Pratt (*Officer Powers*); Lee Phelps (*Steve, the Bartender*); Nanci Price, Helen Parrish and Dorothy Gray (*Little Girls*); Ben Hendricks III (*Bugs as a Boy*); Eddie Kane (*Joe, the Headwaiter*); Douglas Gerrard (*Assistant Tailor*); Sam McDaniel (*Black Headwaiter*); William H. Strauss (*Pawnbroker*); Snitz Edwards (*Hack*); Landers Stevens (*Doctor*); Russ Powell (*Bartender*).

In that popular genre of the gangster film—which, for a long time, seemed virtually patented, owned, copyrighted and supplied only by Warner Bros., that most socially-conscious of Hollywood studios—there remain a pair of early-sound classics that were frequently revived over the years in theatrical double-bills—*Little Caesar* and *The Public Enemy*. And, if the former made a major movie star out of bulldog-faced Edward G. Robinson, the latter definitely gave tremendous impetus to the motion picture career of pugnacious, bantam-sized James Cagney.

Prior to *The Public Enemy*, Cagney had, under his Warners contract, been getting the build-up in secondary roles. Only one had been in a gangster film, *Doorway to Hell*, which starred Lew Ayres. Originally, *The Public Enemy* had been assigned to Warner "house" director Archie Mayo, with Edward Woods in the leading role of incipient mobster Tom Powers and with Cagney in the secondary role of his buddy, Matt Doyle. Actually, the studio had little faith in this project, reasoning that the gangster-film craze had just about run its course. But another Warner Bros. director, William A. Wellman, who had managed to read a copy of the screenplay, convinced producer Darryl F. Zanuck that *he*, Wellman, should direct and that he would make it "the toughest goddamn one of them all." He also argued for Cagney's playing the Powers role, switching places with Woods, and after Wellman made an issue out of it, the change was accomplished. Zanuck later took credit for this inspired stroke of casting, as he also did for the infamous grapefruit scene in which a bored Cagney pushes the fruit into the face of his whining mistress, Mae Clarke. That, too, sprang from the directorial genius of Wellman, who later remarked, "When I made *The Public Enemy*, I was way ahead in thinking. No love story, but loaded with sex and violence."

The sex is chiefly supplied by slinky, platinum-tressed Jean Harlow, then still an actress-in-the-making with her best years ahead of her at MGM. But the natural sexual magnetism is very evidently present, and her scenes with Cagney generate the necessary chemistry. Mae Clarke had much better roles in a number of other movies of that era, especially *Waterloo Bridge*, *Frankenstein* and *The Front Page*. But it would be her unfortunate fate that she would always be remembered mainly for that grapefruit bit with Cagney.

Cagney and Woods play two childhood buddies growing up in a Chicago ghetto that's a natural breeding ground for the petty criminal. They serve a fence for stolen goods as teen-agers, and one day the pair stage a holdup and kill a cop. Their future is mapped out for them. Next they turn to driving trucks for bootleggers, which brings in the money that enables them to wear expensive clothes and attract flashy women. Tom can fool his widowed mother, but his war-vet brother Mike (Donald Cook) disapproves of Tom, and refuses to have anything to do with the rackets.

Dumping his first girlfriend, Kitty (Clarke) for the sexy Gwen (Harlow), Tom settles an old score by killing Putty Nose (Murray Kinnell), as well as a horse that throws and kills his friend Nails (Leslie Fenton). In a gun battle with a rival mob, Matt dies and Tom is wounded. Finally, the other gang members spirit Tom from his hospital bed, riddle his body with bullets and leave him on his mother's

THE PUBLIC ENEMY: Edward Woods, Murray Kinnell and James Cagney.

THE PUBLIC ENEMY: Edward Woods and James Cagney.

THE PUBLIC ENEMY: Edward Woods, Joan Blondell, James Cagney and Mae Clarke.

doorstep. When his brother answers the doorbell, Tom's mummy-wrapped corpse crashes to the hall floor. It's an ending that continues to shock today.

Cagney's natural charisma and cocky charm make his Tom Powers a "public enemy" who's both engaging and repulsive, all at the same time. As such, Cagney obviously did his bit to help establish that now-long-familiar figure of the antihero who possesses enough charm to make an audience root for his lawless triumphs, despite the reprehensibility of his actions.

In his book *Cagney by Cagney*, the actor adds an interesting footnote to *The Public Enemy*, calling it "one of the first low-budget million-dollar grossers in the business." He also reveals, "The whole thing came in for $151,000, and it took us just 26 days to make."

AN AMERICAN TRAGEDY

1931

CREDITS

A Paramount Picture. Director: Josef von Sternberg. Screenwriters: Samuel Hoffenstein and (uncredited) Josef von Sternberg. Based on the novel by Theodore Dreiser. Cinematographer: Lee Garmes. Art Director: Hans Dreier. Running Time: 96 minutes.

CAST

Phillips Holmes (*Clyde Griffiths*); Sylvia Sidney (*Roberta Alden*); Frances Dee (*Sondra Finchley*); Irving Pichel (*Orville Mason*); Frederick Burton (*Samuel Griffiths*); Claire McDowell (*Mrs. Samuel Griffiths*); Wallace Middleton (*Gilbert Griffiths*); Lucille La Verne (*Mrs. Asa Griffiths*); Charles B. Middleton (*Jephson*); Emmett Corrigan (*Belknap*); Albert Hart (*Titus Alden*); Fanny Midgley (*Mrs. Alden*); Arline Judge (*Bella Griffiths*); Evelyn Pierce (*Bertine Cranston*); Elizabeth Forrester (*Jill Trumbell*); Arnold Korff (*Judge*); Imboden Parrish (*Earl Newcomb*); Russell Powell (*Coroner Fred Heit*); Richard Kramer (*Deputy Sheriff Kraut*).

Theodore Dreiser's voluminous 1925 novel was based on the sensational 1906 murder trial of lower-class Chester Gillette, who was sentenced to the electric chair for drowning his girlfriend in order to marry into society. Dreiser's book centers on a youth who attempts to surmount the poverty and hopeless-

AN AMERICAN TRAGEDY: Sylvia Sidney and Phillips Holmes.

ness of his Midwestern background, only to be swept away by his association with the wealth of Eastern society. A dramatization by Patrick Kearney proved a Broadway success in 1926 with Morgan Farley as the young man, Clyde Griffiths, Miriam Hopkins as Sondra, the society girl he wants, and Katherine Wilson as Roberta, the factory girl he loves, leaves and eventually murders.

Paramount paid Dreiser $150,000 for the movie rights and in 1929 engaged the notable Russian filmmaker Sergei Eisenstein as director. But the screenplay that Eisenstein developed in collaboration with Grigori Alexandrov and Ivor Montagu failed to gain the approval of Paramount's Jesse Lasky, and Eisenstein left the country, while others tackled the project. Josef von Sternberg, the flamboyant stylist who had made a sensation of his German discovery, Marlene Dietrich, in *The Blue Angel*, *Morocco* and *Dishonored*, was assigned to direct a low budget version of this already costly property.

Sternberg later claimed that the screenplay he used, employing dialogue from Dreiser's novel, was essentially his own, allowing however that the onscreen-credited Samuel Hoffenstein had collaborated with him on the treatment. While Eisenstein's approach had leaned toward social criticism, Sternberg's film concentrated on Clyde's sexual obsessions and his self-destructive ambitions. Dreiser's contract with Paramount guaranteed him the right to read the screen adaptation of his work, and he was sufficiently displeased to unsuccessfully sue the studio over the results—claiming that the film "outraged" his book.

Josef von Sternberg's films are usually noteworthy for their pictorial exoticism, and are generally recognizable for their atmosphere, the result of the director's imaginative approach to matters of light and shadow. He would frequently shoot through partial obstructions (beaded curtains, Venetian blinds, etc.) or soften the focus of his cameras. As Ephraim Katz eloquently puts it in *The Film Encyclopedia*, "Sternberg used the camera as a painter's brush or a poet's pen."

Coming amidst the six movies he directed with Dietrich, *An American Tragedy* is the least characteristic of Sternberg's works. But with the aid of Lee Garmes' expert photography, his main focus is on his leading actors: moody, introspective Phillips Holmes as Clyde, whose hollow cheeks and deep-set eyes only occasionally begin to disclose the uncertain machinations behind his facade, and pretty Sylvia Sidney, whose expressive face never fails to mirror the glowing happiness that sometimes illuminates Roberta's wan features, or the uncertain frowns that reveal her fears.

We first see good-looking Clyde Griffiths as a furtively opportunistic bellhop in a Midwestern luxury hotel, where his inclination is to service the female guests' every desire, rather than fraternize with his fellow hotelworkers. Sternberg lets us see that women are naturally attracted to Clyde, despite his general indifference to their glances. Using a distant kinship to a more affluent branch of his family, Clyde becomes the department manager of a group of female factory workers, among whom is the naive Roberta. Gradually responding to his callous manipulations, she allows him to come to her rooming-house, despite being told she may not have visitors. In time, Roberta becomes pregnant and begs Clyde to marry her. He stalls, knowing that should such a union become public, he'd lose his job, since factory fraternization is forbidden. She wins from him a promise of "later," but it's a promise he never intends to keep, having since met the rich and vi-

vacious Sondra Finchley (Frances Dee), with whom he's conducting an affair that promises to lead to marriage—but for the quietly insistent presence of Roberta.

Clyde's amorality finally surfaces sufficiently for him to plan Roberta's murder: he'll invite her to a picnic outing, take her out in a rowboat on a remote Adirondack lake, and drown her. Roberta eagerly accepts his invitation but his odd behavior puzzles and frightens her. While in the boat, she demands to know what's wrong. He spouts out the details of his murderous plot, but admits he can't go through with it. In great agitation, Roberta stands up in the boat and, in an attempt to calm her, Clyde upsets the boat plunging both of them into the lake. Faced now with a true accident, he cannot bring himself to rescue the drowning Roberta and instead he swims to shore.

AN AMERICAN TRAGEDY: Sylvia Sidney.

AN AMERICAN TRAGEDY: Phillips Holmes.

Too many clues eventually point District Attorney Orville Mason (Irving Pichel) to Clyde, and he's arrested for murder. A lengthy trial ensues with Clyde mentally divided by the act he had intended to commit and the rescue he was unable to attempt. The sentence is death in the electric chair.

Faced with difficult roles to characterize and within the boundaries of the Hoffenstein-Sternberg script and production, Holmes and Sidney are most effective. Holmes' handsome face projects little emotional display, for this is a calculating and undemonstrative personality he's portraying. But everything he does is right. And Sidney is tremendously appealing as Roberta. Frances Dee has less to do as Sondra—indeed she quite disappears from the film after Clyde's arrest—but her initial demonstration of confident, affluent sexual aggression is entirely appropriate to such a society girl. As the lawyers who virtually take over the dramatic action during the film's final scenes, Irving Pichel and Charles B. Middleton are encouraged to let their sonorous voices and melodramatic tendencies go a bit overboard.

Sternberg's *An American Tragedy* has long been overshadowed by George Stevens' much more rewarding 1951 remake, *A Place in the Sun*, but the 1931 movie fully deserves another look.

THE YELLOW TICKET

1931

THE YELLOW TICKET: Laurence Olivier.

CREDITS

A Fox Film. Director: Raoul Walsh. Screenwriters: Jules Furthman and Guy Bolton. Based on the play by Michael Morton. Cinematographer: James Wong Howe. Editor: Jack Murray. Sound: Donald Flick. Music Director: Carli Elinor. Running Time: 83 minutes.

CAST

Elissa Landi (*Marya Kalish*); Lionel Barrymore (*Baron Igor Andreev*); Laurence Olivier (*Julian Rolfe*); Walter Byron (*Count Nikolai*); Arnold Korff (*Grandfather Kalish*); Mischa Auer (*Melchior*); Edwin Maxwell (*Alexis Balikoff*); Rita LaRoy (*Fania Rubinstein*); Sarah Padden (*Mother Kalish*); Boris Karloff (*Orderly*); Henry Kolker (*Passport Officer*); Gilbert Emery (*Hubert*); Ed Mortimer (*Nightclub Patron*).

Director Raoul Walsh (1887–1981) was usually at his best with action and melodrama, especially with stories of crime, war and the Old West. In his 50-year movie career there were, of course, exceptions. One such was *The Yellow Ticket*, based on an old stage thriller by Michael Morton that had teamed John Barrymore with Florence Reed for a 183-performance run in 1914. The first screen version was in 1916, titled *The Yellow Passport*, a lavish production starring Clara Kimball Young. Another version surfaced two years later (*The Yellow Ticket*), this time with Fannie Ward, Warner Oland and Milton Sills. Because it dealt heavily with prostitution, Jewish persecution and Russian nihilism, *Variety*, while admiring the movie's production values, hesitated to recommend it: "It is doubtful whether it will ever be a popular program feature, as it is hardly a subject which will appeal to the average neighborhood or family picture house."

But *The Yellow Ticket* was to appear yet again in 1931, in a handsome Fox production with an excellent cast topped by Elissa Landi, Lionel Barrymore (in the role his brother John had originated) and the novice British film actor Laurence Olivier.

In 1913 Czarist Russia, Jewess Marya Kalish (Elissa Landi) is confined to the area of Kiev where she teaches school. But a letter arrives informing her that her father lies dying in a St. Petersburg prison. She learns that the only way she will be allowed to travel there is to pose as a prostitute. She pays a madam handsomely to get the needed "yellow passport." Marya reaches her destination, only to find her father dead, an apparent victim of police brutality. She curses his killers and swears revenge. She's briefly "befriended" by Baron Andreev (Lionel Barrymore), head of the Czarist secret police, and his aide Count Nikolai (Walter Byron), who attempt to take advantage of her. Marya is subsequently arrested by the police for failing to "register," and is

THE YELLOW TICKET: Elissa Landi and Laurence Olivier.

THE YELLOW TICKET: Walter Byron, Lionel Barrymore, Laurence Olivier, Elissa Landi and Gilbert Emery.

thrown into prison. Once out of jail, she sets about improving her lot by getting a job selling cosmetics for a German firm. On a train, she meets Julian Rolphe (Laurence Olivier), a handsome, outgoing British journalist who's in Russia to write about social conditions.

The authorities (in this case Andreev and Nikolai) find his articles inflammatory since they expose corrupt police methods, bad prison conditions, etc. They cleverly reason his source for this information must be a woman, and it doesn't take them long to track him down and find he's now keeping steady company with Marya. They all meet one night in a fashionable nightclub and, when Julian leaves to take care of a breaking story, Andreev moves in on Marya, insisting that he's met her somewhere before. He then remembers she's the girl with the yellow ticket, and he begins to plot how he can get her for himself. Meanwhile, back at Marya's apartment, Julian asks her to marry him, and she spills out the whole story of her background and her yellow passport. Julian's feelings about her are unchanged. Later, Andreev has one of his officials bring Marya to his living quarters where he tells her that Julian's articles must stop, but that he, Andreev, can protect her—or he can send her to a fate worse than death:

the quicksilver mines. She's soon convinced of his duplicity, and when he forces himself upon her, she kills him with one of his own pistols.

With the secret police in pursuit, Marya and Julian nevertheless manage to pull some strings and have a plane awaiting them at the airport. And, when last seen, they're winging off into the skies, presumably for a safer future in England.

Much of *The Yellow Ticket* is little more than good, old-fashioned melodrama. What saves it from becoming just another cliffhanging serial is the knowing direction of Raoul Walsh, as well as the excellence of his cast. In a potentially ham-laden role, Lionel Barrymore underplays the villainy (and even finds humor) in Baron Andreev. Elissa Landi is completely believable, and Laurence Olivier, still more at home on stage than on screen, nevertheless delivers with aplomb his romantic-minded journalist. And James Wong Howe's expert camerawork makes them all look beautiful. Films like *The Yellow Ticket* seem dated and rather amusing, but now and then they're fun to spend 83 minutes with.

GIRLS ABOUT TOWN

1931

CREDITS

A Paramount Picture. Director: George Cukor. Screenwriters: Raymond Griffith and Brian Marlow. Based on a story by Zoë Akins. Cinematographer: Ernest Haller. Costumes: Travis Banton. Running Time: 66 minutes.

CAST

Kay Francis (*Wanda Howard*); Joel McCrea (*Jim Baker*); Lilyan Tashman (*Marie Bailey*); Eugene Pallette (*Benjamin Thomas*); Allan Dinehart (*Jerry Chase*); Lucille Webster Gleason (*Mrs. Benjamin Thomas*); Anderson Lawler (*Alex Howard*); Lucille Browne (*Edna*); George Barbier (*Webster*); Robert McWade (*Simms*); Louise Beavers (*Hattie*); Judith Wood (*Winnie*); Adrienne Ames (*Anne*); Claire Dodd (*Dot*); Hazel Howard (*Joy*); Patricia Caron (*Billie*); Katherine DeMille (*Girl*).

Girls About Town is very much a motion picture of its time. Its glamorous, gold-digging tarts put on airs and travel in expensive circles, but never seem to have any visible social background or source of in-

GIRLS ABOUT TOWN: Anderson Lawler and Kay Francis.

come. Zoë Akins had written *Girls About Town*'s original story on a theme similar to her 1930 stage comedy, *The Greeks Had a Word for It*. But while the latter work has its three heroines hunting for husbands, in *Girls About Town* they're simply after money and the stuff that glitters. Director George Cukor puts the blame for the script's ambiguities on the censors of 1931: "They had lovely clothes and lots of money and a succession of rich men who were mad about them, but they always said 'Good night' at the door." In fact, *Girls About Town* goes to elaborate means to cloud the issue. In one sequence, apartment house roommates Kay Francis and Lilyan Tashman successively arrive home with separate escorts from the same party, each to go through the routine of looking up at a high window and exclaiming that she can't invite the gentleman in, since she can see her mother waiting up for her. "Mother" turns out to be their black maid Hattie (Louise Beavers), window-posed like Whistler's Mother in shawl and dust cap.

Marie (Tashman) and Wanda (Francis, with her dialogue practically devoid of those pesky "r" words that still convulse old-movie buffs) are pals who share fancy quarters and frequently double-date well-heeled older men who revel in the attention these enterprising young women are accustomed to dispensing on call. Marie is blonde, vivacious and a life-of-the-party type, while dark-haired Wanda is quieter and more soulful. Both are stylish dressers with wardrobes for all occasions. They're invited aboard a yacht, where Marie is paired with a good-looking but boring young introvert, Jim Baker (Joel McCrea); his paunchy older pal, the tight-wad practical joker Ben Thomas (Eugene Pallette), teams up with the equally disinterested Wanda. However, the women soon agree to switch partners. Meanwhile, a

GIRLS ABOUT TOWN: Lilyan Tashman, Eugene Pallette and Joel McCrea.

GIRLS ABOUT TOWN: Kay Francis and Lilyan Tashman.

genuine love affair develops between Jim and Wanda after he rescues her from drowning while swimming. Marie's sense of humor impresses Ben sufficiently to net her a few glittering baubles.

Complications ensue when it's revealed that Wanda still has a husband named Alex (Anderson Lawler) in her background. Alex arrives and manages

GIRLS ABOUT TOWN: Joel McCrea, Kay Francis and Lilyan Tashman.

to blackmail the disillusioned Jim, who decides he's through with Wanda. She, in turn, has it out with Alex, only to discover that their marriage was legally dissolved long ago. In the interim, Ben's suspicious wife (Lucile Webster Gleason) has also arrived on the scene to complicate *his* life. Eventually, Wanda patches it up with Jim, and Marie's quick wits not only allay the fears of Ben's wife, but they actually end up in a good-natured three-way friendship.

Highlighting this comedic romp are the performances of Lilyan Tashman, Eugene Pallette and Lucile Webster Gleason, all of whom have the brightest lines and situations. Kay Francis has the more serious scenes, although the sequence in which she and Tashman desperately endeavor to raise cash by auctioning off their gowns, furs and jewels is well and energetically played for laughs, and well paced by director George Cukor. It was Cukor who was largely responsible for tailoring this film to showcase the wonderful style and sense of humor of his good friend Tashman, whose prior roles too often had kept her in heavy dramatic situations. Twenty-six-year-old Joel McCrea, in only the second year of his long film career, is handsome and colorless, though already in possession of more poise and style than most young actors of today at his age. But at recent viewings of *Girls About Town*, those who have seen it for the first time all come away raving about Tashman. For them, she's the film's delightful revelation. Unfortunately, she died of cancer in 1934, aged only 35.

FRANKENSTEIN

1931

CREDITS

A Universal Picture. Producer: Carl Laemmle, Jr. Director: James Whale. Screenwriters: John L. Balderston, Robert Florey, Garrett Fort and Francis Edward Faragoh. Based on the novel by Mary W. Shelley and the play by Peggy Webling. Cinematographer: Arthur Edeson. Editor: Clarence Kolster. Art Director: Charles D. Hall. Sound: William Hedgecock. Make-Up: Jack P. Pierce. Technical Advisor: Dr. Cecil Reynolds. Running Time: 71 minutes.

CAST

Colin Clive (*Henry Frankenstein*); Mae Clarke (*Elizabeth*); John Boles (*Victor Moritz*); Boris Karloff (*The Monster*); Edward Van Sloan (*Dr. Waldman*); Frederic Kerr (*Baron Frankenstein*); Dwight Frye (*Fritz*); Lionel Belmore (*Burgomaster Vogel*); Marilyn Harris (*Maria, the Little Girl*);

Michael Mark (*Ludwig*); Arletta Duncan and Pauline Moore (*Bridesmaids*); Francis Ford (*Villager*).

British-born James Whale (1889–1957) began his career as a trained graphics artist who turned newspaper cartoonist during World War I. And after his release from a prisoner-of-war camp, he shifted his interests to the theatre, where he began acting and designing sets. That led him into stage directing in the Twenties, where his greatest success was R.C. Sheriff's play *Journey's End*. He was hired in 1930 to direct the film version. This was followed by Universal's excellent 1931 adaptation of the play *Waterloo Bridge*, a movie overshadowed—and undoubtedly suppressed by—MGM's more glossy and glamorous remake of 1940. Next came the first of four great horror films by which Whale is still best known—*Frankenstein*.

Mary Shelley's classic Gothic novel had first reached the screen in a 1910 silent Edison one-reeler with Charles Ogle as the monster, followed by a lesser-known 1915 adaptation starring Percy Standing. But it was Whale's 1931 *Frankenstein* that set the pattern for monster movies to come. Earlier that year, Universal had chilled audiences with Bela Lugosi's *Dracula*, and when *Frankenstein* was in the planning stage, a lengthy test scene was directed by Robert Florey on *Dracula* sets, employing Lugosi as the Monster. However, when it came to activating the project, James Whale was assigned to *Frankenstein* as director, while Florey was, without explanation, moved to another Lugosi horror project, *Murders in the Rue Morgue*.

Whale selected his friend Colin Clive to play the Monster's tormented creator, Henry Frankenstein, and Mae Clarke—his *Waterloo Bridge* star—to take on the relatively thankless role of Henry's bride Elizabeth (Universal contract player Bette Davis had been tested for Elizabeth, but was rejected as "too aggressive"). But the problem of casting a suitable Monster remained—until Whale recalled being impressed by character actor Boris Karloff's strong acting in a recent picture called *The Criminal Code*. Karloff, who was then on the Universal lot filming *Graft*, was signed for the part, and Whale got together with make-up artist Jack Pierce to devise the Monster's appearance. Mae Clarke, who was intensely interested in the movie's behind-the-scenes preparations, later termed Pierce "a genius," remarking, "I remember him working with the still man, taking pictures of each step as the make-up was applied. He would add here and change there, and then ask Whale's opinion."

Pierce himself talked about that make-up in a 1939 *New York Times* interview: "There are six ways

FRANKENSTEIN: Boris Karloff.

FRANKENSTEIN: Dwight Frye, John Boles, Edward Van Sloan, Mae Clarke and Colin Clive.

FRANKENSTEIN: Boris Karloff and Dwight Frye.

a surgeon can cut the skull, and I figured Dr. Frankenstein, who was not a practicing surgeon, would take the easiest. That is, he would cut the top of the skull off, straight across like a pot lid, hinge it, pop the brain in and clamp it tight. That's the reason I decided to make the Monster's head square and flat like a box and dig that scar across his forehead and have two metal clamps hold it together. The two metal studs that stick out the sides of the neck are inlets for electricity—plugs. Don't forget the Monster is an electrical gadget and that lightning is his life force. The lizard eyes were made of rubber, as was his false head. I made his arms look longer by shortening the sleeves of his coat. His legs were stiffened by steel struts and two pairs of pants. His large feet were the boots asphalt-spreaders wear. His fingernails were blackened with shoe polish, and his

FRANKENSTEIN: Colin Clive and Boris Karloff.

face was coated with blue-green greasepaint, which photographs gray."

Playing the Monster was no picnic for Karloff. He was in agony from start to finish, emotionally as well as physically. Heavy padding and 30-pound weighted boots made movement difficult, in addition to the built-up head and heavy make-up designed to increase the actor's size to a massive seven feet, six inches. And there was little sympathy from director Whale, who insisted on endless takes of a scene in which the Monster carries Henry Frankenstein uphill to the mill for the film's exciting climax.

Despite the technical improvements in motion pictures in the nearly 60 years since *Frankenstein* was made, there is no denying that it remains Hollywood's quintessential monster movie. A dearth of background music helps date it, of course, as well as some of its overwrought performances. But its overall impact remains considerable, and much of that effect is attributable to Karloff's acting. In a role that might have swamped a lesser performer—especially under all that make-up—Karloff's innate gentleness and intelligent approach to that tragic creature make his performance classic. As the actor has said of this role, "His master, the only person he knew, had turned on him; he was helpless, confused and terrified. How could one not feel sympathy?"

Fortunately, *Frankenstein* now lives on on videocassette in a restored version containing footage that was long unseen for censorship reasons—including that sequence involving the Monster's inadvertent drowning of a little girl. Whale's 1935 sequel, *The Bride of Frankenstein*, also with Clive and Karloff, stands as an even better picture than this one, with so many subsequent sequels to follow that the general public has long since lost sight of the fact that it's not the *Monster* who's named "Frankenstein," but his *creator*!

56

PRIVATE LIVES

1931

CREDITS

A Metro-Goldwyn-Mayer Picture. Producer: Albert Lewin. Director: Sidney Franklin. Screenwriters: Hans Kraly, Richard Schayer and Claudine West. Based on the play by Noël Coward. Cinematographer: Ray Binger. Editor: Conrad A. Nervig. Art Director: Cedric Gibbons. Costumes: Adrian. Sound: Douglas Shearer. Song: "Some Day I'll Find You" by Noël Coward. Running Time: 92 minutes.

CAST

Norma Shearer (*Amanda Chase Prynne*); Robert Montgomery (*Elyot Chase*); Reginald Denny (*Victor Prynne*); Una Merkel (*Sibyl Chase*); Jean Hersholt (*Oscar*); George Davis (*Bellboy*).

This most farcially sophisticated of all Noël Coward's comedies was devised as a stage vehicle for himself and Gertrude Lawrence. These two luminaries played it together first in London and then on Broadway, where it ran for 248 performances. The only important supporting roles were filled by a young Laurence Olivier and his first wife Jill Esmond.

MGM production chief Irving Thalberg sensed that *Private Lives* would be an apt vehicle for his wife Norma Shearer. He teamed her with Robert Montgomery, with whom she had previously worked in the more dramatic *Their Own Desire*, *The Divorcee* and *Strangers May Kiss*. Thalberg had a performance of the play photographed, to help his cast and director Sidney Franklin maintain Coward's impeccable style and pace. The play was "opened up" for the screen to include brief scenes of weddings and mountain climbing.

Montgomery was already identified with comedy, but Shearer had spent most of her career confined to heavy dramatics. With the actual play as their guide, one can better understand then how Shearer, in particular, so well manages to depart from her usual dramatic posings and enters into the abandoned fun of this stylish farce.

Coward's plot is thin, but deliciously amusing. The filmed *Private Lives* begins with short introductory segments introducing the characters and estab-

PRIVATE LIVES: Robert Montgomery and Norma Shearer.

lishing their relationships by showing us a full church wedding for Montgomery and whiney and boring Una Merkel, and a modest civil ceremony for Shearer and dull and stuffy Reginald Denny. Previously, Shearer had been wed to Montgomery, a fact known to both of their new spouses. But what no one yet knows is that they've booked adjoining suites at the same French honeymoon hotel. Shearer is first to discover Montgomery on their mutual balcony, while Denny and Merkel are elsewhere, each having already begun quarreling with their respective bride and bridegroom. Discovering that not only are they compatible but also

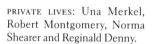
PRIVATE LIVES: Norma Shearer and Robert Montgomery.

still in love with one another, Shearer and Montgomery pack their bags and steal away together, just missing their returning mates, who are left to commiserate over mutual notes of farewell.

The scene changes to a Swiss chalet in the mountains, where Shearer and Montgomery have retreated to live in sin, but where, as before, their tempestuous natures soon clash. And as they engage in a knockdown-dragout battle that lays waste to their living room, Merkel and Denny enter. After things simmer down, the couples manage to sort things out and resume their ill-matched legal ties at the next day's breakfast. But then, as Denny and Merkel enter into an intense quarrel, Shearer and Montgomery once again steal away, this time presumably for good.

Sidney Franklin's firm directorial hand allows the movie to start slowly; but as soon as Shearer discovers ex-hubby Montgomery is present for her second honeymoon, all hell breaks loose, and the pace noticeably quickens, never to slacken until the film's close. Norma Shearer and Robert Montgomery were probably the closest match that Hollywood could then cast to equal Gertrude Lawrence and Noël Coward. Their delightful interacting is still a pleasure to watch on TV many years later. To date, *Private Lives* has never again been filmed.

PRIVATE LIVES: Una Merkel, Robert Montgomery, Norma Shearer and Reginald Denny.

A HOUSE DIVIDED

1931

A HOUSE DIVIDED: Helen Chandler and Walter Huston.

CREDITS

A Universal Picture. Producer: Paul Kohner. Director: William Wyler. Screenwriters: John B. Clymer, Dale Van Every and John Huston. Based on the story *Heart and Hand* by Olive Edens. Cinematographer: Charles Stumar. Editor: Ted Kent. Running Time: 70 minutes.

CAST

Walter Huston (*Seth Law*); Kent Douglass (*Matt Law*); Helen Chandler (*Ruth Evans*); Vivian Oakland (*Bess*); Frank Hagney (*Mann*); Mary Foy (*Mary*); Lloyd Ingraham (*Doctor*); Charles Middleton (*Minister*); Walter Brennan (*Man*).

This early and rarely seen William Wyler talkie (his third) has always been written about in terms of Eugene O'Neill and Lon Chaney. It is easy to see

A HOUSE DIVIDED: Walter Huston and Kent Douglass (Douglass Montgomery).

why. The plot's basic structure—though it derives from an Olive Edens magazine story called *Heart and Hand*—bears an uncanny resemblance to O'Neill's prize-winning play *Desire Under the Elms*. In reviewing *A House Divided*, *Variety*'s critic naively wrote, "Thematically, it's the sort of thing Eugene O'Neill would doubtless like to have tackled," perhaps unmindful of the fact that the playwright had already done so eight years earlier. In both cases, a middle-aged widower with contempt for his grown offspring takes a young, second wife, only to find his new bride involved with his son—all of which leads to a tragic ending.

References to Lon Chaney obviously spring from the strong central performance of Walter Huston, the film's rugged New England fisherman, who believes in passing his leisure time in the company of straight liquor and whatever women he can find. But it's the accident that cripples Huston's character halfway through the movie that most likely resembles many of Chaney's more memorable performances in which that actor was often given to depicting physically crippled men. As Huston's angry, undefeated Seth Law drags himself about his home, refusing help and even mounting a staircase the hard way, it is Chaney who most readily comes to the viewer's mind.

None of these similarities should be allowed to spoil the enjoyment of *A House Divided*, should one get the opportunity to see it. Today, undoubtedly its chief appeal is that it's a Wyler film, made in the years before that major director began winning awards, not only for himself but also for the actors and actresses who usually delivered their best work under his difficult but inspiring guidance.

Walter Huston was always an impressive actor. Following years of dedicated theatrical performances, he entered motion pictures with the beginnings of sound, when he was already past 40. Although still a handsome and youthful man, he was more given to assuming what is generally referred to as "character acting." In *A House Divided*, his Seth Law is a man at once simple and complex. The story begins with the funeral of Law's first wife and the mother of his son Matt, a difficult role well enacted by Kent Douglass (perhaps better known today by the name he later used, Douglass Montgomery). Sensitive and disinterested in the family fishing tradition, Matt longs to leave his rugged surroundings for a more civilized future. There's little understanding between this father and son, and no love lost. But without a woman in the house (their most recent housekeeper has left in a huff, unable to cope with Seth's rough demands), Matt agrees to take on

A HOUSE DIVIDED: Helen Chandler, Walter Huston and Kent Douglass (Douglass Montgomery).

the cooking while his father answers responses to a magazine advertising mail-order brides.

Seth's bride arrives, not in the form of the middle-aged woman he was expecting. Young, pretty, shy and blonde Ruth Evans (Helen Chandler) soon realizes the impossible situation into which she's walked. And she nearly leaves to return to the farming community from which she's come—only to be deterred by Matt, who begs her to stay. The loveless marriage of Seth to Ruth takes place, but before it can be consummated, Seth and Matt engage in a brutal fight, and Seth is crippled in an accidental fall. As time passes, Matt and Ruth fall in love and plan to run away together. But before they can do so, a fierce storm arrives and breaks the mooring of the fishing vessel on which Ruth is waiting for Matt. As father and son unite in an effort to rescue her, Seth's rowboat capsizes and he is drowned, while Matt saves Ruth for a happier ending to the grim story.

Wyler's already firm hand is evident in the strong, atmospheric fashion in which this moody tale unfolds, as well as in the uniform excellence of the acting. Kent Douglass, faced with depicting sensitivity that must nevertheless mask a character with quiet backbone, succeeds in preventing audience alienation by walking a thin line between the artistic and the basic. We are asked to believe that his lack of coordination keeps him from scoring as a fisherman, not the fact that his heart isn't in that profession. Yet he *seems* quietly capable of manual labor. From his father's derisive attitude toward Matt, one might at first take him for homosexual, an angle that would hardly fit into such a drama from its era. Nor does Matt's interest in Ruth seem anything but genuine. He's willing to be her man, but not his father's, and perhaps that's because *no* son could likely meet Seth's demanding expectations.

In a role for which Bette Davis remembers testing (Wyler's insulting attitude toward her was recalled to the director when they united seven years later for the Oscar-winning *Jezebel*), mystic-eyed Helen Chandler gradually reveals the spunk that lies beneath her sweet, demure facade. That Wyler's three leading actors came to him with stage experience is evident in the details of their playing. A *House Divided* remains a worthwhile drama, undeserving of its present obscurity.

MATA HARI

1931

MATA HARI: Greta Garbo.

CREDITS

A Metro-Goldwyn-Mayer Picture. Producer: Irving Thalberg. Director: George Fitzmaurice. Screenwriters: Benjamin Glazer, Leo Birinski, Doris Anderson and Gilbert Emery. Cinematographer: William Daniels. Editor: Frank Sullivan. Costumes: Adrian. Running Time: 90 minutes.

CAST

Greta Garbo (*Mata Hari*); Ramon Novarro (*Lt. Alexis Rosanoff*); Lionel Barrymore (*Gen. Serge Shubin*); Lewis Stone (*Andriani*); C. Henry Gordon (*Dubois*); Karen Morley (*Carlotta*); Alec B. Francis (*Caron*); Blanche Frederici (*Sister Angelica*); Edmund Breese (*Warden*); Helen Jerome Eddy (*Sister Genevieve*); Frank Reicher (*The Cook*); Sarah Padden (*Sister Theresa*); Harry Cording (*Ivan*); Gordon De Main (*Aide*); Mischa Auer (*Executed Man*); Michael Visaroff (*Orderly*); Cecil Cunningham (*Gambler*).

Mata Hari, that near-mythical, exotic dancer/spy of World War I, has long been a creature that fascinates filmmakers. In 1921, Denmark's Asta Nielsen starred in a German production entitled *Die Spionin* (*The Spy*). And there followed Germany's 1927 *Mata Hari, die Rote Tanzerin* (*Mata Hari, the Red Dancer*) with Magda Sonja. In more recent times, Jeanne

MATA HARI: Lewis Stone and Karen Morley.

Moreau portrayed the legend in the 1965 French film *Mata Hari, Agent H-21*, and soft-core porn star Sylvia Kristel did what was expected of her in 1985's *Mata Hari*. But, for exotic mystery and genuine star quality, none has outdone Greta Garbo's 1931 *Mata Hari*, bizarrely costumed by Adrian and lovingly photographed by William Daniels.

Without question, Garbo's Mata Hari bears little resemblance, beyond the barest outlines, to the real story of the fortyish Dutch dancer whose real name was Margaretha Geertruida Zelle (1876–1917), and who spied for Germany during The Great War. True, she betrayed vital military secrets confided to her by the many Allied officers with whom she was intimate. And it's also a fact that she was arrested, condemned and executed by a French firing squad in 1917. But from there, a quartet of Metro writers (Benjamin Glazer, Leo Birinski, Doris Anderson and Gilbert Emery) wove their own fanciful tale of a Mata Hari that could only have come from Hollywood.

Like Josef von Sternberg's similarly themed *Dishonored*—filmed at the same time as *Mata Hari*,

MATA HARI: Greta Garbo and Lionel Barrymore.

with Paramount's answer to Garbo, Marlene Dietrich—the MGM spy story blends sex, intrigue and exotic atmosphere to deliver what some might term movieland "camp." Dietrich would undoubtedly dismiss it all as *kitsch*. *Mata Hari* opens in Paris, where that lady (Garbo) disguises her spying by masquerading as an Oriental dancer. Under the orders of Andriani (Lewis Stone), she's assigned to intercept Russian messages concerning Allied troop maneuvers. She's also a longtime mistress of the indiscreet General Shubin (Lionel Barrymore) until she encounters Lieutenant Rosanoff (Ramon Novarro), a handsome young Russian flier, to whom she's immediately attracted—and he to her.

When she discovers that Rosanoff has the information she needs, Mata Hari puts duty before love and seduces him, while her colleagues copy down the information. Shubin finds out about their night together, and he jealously threatens to expose her activities and Rosanoff as well. In desperation, Mata Hari kills her former protector and sends Rosanoff back to Russia. But his plane is shot down, blinding him in the crash. When she hears of his misfortune, she hurries to his side to assure him of her love. Andriani then directs a henchman to kill her, but his mission is foiled. However, Mata Hari is unmasked and arrested, tried and sentenced to die. Before her execution, she arranges for a last meeting with Rosanoff, managing to shield him from the truth by leading him to believe she's dying in a prison hospital. She's then killed by a firing squad.

George Fitzmaurice, who also directed Garbo in the less successful *As You Desire Me*, released the following year, was known as a specialist in the lush romanticism of which *Mata Hari* remains a prime example. Garbo is first seen, albeit none too clearly, executing a dance of erotic mystery, attired in veils and a Javanese headdress. As photographed by her pet cameraman William Daniels, she's either partially obscured by the decor or shot at an extreme distance, while an intrigued gaggle of military men looks on. And there appears to be some doubt as to how much of that dancing is actually Garbo's, especially as it's a known fact that a double named Geraldine Dvorak occasionally pinch-hit for Garbo in long shots.

It would be interesting to know what personal fantasies inspired MGM's house designer Adrian to create the various extreme costumes in which he showcases Garbo here, for never in her entire 17-year career did she wear such a stunningly unusual array of bejewelled silks, sequinned lamés, velvets and brocades. Each outfit seems more outlandish than the one before, with headgear and earrings to match—until Mata Hari is ultimately reduced, in the final scenes, to stark black clothing and severely slicked-down hair. Obviously, Adrian was allowed his complete freedom, and the results are spectacular in the extreme.

With his Hispanic features and slight Mexican accent, Ramon Novarro's Russian flier seems like odd casting. And he's no match for Garbo in the romance department. But Lionel Barrymore and Lewis Stone offer solid acting support, and the

MATA HARI: Ramon Novarro and Greta Garbo.

63

memorably intense visage of C. Henry Gordon adds an appropriately sinister note to his scenes as Mata Hari's French nemesis, Dubois. In a black wig, blonde Karen Morley is seen to advantage as another spy named Carlotta, who's ordered to be killed when she allows her business sense to be swayed by love; obviously, this character is included as an object lesson for any woman who dares act so boldly as to proclaim—as does our heroine—"I am Mata Hari—and my own master."

THE MAN WHO PLAYED GOD

1932

CREDITS

A Warners Bros. Picture. Producer: Jack L. Warner. Director: John G. Adolfi. Screenwriters: Julien Josephson and Maude Howell. Based on a short story by Gouverneur Morris and the play *The Silent Voice* by Jules Eckert Goodman. Cinematographer: James Van Trees. Editor: William Holmes. Music and piano solos: Salvatore Santaella. Running Time: 81 minutes.

CAST

George Arliss (*Montgomery Royale*); Violet Heming (*Mildred Miller*); Ivan Simpson (*Battle*); Louise Closser Hale (*Florence Royale*); Bette Davis (*Grace Blair*); Andre Luguet (*The King*); Donald Cook (*Harold Van Adam*); Charles E. Evans (*The Doctor*); Oscar Apfel (*The Lip Reader*); Paul Porcasi (*French Concert Manager*); Raymond Milland (*Eddie*); Dorothy Libaire (*Jenny*); William Janney (*First Boy*); Grace Durkin (*First Girl*); Russell Hopton (*Reporter*); Murray Kinnell (*King's Aide*); Harry Stubbs (*Chittendon*); Hedda Hopper (*Alice Chittendon*); Wade Boteler (*Detective*); Alexander Ikonikoff, Michael Visaroff and Paul Panzer (*Russian Officers*).

As with *The Green Goddess* and *Disraeli*, the distinguished character actor George Arliss (he was often billed as *Mr.* George Arliss) filmed both silent and talkie versions of *The Man Who Played God*, which was based on Gouverneur Morris' short story and the 1914 stage play by Jules Eckert Goodman, *The Silent Voice*. Arliss was then a prestigious star at Warner Bros., at the same time that young, stage-trained Bette Davis was circulating about Hollywood, taking ingenue roles in pictures of steadily decreasing importance like *Way Back Home*, *The*

Menace and *Hell's House*—all released in 1932. After six motion pictures, the actress believed she was a failure in movieland and should return to New York to salvage the remains of her once-promising acting career. But the day before she and her mother were to return East, there was a telephone call from George Arliss. Because Murray Kinnell, a fellow player in *The Menace*, had recommended her, Arliss was interested in considering her for the female lead in his next picture, *The Man Who Played God*. Could she, he asked, meet with him the next day to discuss the possibilities?

Despite his age (64), his wizened appearance and his eccentric acting style, George Arliss was then a popular star. At Warner Bros., he had won an Academy Award for *Disraeli*, and such other Arliss vehicles as *The Green Goddess*, *Old English* and *Alexander Hamilton* were financially successful for the studio. So the prospect of playing opposite Arliss was exciting for Davis.

The two realized immediate rapport. Their training in live theatre and their dedication to the craft of acting helped them establish a unity of approach that assured Arliss he was right in selecting her for the film. Davis had called *The Man Who Played God* her most important picture. "I did others I liked better," she later recalled. "But there was something about appearing as Mr. Arliss' leading lady which gave me standing. I owe him the career that finally emerged." Indeed, Arliss liked her well enough to cast her opposite him again the following year in *The Working Man*.

THE MAN WHO PLAYED GOD:
Bette Davis.

The Man Who Played God centers on Montgomery Royale (Arliss), a celebrated, middle-aged concert pianist who loses his hearing in a bombing incident, and eventually comes to help others by reading lips. His admiring young fiancée Grace (Davis) remains faithful to the musician after his career is suddenly finished, despite her actual love for Harold (Donald Cook), a youth of her own age. The predicament is resolved when Royale lip-reads a meeting between Grace and Harold, and realizes that the girl plans to give up her future for him. He breaks their engagement to find happiness with Mildred Miller (Broadway actress Violet Heming in a rare movie role), a mature woman who has always loved him. And Royale finds musical rewards playing "Onward, Christian Soldiers" on a church organ.

In his autobiography *My Ten Years in the Studio*, George Arliss wrote: "I think that only two or three times in my experience have I ever got from an actor at rehearsal something beyond what I realized in the part. Bette Davis proved to be one of the exceptions. I did not expect anything but a nice little performance. But when we rehearsed, she startled me; the nice little part became a deep and vivid creation, and I felt rather humbled that this young girl had been able to discover and portray something that my imagination had failed to conceive. She startled me because, quite unexpectedly, I got from her a flash

THE MAN WHO PLAYED GOD: Bette Davis and George Arliss.

THE MAN WHO PLAYED GOD: Bette Davis, George Arliss, Louise Closser Hale, Donald Cook and Violet Heming.

65

that illuminated mere words and inspired them with passion and emotion."

For Bette Davis, George Arliss truly played God. Not only did he assist John Adolfi in her direction (Davis claims that Arliss was the film's *real* director—as with all his films), but he also saw that exceptional care was taken with her make-up, hairdo and wardrobe. Her natural ash-blonde hair was lightened; she emerged a stylish golden-blonde whose intense performance impressed Warners enough to win her a five-year studio contract with yearly options.

Those who look closely at *The Man Who Played God* will spot future star Ray (then billed as "Raymond") Milland as the male half of a troubled young couple on whom Royale spies from his park-side window, and whose lips he reads sufficiently to be able to give them aid.

The Man Who Played God was ineffectually remade in 1955 as *Sincerely Yours*, the only starring vehicle Hollywood ever produced as a showcase for the flamboyant pianist Liberace. With Dorothy Malone and Joanne Dru as his leading ladies, it was neither an artistic nor financial success.

TARZAN THE APE MAN: Johnny Weissmuller.

TARZAN THE APE MAN

1932

CREDITS

A Metro-Goldwyn-Mayer Picture. Producer: Irving Thalberg. Director: W.S. Van Dyke. Screenwriters: Cyril Hume and Ivor Novello. Based on the character created by Edgar Rice Burroughs. Cinematographers: Harold Rosson and Clyde DeVinna. Editors: Ben Lewis and Tom Held. Art Director: Cedric Gibbons. Running Time: 99 minutes.

CAST

Johnny Weissmuller (*Tarzan*); Neil Hamilton (*Harry Holt*); Maureen O'Sullivan (*Jane Parker*); C. Aubrey Smith (*James Parker*); Doris Lloyd (*Mrs. Cutten*); Forrester Harvey (*Beamish*); Ivory Williams (*Riano*).

Prior to 1932, the year Tarzan became both a radio serial and a United Features comic strip, Edgar Rice Burroughs' magazine jungle hero of 1912 had become widely known to the public via some 26 books and eight feature films. MGM had realized sufficient profit from 1931's *Trader Horn* (shot largely on location in Africa) to seek out further movie projects in a similar vein, with the result that rights to the Burroughs stories were obtained. Recycling unused footage from *Trader Horn* and assigning its director, W.S. Van Dyke, to follow up with *Tarzan the Ape Man*, the studio tested—or seriously considered—a succession of candidates for the athletic hero, ranging from the fast-rising likes of Clark Gable, Charles Bickford and Joel McCrea to such prize-winning athletes as Larry "Buster" Crabbe and Herman Brix (later to be known in films as Bruce Bennett), before settling on Johnny Weissmuller.

Weissmuller was a six-foot-three, 190-pound swimming champ and the winner of five gold medals from the Olympic Games of 1924 and 1928, whose only previous motion picture experience had been a fleeting appearance in Paramount's 1929 *Glorifying the American Girl*. But his tall, slim good looks and natural athleticism made him ideal for a role requiring more physical presence than acting ability. And, indeed, Weissmuller found the Tarzan character so congenial that he subsequently forged a lengthy film career out of merely repeating that role in a succession of sequels until, finally, age and weight-gain forced him to relinquish the part to others in 1948 and move into the less-demanding and lower-budgeted *Jungle Jim* series.

The 1932 *Tarzan the Ape Man* may look a bit quaint today, with its obvious use of occasional fake sets, phony animals, process photography and speeded-up action scenes. But there's also sufficient location photography (blending rural Southern California in with the *Trader Horn* out-takes) and exciting narrative action to maintain viewer interest. Its storyline is simple and direct, involving an African safari in quest of the ivory to be found in a sacred elephant burial ground by C. Aubrey Smith, daughter Maureen O'Sullivan (the inevitable "Jane") and her fiancé, stolid Neil Hamilton. The dangers of mountains and jungle make up the movie's initial half-hour, before Tarzan's famed yodeling yell is first heard (a technical blending of sounds which Weissmuller later found he could emulate "live"). And the film's middle portion is concerned with Tarzan's abduction of Jane and their subsequent jungle idyll of getting to know one another, as he introduces her to the pleasures of vine-swinging, pool-swimming and tree-climbing, as well as the skills of surviving the locale's more life-threatening denizens. This segment of the movie treats the viewer's ears to as much screaming as Fay Wray in the following year's *King Kong*, as O'Sullivan is roughly dunked and knocked about like a rag doll by the far-from-gentle Weissmuller. In fact, one now marvels that the actress had the pluck and fortitude to take her through five Tarzan sequels, before eventually leaving him to find another "Jane."

Of course, much of the film's tremendous box-office success was due to the excitement raised by such provocative advertising slogans as . . . "Girls— would you live like Eve if you found the right Adam?" and photos that previewed the movie's skimpy, pre-Code costuming of its male star, whose barely adequate loincloth relied on the strength of a single thong.

At its denouement, *Tarzan the Ape Man*'s ideal couple elects to set up jungle housekeeping, while Jane's father conveniently expires in the elephant graveyard, thus leaving her now-ex-fiancé to return to civilization on his own. This he does with remarkable resignation, clambering aboard an elephant to ride off as Tarzan, Jane and Cheetah the chimp wave him goodbye from a near-by hilltop—all to a sudden burst of unexpected Tchaikovsky on the soundtrack!

MGM attempted a half-hearted *Tarzan the Ape Man* remake with Denny Miller in 1959, but it wasn't successful. And when that title resurfaced again in 1981 with an unknown named Miles O'Keeffe and a breast-baring Bo Derek as Jane, the results were dismally exploitative.

TARZAN THE APE MAN: Maureen O'Sullivan, Neil Hamilton and Johnny Weissmuller.

TARZAN THE APE MAN: Maureen O'Sullivan and Johnny Weissmuller.

67

NIGHT WORLD

1932

CREDITS

A Universal Picture. Producer: Carl Laemmle, Jr. Director: Hobart Henley. Screenwriter: Richard Schayer. Based on a story by P.J. Wolfson and Allen Rivkin. Cinematographer: Merritt Gerstad. Editor: Maurice Pivar. Composer: Alfred Newman. Choreographer: Busby Berkeley. Running Time: 58 minutes.

CAST

Lew Ayres (*Michael Rand*); Mae Clarke (*Ruth Taylor*); Boris Karloff ("*Happy" MacDonald*); Dorothy Revier (*Mrs. "Mac"*); Russell Hopton (*Klauss*); Bert Roach (*Tommy*); Dorothy Peterson (*Edith Blair*); Paisley Noon (*Clarence*); Hedda Hopper (*Mrs. Rand*); Clarence Muse (*Tim Washington, the Doorman*); George Raft (*Ed Powell*); Robert Emmett O'Connor (*Policeman*); Florence Lake (*Miss Smith*); Huntley Gordon (*Jim*); Gene Morgan (*Joe*); Greta Granstedt (*Blonde*); Louise Beavers (*Maid*); Sammy Blum (*Salesman*); Harry Woods (*Gang Leader*); Jack La Rue (*Henchman*); Eddie Phillips (*Vaudevillian*); Tom Tamarez (*Gigolo*); Arletta Duncan (*Cigarette Girl*); Geneva Mitchell (*Florabelle*); Pat Somerset (*Guest*); Hal Grayson's Recording Orchestra (*Themselves*); Frankie Farr (*Trick Waiter*); Amo Ingraham and Alice Adair (*Chorines*).

NIGHT WORLD: Mae Clarke.

Night World has been called a minor league *Grand Hotel*, and sure enough, there are similar elements in the basic plot structure of a single setting (here, it's a night club) where the events of a 24-hour period effect changes in the lives of various interrelated people. We share the minor and major crises of the club's owner (Boris Karloff), his erring wife (Dorothy Revier), her dance-director lover (Russell Hopton), an alcoholic playboy (Lew Ayres), a good hearted chorus girl (Mae Clarke) and the garrulous black doorman (Clarence Muse). But "Happy's Club" is anything but that during the time period of this story. When the next day dawns, several people are dead, others' lives are forever altered, and the playboy and the chorine appear to be together headed for a more hopeful future.

Though hardly a Thirties classic, *Night World*, at a compact 58 minutes, is a programmer that sustains itself surprisingly well in the Eighties, as witnessed by its surprise reappearance on cable TV. In a reasonably good-guy role, Boris Karloff, as always, pro-

jects a commanding screen presence, and the suave, tailored moustache gives his "Happy" MacDonald more sex appeal than one would ever expect to find in this master of the sinister and macabre. Two years after his breakthrough success as the star of *All Quiet on the Western Front*, Lew Ayres makes a convincing young society lush, but his Universal contract appears predictably unable to give him the boost that would ensure more permanent stardom. Although steadily employed throughout the decade (and beyond), Ayres would wait six more years before MGM's *Young Dr. Kildare* would start him on a nine-picture series of popular medical stories.

As for *Night World*'s talented distaff star, this was the last of five movies Mae Clarke made for Universal, which had cast her to great advantage as the prostitute heroine of James Whale's 1931 *Waterloo Bridge* and as the monster-menaced bride in his *Frankenstein*. One can still marvel at the fresh and natural charm of her performance here. Considering that Clarke's acting style hasn't dated, and that she's obviously as at home on the cabaret dance floor as in the film's more dramatic moments, the mystery remains why this attractive and versatile actress didn't go further than a future that centered on leads in B-pictures and smaller roles in A-productions before descending to unbilled bits in the Fifties and Sixties.

In the supporting cast, Hedda Hopper contributes an effective performance as Lew Ayres' estranged mother who, in a strong (if undeveloped) confrontation scene, airs her selfish true emotions about her lack of love for him or for the husband of whose murder she was acquitted. Stonefaced George Raft has less to do than Hopper, but his steely presence, as always, adds to the appropriately underworld-like atmosphere of the night club. And a similar type, the popeyed Jack La Rue, is immediately recognizable in an unbilled bit as a sidekick of the mobster who wipes out Karloff and Revier in the film's climax.

Night World's director, Hobart Henley, whose 20-year career would end two years—and one picture—later with 1934's poverty-row quickie *Unknown Blonde*, works well to pull screenwriter Richard Schayer's slice-of-life script into a reasonably cohesive whole. And the local color of the setting is suitably enhanced by the choreographic contribution of Busby Berkeley (a year before his breakthrough *42nd Street*), whose signature of overhead dance formations and kaleidoscopic groupings have become so integral a part of Thirties Hollywood musicals. For an unambitious "program" picture, *Night World* is a neat little entertainment, underrated in the reference books and worthy of rediscovery.

NIGHT WORLD: Mae Clarke, Lew Ayres and Geneva Mitchell.

NIGHT WORLD: Boris Karloff and Dorothy Revier.

NIGHT WORLD: Mae Clarke and Dorothy Revier.

SCARFACE

1 9 3 2

CREDITS

A United Artists Picture. Producers: Howard Hughes and Howard Hawks. Director: Howard Hawks. Screenwriters: Ben Hecht, Seton I. Miller, John Lee Mahin, W.R. Burnett and Fred Palsey. Based on the novel by Armitage Trail. Cinematographers: Lee Garmes and L. William O'Connell. Editor: Edward Curtiss. Production Designer: Harry

69

SCARFACE: Paul Muni.

SCARFACE: Maurice Black, Osgood Perkins, Paul Muni and Karen Morley.

Oliver. Sound: William Snyder. Music: Adolph Tendler and Gus Arnheim. Running Time: 99 minutes.

CAST

Paul Muni (*Tony Camonte*); Ann Dvorak (*Cesca Camonte*); Karen Morley (*Poppy*); Osgood Perkins (*Johnny Lovo*); Boris Karloff (*Gaffney*); C. Henry Gordon (*Inspector Guarino*); George Raft (*Guido Rinaldo*); Purnell Pratt (*Publisher*); Vince Barnett (*Angelo*); Inez Palange (*Mrs. Camonte*); Harry J. Vejar (*Big Louis Costillo*); Edwin Maxwell (*Chief of Detectives*); Tully Marshall (*Managing Editor*); Henry Armetta (*Pietro*); Charles Sullivan and Harry Tenbrook (*Bootleggers*); Maurice Black (*Sullivan*); Hank Mann (*Worker*); Paul Fix (*Gaffney Hood*); Bert Starkey (*Epstein*); Howard Hawks (*Man on Bed*); Dennis O'Keefe (*Dance Extra*).

Howard Hughes had a reputation for taking great pains and much time producing those few motion pictures that he cared enough to put his personal stamp on. *Scarface*'s length of production, while briefer than his previous blockbuster *Hell's Angels*, was preceded in release by two other landmark gangster melodramas, *Little Caesar* and *The Public Enemy*. Part of the problem was censorship, for *Scarface* went further in areas of sex and violence than had previously been attempted. Killings were depicted more graphically, and sexual attraction became somewhat more specific in the film Hughes co-produced with its director, Howard Hawks. So it was necessary to make a number of cuts and compromises before the film could be released.

For its star, Paul Muni, *Scarface* was a milestone. On the stage, Muni was a star who felt secure and comfortable. But on screen, he had only been seen in two unsuccessful early-sound pictures, *The Valiant* and *Seven Faces*, both released in 1929. It was the actor's wife and business manager, Bella, who sensed something in the *Scarface* script that seemed worth exploring, and she urged a reluctant Muni to accept the role of Tony Camonte, a Chicago mobster who was obviously a thinly-disguised Al Capone (although everyone connected with this production took pains to deny the likeness).

Scarface not only made Paul Muni a major film star, but it also hit the public with a terrific impact, moving *The New York Times* to comment: "It is a stirring picture, efficiently directed and capably acted." The easily outraged industry bulletin *Harrison's Reports* waxed true to form, calling *Scarface* "The most vicious and demoralizing gangster pic produced." *Variety* was more circumspect: "Regardless of the moral issues, *Scarface* is entertainment on an important scale."

Paul Muni also brought to his characterization of

SCARFACE: Paul Muni and Ann Dvorak.

a potentially dangerous, frequently pleasant-mannered gang boss the kind of animal sex appeal seldom seen in the Thirties. And he's far more attractive a nonhero than the hard-as-nails characters already witnessed in Edward G. Robinson's *Little Caesar* and James Cagney's *The Public Enemy*. In fact, Muni was that rarity in Thirties Hollywood, a sexy character actor. The tensions that surface between Muni's Tony Camonte and his onscreen paramour Poppy (Karen Morley) and sister Cesca (Ann Dvořak) are strongly evident of the palpable sensuality that the actor brought to those relationships. It is a quality that an actor either has or doesn't have—and Muni had it.

Scarface may seem overly familiar today, considering the many intervening films that have copied and borrowed from it, up to and including Brian De Palma's 1983 blood-spattered remake with the intense Al Pacino. Tony Camonte is an immigrant who starts out as a smalltime bootlegger's bodyguard. It's a business he soon takes over, moving onward and upward to wipe out both his boss Johnny Lovo (Osgood Perkins) and a rival named Gaffney (Boris Karloff). In so doing, Tony wins Lovo's girlfriend Poppy at the same time the movie subtly weaves in an incest theme involving Tony's young sister Cesca, of whom he's overly protective. In fact, he's particularly jealous of her relationship with his own coin-flipping sidekick Guido Rinaldo (George Raft), whom he kills when he finds the pair in a hotel room together. Explosive Tony doesn't wait to find out that they'd just been married. Cesca later forgives her brother, before they're gunned down together in a final shootout.

Scarface, as expected, ran into censorship problems everywhere. Shot with three different endings, in an effort to appease those who tried to suppress the movie, it was most widely seen with the ending made popular by *Little Caesar*, where Edward G. Robinson is hunted and gunned down as he cries out, "Mother of mercy! Is this the end of Rico?" *Scarface*, too, closes with Tony Camonte pleading in vain for mercy.

Paul Muni went on to become one of the Thirties' most successful and distinguished movie actors, winning an Academy Award nomination for *I Am a Fugitive From a Chain Gang*, an Oscar for *The Story of Louis Pasteur* and the New York Film Critics Award for *The Life of Emile Zola*. He and the underrated Ann Dvorak were reunited in 1935's *Dr. Socrates*.

The movie is frequently listed as bearing the moralistic subtitle "The Shame of a Nation." However, no such wording is carried on the *Scarface* print available on cassette from MCA Home Video.

SCARFACE: Paul Muni and Osgood Perkins.

RAIN: Walter Catlett, Joan Crawford and Matt Moore.

RAIN: Beulah Bondi and Joan Crawford.

RAIN

1932

CREDITS

A United Artists Picture. Producer: Joseph M. Schenck. Director: Lewis Milestone. Screenwriter: Maxwell Anderson. Based on the play by John Colton and Clemence Randolph, and the story *Miss Thompson* by W. Somerset Maugham. Cinematographer: Oliver T. Marsh. Editor: W. Duncan Mansfield. Art Director: Richard Day. Running Time: 92 minutes.

CAST

Joan Crawford (*Sadie Thompson*); Walter Huston (*Alfred Davidson*); William Gargan (*Sergeant O'Hara*); Guy Kibbee (*Joe Horn*); Walter Catlett (*Quartermaster Bates*); Beulah Bondi (*Mrs. Davidson*); Matt Moore (*Dr. MacPhail*); Kendall Lee (*Mrs. MacPhail*); Ben Hendricks (*Griggs*); Frederic Howard (*Hodgson*).

The character of Sadie Thompson first turned up in a Somerset Maugham short story he called simply *Miss Thompson* and was first brought to life in 1922 in the stage adaptation *Rain*, by John B. Colton and Clemence Randolph.

Borrowed by United Artists president Joseph Schenck for the juicy role of the South Seas trollop, Joan Crawford was intimidated by Sadie. After all, it was the role which had brought Broadway glory to Jeanne Eagels and silent-screen accolades to Oscar-nominated Gloria Swanson in 1928, when it was initially filmed as *Sadie Thompson*.

But by 1932, the ambitious and talented Crawford had moved up from chorus dancer and bit player to become one of MGM's most promising young dramatic actresses. In 1930, she proved she could really act in *Paid*, and earlier in 1932, she scored a personal triumph among formidable company in the all-star *Grand Hotel*.

Lewis Milestone, *Rain*'s director, was riding high on the reputation of *All Quiet On The Western Front* and *The Front Page* when he was assigned to direct Crawford. The fact that her supporting company were stage-trained actors also made her feel inferior. And, since this was the star's first movie away from seven years of careful protection under exclusive service to MGM studios, she was concerned—even after the concession that she would have the benefit of her favorite cameraman, Oliver T. Marsh.

RAIN: William Gargan and Joan Crawford.

Milestone's reputation with actors was good, but Crawford felt at odds with his methods ("we rehearsed interminably"). As she later explained, "What I do on the screen is more instinctive than calculated. The first take of any scene of mine is the best. Since I am not a studied craftsman, rehearsals rob me of spontaneity."

Exteriors were shot on Catalina Island, deemed suitably similar to the story's actual locale of Pago Pago, the Samoan island at which a tramp steamer is forced to dock because of a minor epidemic on board. Among the passengers deposited at the island's hotel/general store run by affable Joe Horn (Guy Kibbee) are the flashy Sadie, a zealous lay-missionary couple named Davidson (Walter Huston and Beulah Bondi), and a doctor and his wife (Matt Moore and Kendall Lee). Sadie quickly attracts the attention of some Marines stationed on the island, especially Sergeant O'Hara (William Gargan), as well as the intense disapproval of Mr. Davidson, who attempts to reform her while the island's seasonal rains confine the reluctant hotel guests to one another's company.

Despite Sadie's past, the love-smitten O'Hara naively wants to marry her, while Davidson's religious persistence annoys her. Finally, his threats to see her imprisoned for past sins chip away at her tough,

RAIN: Walter Huston, Joan Crawford and William Gargan.

73

wise-cracking facade and Sadie begins to concede to his tactics. Devoid of her customary heavy make-up and extravagant attire, she appears a successful convert. But one night, Davidson's self-control gives way to lust and he rapes her, shattering all of her new-found illusions. The next day, he's discovered in the surf, a suicide, while Sadie's jazzy phonograph music signals her return to a more familiar personality. She leaves the island on a ship bound for Australia, and one is left to believe that O'Hara will soon join her there when his tour of duty ends.

Audiences used to seeing Joan Crawford in roles with which they could more easily identify didn't care for her blatant appearance in *Rain*. Nor did most of the film's critics, who responded negatively to it. Even the usually esteemed Walter Huston escaped much praise. Milestone's direction tried admirably to give cinematic variety to *Rain*'s naturally claustrophobic atmosphere by keeping his cameras constantly on the move.

Years later, and long after Rita Hayworth's so-so remake of the film in 3D as *Miss Sadie Thompson*, and perhaps convinced by the painfully remembered negative response of 1932's critics and audiences, Joan Crawford continued to downgrade her performance of Sadie Thompson: "I don't understand how I could have given such an unpardonably bad performance." Her comment was as unfortunate as those of critics of today who continue to judge *Rain* by the standards of 1932. An unbiased retrospective look at this movie reveals not only a very respectable piece of vintage filmmaking, but a Crawford performance that continues to hold up as one of her most effective. To realize that this was the relatively early work of a determined, self-made film star, whose dramatic experience (up to that time) had all been gleaned behind the encouraging walls of MGM, is sufficient to make one appreciate the excellence of a totally uncharacteristic and risk-taking performance. It is one she need never have been ashamed of.

VIRTUE

1932

CREDITS

A Columbia Picture. Directed by Edward Buzzell. Screenwriter: Robert Riskin. Based on the story by Ethel Hill.

VIRTUE: Carole Lombard.

Cinematographer: Joseph Walker. Editor: Maurice Wright. Running Time: 68 minutes.

CAST

Carole Lombard (*Mae*); Pat O'Brien (*Jimmy Doyle*); Ward Bond (*Frank*); Shirley Grey (*Gert Hanna*); Mayo Methot (*Lil Blair*); Jack La Rue (*Toots*); Willard Robertson (*MacKenzie*); Lew Kelly (*Magistrate*); Fred Santley (*Hank*); Arthur Wanzer (*Flanagan*); Jessie Arnold (*Landlady*); Edwin Stanley (*District Attorney*).

By 1932, Columbia—under the infamous dictatorship of tough, foul-mouthed Harry Cohn—was slowly achieving begrudging respect in an industry which still tended to think of his studio as a part of the so-called Poverty Row of filmdom. Frank Capra's movies were making great strides in changing Columbia's image, but, for a star, being loaned out to that studio still had the connotation of a humiliating jail sentence.

Like many of Paramount's early-Thirties contractees, Carole Lombard occasionally balked at accepting roles she considered less than worthy of her talent and experience. Such was the case that resulted in her landing at Columbia in 1932 to team with Pat O'Brien in a program melodrama entitled *Virtue*. But the platinum-haired starlet's beauty belied a tough mind and a brainy sense of humor that well enabled her to cope with intimidating studio heads like Cohn. Reportedly, their first meeting began with Cohn bluntly telling Lombard, "Your hair's too white. You look like a whore." To which she retorted, "I'm sure *you* know what a whore looks like, if anyone does!" All of which put the pair on such good footing that Lombard ended up making five pictures for Cohn's studio, including one classic—1934's *Twentieth Century.*

Virtue is hardly a classic, even as a program picture. But it's well written by Robert Riskin, whose script packs a lot of plot into its 68 minutes. And both Lombard and O'Brien deliver solid, interesting characterizations, under the steady hand of director Edward Buzzell. Buzzell had begun his career as a musical-comedy performer, before graduating to directing early sound comedy shorts, several of which he also starred in. Buzzell began directing feature films at Columbia in 1932, and *Virtue*'s lighter moments underscore his background in comedy.

VIRTUE: Shirley Grey and Carole Lombard.

The movie's plot—about a bad girl's efforts to "go straight"—shows its pre-Code origins, since she never has to pay "the ultimate price" for her earlier transgressions. In fact, we never learn what set Mae (Lombard) on a streetwalking career. But, as the film begins, she's one of several Manhattan hookers given a suspended sentence, on the condition that they leave town. Thus Mae's given a one-way train ticket to New Haven, Connecticut. But it's a trip she never completes. Disembarking at 125th Street, she

hails a cab driven by a friendly, humorous fellow named Jimmy Doyle (O'Brien), whom she ultimately hoodwinks out of her fare before running off. However, a short time later, Mae somehow finds him and hands him the money she earlier cheated him out of. A begrudging friendship blossoms into love, as Mae takes on a legitimate job as a lunch-counter waitress. After a short courtship, the two marry— only to have the authorities arrive on the wedding night to arrest Mae for violating the court order—

VIRTUE: Carole Lombard and Pat O'Brien.

VIRTUE: Carole Lombard and Pat O'Brien.

which reveals her past to a shocked Jimmy. Nevertheless, he stands by her and produces the marriage license that appeases the law.

But wedded bliss is brief for Jimmy and Mae. He's trying to save enough to buy a filling station. Mae jeopardizes that ambition when she sneaks $200.00 to her friend Gert (Shirley Grey), who appears in desperate need of funds for an operation. Soon afterward, Mae learns that Gert pulled the same ruse on other friends, and has disappeared with all of their money. This, it turns out, is to satisfy her sleazy boyfriend Toots (Jack La Rue), who's playing Gert against his old lover Lil (Mayo Methot, impressive in a fine supporting performance). The desperate Mae manages to track Gert to a disreputable transient hotel she once frequented herself. Jimmy, suspicious of his wife's absences, follows her and spies her silhouetted figure behind a window, and jumps to the wrong conclusion. Inside the hotel, Mae confronts Gert and demands her money, while Toots appears with a gun. Mae gets away with her money, but Toots accidentally kills Gert, and only Lil—who supplies Toots' alibi—knows the whole truth. None of which comes out until after Mae goes to jail, with Jimmy thinking she's gone back to hustling to raise the money they need.

But *Virtue*'s 68-minute length doesn't allow for wasted footage, and before we know it, Jimmy has his filling station, and guess who's his gas-pump girl? Well, Mae, of course! With a rosy future ahead for them both . . .

If the above story sounds like a lot of familiar nonsense, don't believe it! Lombard, O'Brien and company give it all they've got, and deliver a nice little melodrama—tough, hard and clean, with a minimum of the sentimentality that often clung to early-Thirties movies. With her luminous blend of looks and talent, it's easy to see why Carole Lombard soon became one of the decade's major stars. And Pat O'Brien isn't far behind her here. Director Edward Buzzell would seldom rise above B-picture competence, although several of his Forties MGM comedies (*Best Foot Forward, Easy to Wed*) are still worth revisiting.

HOT SATURDAY

1 9 3 2

CREDITS

A Paramount Picture. Director: William A. Seiter. Screenwriter: Seton I. Miller. Adaptation: Josephine Lovett and Joseph Moncure March. Based on the novel by Harvey Fergusson. Cinematographer: Arthur L. Todd. Running time: 73 minutes.

CAST

Cary Grant (*Romer Sheffield*); Nancy Carroll (*Ruth Brock*); Randolph Scott (*Bill Fadden*); Edward Woods (*Conny Billop*); Lillian Bond (*Eva Randolph*); William Collier, Sr. (*Harry Brock*); Jane Darwell (*Mrs. Brock*); Rita La Roy (*Camille*); Rose Coghlan II (*Annie Brock*); Oscar Apfel (*Ed W. Randolph*); Jessie Arnold (*Aunt Minnie*); Grady Sutton (*Archie*).

In *Hot Saturday*, his sixth feature film, Cary Grant received top billing for the first time, co-starring with Nancy Carroll, once one of Paramount's leading stars, but whose career was now sadly waning. Clearly, the studio heads deemed their handsome

HOT SATURDAY: Cary Grant and Nancy Carroll.

76

new actor destined for a brighter future than Miss Carroll, though *Hot Saturday* is strictly her story. Under William A. Seiter's direction, she plays Ruth Brock, a small-town bank clerk who is believed by the local gossips to have been compromised by Romer Sheffield (Grant), a notorious playboy whose chauffeured car brings her home at a scandalously late hour from a party at his lakeside home. The girl's innocence is eventually proven, but at the party announcing her engagement to Bill Fadden (Randolph Scott), her childhood sweetheart, the scandal reaches *his* ears. When her angered fiancé breaks off with her, Ruth retaliates by boldly running to Romer and spending the night with him. The next day, she returns to inform Bill and her family that she is now *truly* guilty of the misconduct they had once all too easily believed. At the fadeout, Ruth and Romer are driving to New York and, presumably, a minister. In *Hot Saturday*'s altered remake—the 1941 Deanna Durbin vehicle, *Nice Girl?*—the young lady ends up with the boy-next-door (Robert Stack), over her more sophisticated swain (Franchot Tone, in the Grant role).

In his first nominal lead, Grant was rather wooden, particularly in contrast to the over-exuberant playing of Nancy Carroll at her most Clara Bow-like. As the small-town rake, he is appropriately sophisticated and convincingly smooth with the ladies (Ruth tells him, "You're considered too dangerous for local consumption"). And he is an

HOT SATURDAY: Nancy Carroll and Jane Darwell.

unquestionably natty dresser, whether in white suit, fedora and two-tone shoes, or Japanese samurai dressing gown. But the script allows him no opportunity for the obligatory character transition.

It is interesting to note the camerawise naiveté of Grant in 1932. He often allows a fellow player to enjoy the full benefit of the lens, while showing the audience only the *under*-side of his upturned jaw or a three-quarters *rear* profile of his face. But it wasn't long before he would learn the full value to the actor of light and camera placement.

Seiter's direction of the sophisticated Seton I. Miller screenplay manages to keep *Hot Saturday*'s rather free-wheeling pre-Code story well within the bounds of good taste, while certainly taking an adult attitude toward sex and the yearnings of small-town youth. Unfortunately for Nancy Carroll, this was her last good film for Paramount, her home studio for five years. Dissatisfied with the scripts offered her, Carroll was generally considered "troublesome" at Paramount. The following year, she was better served at Columbia with *Child of Manhattan*, and even better with Universal's compelling melodrama *The Kiss Before the Mirror*, directed by James Whale.

RED DUST: Clark Gable and Jean Harlow.

RED DUST

1932

CREDITS

A Metro-Goldwyn-Mayer Picture. Supervising Producer: Hunt Stromberg. Director: Victor Fleming. Screenwriters: John Lee Mahin and (uncredited) Howard Hawks; Based on the play by Wilson Collison. Cinematographer: Harold G. Rosson. Editor: Blanche Sewell. Art Director: Cedric Gibbons. Gowns: Adrian. Sound: Douglas Shearer. Running Time: 83 minutes.

CAST

Clark Gable (*Dennis Carson*); Jean Harlow (*Vantine*); Gene Raymond (*Gary Willis*); Mary Astor (*Barbara Willis*); Donald Crisp (*Guidon*); Tully Marshall (*McQuarg*); Forrester Harvey (*Limey*); Willie Fung (*Hoy*).

For a play that lasted a mere eight performances on Broadway in 1928, Wilson Collison's *Red Dust* has had a surprisingly resilient life on the screen: in 1932, it provided the basis for a highly combustible teaming of Clark Gable and Jean Harlow, was recycled eight years later as an Ann Sothern series programmer entitled *Congo Maisie*, and was re-

tailored in 1953 for Gable and (in perhaps her finest performance) Ava Gardner under the title *Mogambo*, with the added prestige of Grace Kelly (in a role played in 1932 by Mary Astor) and direction by John Ford.

But the 1932 *Red Dust* still holds up very well on its own. John Lee Mahin's screenplay (with uncredited input from Howard Hawks) retains the stage play's French Indochina jungle setting and its basic triangular-romance situation. Otherwise, it's a vast improvement over mediocre material, with Gable as the rough-and-ready rubber planter who reluctantly becomes involved with Jean Harlow, as a good-humored prostitute-on-the-lam from Saigon, forced to stay at his plantation until the next boat arrives. When it does, it also brings Gable's fever-ridden new assistant, engineer Gene Raymond, and his aristocratic bride, Mary Astor. Antagonistic at first, Astor and Gable soon realize a mutual attraction, as Raymond is nursed back to health. Meanwhile, Harlow rejoins the household, her ship having run aground downriver. No dummy, she immediately senses Gable's new interest in Astor, while the recovered Raymond is supervising the construction of a jungle bridge. Trying to save Astor's marriage to Raymond, Gable, feeling guilty over his liaison with her, turns her against him. Then he directs his attentions to Harlow, with the result that Astor shoots him in a jealous rage. Harlow tells Raymond that it was Gable's own fault, and that Astor was only defending herself against his advances. At the fadeout, Harlow's nursing the wounded Gable back to health, as Astor and Raymond move on to redefine their marriage vows elsewhere.

Harlow and Gable had previously worked together in supporting roles in 1931's *The Secret Six*, and when she was first suggested to the actor as his *Red Dust* co-star, he balked with recollections of her inexperience. But leading roles in six subsequent movies, added to an ambitious drive to learn and improve, had helped the sexy platinum blonde to

RED DUST: Gene Raymond, Clark Gable and Mary Astor.

RED DUST: Jean Harlow and Mary Astor.

RED DUST: Mary Astor, Gene Raymond, director Victor Fleming, Clark Gable and Donald Crisp on the set.

develop formidable star quality. From what had once looked like little more than another cheap floozy, Jean Harlow now emerged as a genuine star—and a talented comedienne into the bargain. It didn't take Gable long, not only to accept her, but to appreciate the chemistry that was soon made manifest by their teaming. Of course, this film preceded the formation of Hollywood's intimidating Production Code by two years, and so relationships could be more frankly expressed and innuendos could circulate more freely. But, although there's little doubt left in

any adult mind as to what's going on between Gable and his leading ladies in this movie, it's more than tame by Eighties screen standards: language is mild, sex is only implied and there's no nudity—not even when Harlow bathes in an outdoor barrel bathtub. But it's the uninhibited sexual energy that both stars bring to their scenes together that creates the magic here, resulting in a box-office attraction that cost a reported $408,000 to shoot and brought in a profit of $399,000. Gable and Harlow were subsequently re-teamed in *Hold Your Man, China Seas, Wife vs. Secretary* and *Saratoga,* the picture she left not quite completed at her death in 1937, aged 26.

It's interesting to note that, when Harlow's husband, producer Paul Bern, became a suicide while *Red Dust* was in production, MGM honcho Louis B. Mayer considered replacing her with Tallulah Bankhead, in the event that Harlow's career might collapse through her possible implication in the tragedy. Fortunately for Harlow, her career didn't suffer. Nor would Bankhead seriously entertain any ideas of replacing the irreplaceable Harlow. Having failed to impress movie audiences earlier that year in five previous Paramount movies or opposite Robert Montgomery in Metro's *Faithless,* "Tallu" left Hollywood to return to the Broadway stage. Conjuring up the possibility of a Gable-Bankhead *Red Dust,* however, is a bit dismaying. Somehow, Tallulah's sardonic, world-weary humor vs. Gable's tough-tempered male chauvinism would never have created the special chemistry of his teaming with Jean Harlow.

CALL HER SAVAGE: Clara Bow.

CALL HER SAVAGE

1932

CREDITS

A Fox Film. Associate Producer: Sam E. Rork. Director: John Francis Dillion. Screenwriter: Edwin Burke. Based on the novel by Tiffany Thayer. Cinematographer: Lee Garmes. Art Director: Max Parker. Running Time: 88 minutes.

CAST

Clara Bow (*Nasa*); Monroe Owsley (*Lawrence Crosby*); Gilbert Roland (*Moonglow*); Thelma Todd (*Sunny De Lan*); Estelle Taylor (*Ruth Springer*); Willard Robertson (*Peter Springer*); Weldon Heyburn (*Ronasa*); Arthur Hoyt (*Attorney*); Hale Hamilton (*Cyrus Randall*); Katherine Perry (*Maid*); John Elliott (*Hank*); Anthony Jowitt (*Jay Randall*); Mischa Auer (*Agitator in Restaurant*); Mary Gordon (*Tenement Lady*).

The movie career of the vivacious and inimitable Clara Bow spanned only the 11 years between 1922

and 1933, during which she made few films worth remembering. Plagued by personal scandal, weight problems and uneven mental health as silent pictures gave way to sound, Clara lost favor with her studio, Paramount, and suffered a breakdown during the production of her 1931 film *Kick-In.* She was off the screen for well over a year, an unusual hiatus in that era when a star might normally be seen in anywhere from five to 10 pictures during a 12-month period. And, when she returned, it was under a new contract with a different studio (Fox), in this wild 1932 melodrama. *Call Her Savage* served its star handsomely, did well at the box-office and held out future promise for Clara Bow as a screen attraction. In later years, she would list this movie along with her silent vehicles *Mantrap* and *It* as her three favorites.

Call Her Savage was adapted by Edwin Burke from Tiffany Thayer's trashy but popular novel of that name. There's plot enough for three pictures in the lively story of restless, tempestuous Texas heiress Nasa Springer (Bow), who eventually learns that her uninhibited nature is the result of a brief indiscretion by her mother (Estelle Taylor) with an Indian chief. Nasa is initially seen in a love-hate relationship with a handsome young half-breed Indian named Moonglow (Gilbert Roland). Though she bullwhips him when he laughs at her encounter with a rattlesnake (which she whips to death), she also ministers tenderly to the wounds she's inflicted. A sexy and unmanageable vixen, Nasa is sent away to finishing school by her stern and wealthy father (Willard Robertson), a ploy that fails to tame her nature. Two years pass, and we learn that she's been leading a scandalous life that only *appears* to take a turn for the respectable when she impulsively weds wastrel Lawrence Crosby (Monroe Owsley). Crosby is less concerned with love for Nasa than to defy his faithless mistress Sunny (Thelma Todd). Nasa's father disowns her, which causes Crosby to leave her and resume his liaison with Sunny. Nasa recklessly gambles away what remains of her fortune, before facing the fact that Crosby has made her pregnant and she's on her own. An unpleasant confrontation with her now ill and penniless husband nearly results in her rape, as Nasa rapidly descends the social

CALL HER SAVAGE: Clara Bow and Gilbert Roland.

CALL HER SAVAGE: Clara Bow and Monroe Owsley.

ladder. After she gives birth in a charity ward, her ailing baby perishes in a tenement fire while Nasa is streetwalking to afford medicine.

But when Nasa's father dies, she is left the money that enables her to seek a new life in New York City, where she takes a new, socially upscale lover, Jay Randall (Anthony Jowitt) and, incredibly, runs into a recovered Crosby. This results in a battle-royal with his girlfriend Sunny. Jilted by Jay, Nasa then temporarily "goes off the deep end," before pulling herself together for a return to her Texas roots, and the only man with whom she's ever realized reciprocal affection—Moonglow!

Call Her Savage is little more than highly enter-

CALL HER SAVAGE: Clara Bow and Anthony Jowitt.

taining hokum, with its racy script contrived simply as a run-the-gamut vehicle for Clara Bow. And, under John Francis Dillion's knowing direction, she plays the material for much more than it's worth, holding the incredulous viewer's attention at every convoluted plot juncture. One can only admire her energy, her talent and her brazen charm, while marveling that this unique star made only one more movie—the nearly forgotten *Hoopla*—before calling it a career and retiring to private life.

THE ANIMAL KINGDOM

1932

CREDITS

An RKO Radio Picture. Producer: David O. Selznick. Directors: Edward H. Griffith and (uncredited) George Cukor. Screenwriter: Horace Jackson. Based on the play by Philip Barry. Cinematographer: George Folsey. Editor: Daniel Mandell. Art Director: Van Nest Polglase. Sound: Daniel Cutler. Running Time: 90 minutes.

CAST

Ann Harding (*Daisy Sage*); Leslie Howard (*Tom Collier*); Myrna Loy (*Cecilia Henry*); Neil Hamilton (*Owen Arthur*); William Gargan (*Richard Regan*); Henry Stephenson (*Rufus Collier*); Ilka Chase (*Grace Macomber*); Leni Stengel (*Franc Schmidt*); Donald Dillaway (*Joe Fisk*).

Director Edward H. Griffith (1888–1975) is scarcely remembered today. But from the late Twenties to the early Forties, he guided many a female star through her paces in comedies of sophistication, to the extent that he might now be thought of as a minor league George Cukor. In addition to six Madeleine Carroll features, two with Loretta Young and one each with Margaret Sullavan, Constance Bennett and Joan Crawford, he worked in great harmony on no less than four occasions with Ann Harding, and chiefly in vehicles adapted from Philip Barry's stage hits: *Paris Bound, Holiday* and *The Animal Kingdom*. After their initial successes together, it was only natural that Harding should request him—a move that served to prolong her career until inferior scripts and changing public tastes would eventually send her back to the theatre, where she had gotten her start.

The Animal Kingdom, with its glittering cast surrounding Harding, turned out to be the most successful and well-liked of all her movies. Recreating their roles from the stage play were Leslie Howard, William Gargan and Ilka Chase. Producer David O. Selznick wanted to cast Karen Morley as Howard's proper wife but, after passing the demanding eye of Howard, Myrna Loy was cast as the lady he marries to gain respectability. For her he abandons a liaison with the free-spirited artist (Harding) he really loves; in exchange he finds only ennui with his wife's circle of friends, in particular the man (Neil Hamilton) who most admires her. In turn, the wife has a difficult time accepting the boozy ex-fighter (Gargan) her husband keeps on as a rather unorthodox butler (he likes to party with their guests). All of which helps reunite husband and mistress for a decidedly pre-Production Code finale, handled with such taste by director Griffith that the movie's critics were nearly united in their praise. In New York City, where it inaugurated the opening of the new RKO Roxy, *The Animal Kingdom* did good business, although its subsequent failure apparently indicated that moviegoers in general were not interested in the romantic dalliances of the privileged class.

An interesting sidelight occurred in the original stage casting. A young and rising Katharine Hepburn was selected for the role of the mistress. But before its Boston tryout engagement, Hepburn was

THE ANIMAL KINGDOM: Leslie Howard and Ann Harding.

replaced by Frances Fuller, due to differences involving her, Leslie Howard (who was also co-producer) and playwright Philip Barry. Already a Hepburn champion, Barry wanted to enlarge her role—until Howard intervened.

In 1943, Warner Bros. filmed an inferior remake of *The Animal Kingdom* which suffered partly from attempts to appease a then-stricter Production Code. With Alexis Smith, Dennis Morgan and Ann Sheridan in the respective roles of wife, husband and mistress (or what passed for a mistress in Hollywood's sanitized Forties), the movie was released 2½ years after completion under the title *One More Tomorrow*. It entertained no one and was quickly forgotten.

THE ANIMAL KINGDOM: Myrna Loy, William Gargan and Leslie Howard.

THE ANIMAL KINGDOM: Neil Hamilton, Henry Stephenson and Myrna Loy.

THE ANIMAL KINGDOM: Leslie Howard, Leni Stengel and Ann Harding.

CAVALCADE: Herbert Mundin, Diana Wynyard, Clive Brook and Una O'Connor.

CAVALCADE

1933

CREDITS

A Fox Film. Producer: Winfield Sheehan. Director: Frank Lloyd. Screenwriter: Reginald Berkeley. Based on the play by Noël Coward. Cinematographer: Ernst Palmer. Editor: Margaret Clancy. Art Director: William S. Darling. Women's Costumes: Earl Luick. Men's Costumes: A. McDonald. Special Effects (war scenes): William Cameron Menzies. Technical Advisor: Lance Baxter. Dialogue Director: George Hadden. Assistant Director: William Tummel. Sound: Joseph E. Aiken. Dances: Sammy Lee. Music: Noël Coward. Song: "Twentieth Century Blues" by Noël Coward. Running Time: 110 minutes.

CAST

Diana Wynyard (*Jane Marryot*); Clive Brook (*Robert Marryot*); Ursula Jeans (*Fanny Bridges*); Herbert Mundin (*Alfred Bridges*); Una O'Connor (*Ellen Bridges*); Merle Tottenham (*Annie*); Irene Browne (*Margaret Harris*); Beryl Mercer (*Cook*); Frank Lawton (*Joe Marryot*); John Warburton (*Edward Marryot*); Margaret Lindsay (*Edith Harris*); Tempe Pigott (*Mrs. Snapper*); Billy Bevan (*George Grainger*); Desmond Roberts (*Ronnie James*); Frank Atkinson (*Uncle Dick*); Ann Shaw (*Mirabelle*); Adele Crane (*Ada*); Will Stanton (*Tommy Jolly*); Stuart Hall (*Lieutenant Edgar*); Mary Forbes (*Duchess of Churt*); C. Montague Shaw (*Major Domo*); Lionel Belmore (*Uncle George*); Dick Henderson, Jr. (*Edward, Age 12*); Douglas Scott (*Joey, Age 8*); Sheila MacGill (*Edith, Age 10*); Bonita Granville (*Fanny, Ages 7–12*); Howard Davies (*Agitator*); David Torrence (*Man at Disarmament Conference*); Lawrence Grant (*Man at Microphone*); Winter Hall (*Minister*); Claude King (*Speaker*); Pat Somerset (*Ringsider*); Douglas Walton (*Soldier*); Tom Ricketts (*Waiter*); Betty Grable (*Girl on Couch*); Harry Allen and John Rogers (*Buskers*); Brandon Hurst (*Gilbert & Sullivan Actor*).

To the familiar, stirring strains of "Land of Hope and Glory," this Hollywood-made adaptation of Noël Coward's episodic 1931 British play opens on New Year's Eve as the 19th century is about to become the 20th. True to the Coward stage pageant, we're taken through three decades of English life as it effects the residents of a well-to-do London household, both upstairs and downstairs—as in the 1970s British TV series of that name. And Fox, by using a cast of mostly English performers, gives this production the illusion of having come to us from across the sea. Spanning the years from 1899 and the outbreak of the Boer War to 1932, *Cavalcade* tends to overlap the period and theme of Coward's later play, *This Happy Breed,* which took one working-class family from 1919 to 1939. However, *Cavalcade*'s family, the Marryots, is strictly upper crust, with the balance offered by the script's occasional shift downstairs to visit the Bridges (Una O'Connor and Herbert Mundin), the servant couple who eventually save enough money to leave service and open their own pub.

CAVALCADE: John Warburton, Margaret Lindsay, Irene Browne, Frank Lawton and Diana Wynyard.

CAVALCADE: Herbert Mundin and Bonita Granville.

And so *Cavalcade* takes us through the years in vignette style, as Jane and Robert Marryot (Diana Wynyard and Clive Brook) pass from that momentous New Year's Eve through the pain of seeing Britain's adult males off to serve in the faraway Africa Boer War, through Queen Victoria's death. And then there's the raising of the children, followed by the Marryots' tragedy of losing their honeymooning son Edward (John Warburton) and his bride (Margaret Lindsay) on the Titanic, and through the monumental disruption of The Great War (depicted in montage by special-effects director William Cameron Menzies) and the social ferment of the Jazz Age. And always there's the music (much of it written by Coward) of the changing eras to underscore the action of the story, from Strauss waltzes to martial band music to the popular tunes of war and peace ("I'm Only a Bird in a Gilded Cage," "Pack Up Your Troubles," "Beside the Sea," "Take Me Back to Yorkshire," "Nearer My God to Thee," "Twentieth Century Blues," etc).

By *Cavalcade*'s sentimental conclusion, Jane and Robert Marryot have lost both their sons (the second is killed in the war), and have progressed into early old age, along with their old, socially-active friend Margaret Harris (Irene Browne). Another New Year's Eve closes the story as they toast the future.

Criticism directed at the film, both in 1933 and more recently, has centered on *Cavalcade*'s slowness of development. However, today's Anglophile Amer-

CAVALCADE: Clive Brook, Diana Wynyard and Irene Browne.

icans, used to following the episodic dramas of Public Television's "Masterpiece Theatre," will surely have no problems with this movie, should they be fortunate enough to encounter it. Hollywood was sufficiently impressed with the painstaking detail of this hands-across-the-sea gesture to Britain to award it the Academy Award for Best Picture, as well as Oscars to the picture's director, Frank Lloyd, and art director William S. Darling. For her much-admired performance as Jane Marryot, the family matriarch who holds much of the continuity together, Diana Wynyard (in her graceful film debut) won a nomination, though she lost the award to Katharine Hepburn's delineation of a self-enchanted young actress in *Morning Glory*.

FRISCO JENNY

1933

CREDITS

A Warner Bros./First National Picture. Production Supervisor: Raymond Griffith. Director: William A. Wellman. Screenwriters: Wilson Mizner and Robert Lord. Based on a story by Gerald Beaumont, Lillie Hayward and John Francis Larkin. Cinematographer: Sid Hickox. Editor: James Morley. Art Director: Robert Haas. Costumes: Orry-Kelly. Sound: Vitaphone. Running Time: 70 minutes.

CAST

Ruth Chatterton (*Jenny Sandoval*); Louis Calhern (*Steve Dutton*); Donald Cook (*Dan Reynolds*); James Murray (*Dan McAllister*); Helen Jerome Eddy (*Amah*); Hallam Cooley (*Willie Gleason*); Pat O'Malley (*O'Houlihan*); Robert Warwick (*Kelly*); Harold Huber (*Weaver*); Frank McGlynn, Sr. (*Good Book Charlie*); J. Carrol Naish (*Ed Harris*); Noel Francis (*Rose*); Robert Emmett O'Connor (*Jim Sandoval*); Sam Godfrey (*Kilmer*); Franklin Parker (*Martel*); Willard Robertson (*Police Captain*); Edwin Maxwell (*Tom Ford*); Nella Walker (*Mrs. Reynolds*); Berton Churchill (*Mr. Reynolds*); Buster Phelps (*Dan as a Child*); William Wellman (*Reporter*).

During her mid-Thirties years as a Warner Bros. star, stage-trained Ruth Chatterton often played roles that were interchangeable with those of fellow studio contractee Kay Francis. Whether in period costume or chic modern dress, they were usually dramas of suffering women who inevitably had romantic problems. But, for the most part, these were women of class and independence, and one of Chatterton's best was *Frisco Jenny*, a period piece that began in old San Francisco, just prior to the 1906 cataclysm. It's a tale that spans the years between then and 1933, and its star is required to age from a young girl to a prematurely-old middle-aged woman. She manages to do this amazingly well, despite the fact the actress herself was fortyish when *Frisco Jenny* was filmed. It's a metamorphosis subtly achieved through costume, make-up and, of course, the innate ability of a performer whose skills were always under-utilized during the relatively brief span (1928–1936) of her Hollywood career.

Frisco Jenny is little more than a variation on that hoary and much-filmed melodrama *Madame X*, as it shows us a young Jenny Sandoval from her beginnings as the cashier in her father's tough Barbary Coast joint, a place where, apparently, just about anything goes that will bring in cash. Here Jenny learns from the other girls how to take the male customers for all they can get, by whatever means necessary. Jenny seems like a good little girl, but she's really been having a love affair with the beer hall's pianist, Dan McAllister (James Murray), and is expecting a child. They plan to wed, but this idea is loudly vetoed by Jenny's intimidating father Jim (Robert Emmett O'Connor), who threatens to shoot the piano player if he as much as talks with Jenny again. But before she can run away with Dan, the earth tremors begin, and in fast order the building is a shambles, her father and would-be husband are dead, and Jenny is on the streets with her Chinese friend Amah (Helen Jerome Eddy in none-too-convincing Oriental make-up). Jenny is shattered and decides that from then on, the name of her

FRISCO JENNY: Robert Emmett O'Connor and Ruth Chatterton.

FRISCO JENNY: Ruth Chatterton and Louis Calhern.

FRISCO JENNY: James Murray, Ruth Chatterton and Hallam Cooley.

game is survival, first for herself and then for the son she bears out of wedlock.

As the years pass, Jenny becomes successful in gambling and prostitution, and gains a reputation as the most notorious woman in all San Francisco. Later, when she must release her son for adoption, he's raised by a respectable couple under the name of Dan Reynolds (Donald Cook plays the adult Dan), with no knowledge of who his real mother is. Mean-

87

FRISCO JENNY: Louis Calhern and Ruth Chatterton.

THE BITTER TEA OF GENERAL YEN

1933

CREDITS

A Columbia Picture. Producer: Walter Wanger. Director: Frank Capra. Screenwriter: Edward Paramore. Based on the novel by Grace Zaring Stone. Cinematographer: Joseph Walker. Editor: Edward Curtis. Sound: E.L. Bernds. Musical Score: W. Frank Harling. Costumes: Edward Stevenson and Robert Kalloch. Running Time: 89 minutes.

CAST

Barbara Stanwyck (*Megan Davis*); Nils Asther (*General Yen*); Gavin Gordon (*Dr. Robert Strike*); Walter Connolly (*Jones*); Toshia Mori (*Mah-Li*); Lucien Littlefield (*Mr. Jackson*); Richard Loo (*Captain Li*); Clara Blandick (*Mrs. Jackson*); Molly Ming (*Dr. Lin*); Robert Wayne (*Reverend Bostwick*); Knute Erickson (*Dr. Hansen*); Ella Hall (*Mrs. Hansen*); Arthur Millette (*Mr. Pettis*); Helen Jerome Eddy (*Miss Reed*); Martha Mattox (*Miss Avery*); Jessie Arnold (*Mrs. Blake*); Emmett Corrigan (*Bishop Harkness*); Willie

while, Jenny's become associated with a rather slippery lawyer named Steve Dutton (Louis Calhern), whom she's eventually forced to shoot when he threatens to expose her secret life to save himself from a bribery indictment. Charged with Dutton's murder, Jenny now goes up against the D.A., who is, incredibly, her illegitimate son. Sentenced to the gallows, Jenny is visited by a sentimental Dan, but she controls any impulse to reveal her secret to him, nor will she allow the willing Amah to do so on her behalf. The film ends on this tragic note, Jenny's final sacrifice designed to meet all the censorship requirements of the 1933 screen.

Frisco Jenny was Ruth Chatterton's favorite among all her movies, even excluding the excellent 1936 *Dodsworth*. Perhaps this is partially attributable to the size and scope of her Jenny role, admittedly a longer one, in screen time, than Fran Dodsworth. More likely, Chatterton preferred working with director William A. Wellman to *Dodsworth*'s demanding William Wyler. Ironically, she and Wellman started off badly, with each resenting the other's attitude. As Wellman later described it: "At the end of three days, she said 'Truce?' I said, 'Yep. Truce.' She said, 'These have been the most enjoyable three days I've ever spent.' I said, 'It's gonna be enjoyable every time, because you're a great artist and you're a lot of fun to work with and you're in love with a guy I'm crazy about—George Brent.' And from that moment we became nothing but pals. We made a hell of a picture together."

88

THE BITTER TEA OF GENERAL YEN: Nils Asther and Barbara Stanwyck.

Fung (*Officer*); Ray Young (*Engineer*); Miller Newman (*Dr. Mott*); Lillianne Leighton, Harriet Lorraine, Nora Cecil and Robert Bolder (*Missionaries*); Arthur Johnson (*Dr. Schuler*); Adda Gleason (*Mrs. Bowman*); Daisy Robinson (*Mrs. Warden*); Doris Louellyn (*Mrs. Meigs*); Milton Lee (*Telegrapher*).

The Bitter Tea of General Yen marked the end of Barbara Stanwyck's association with Columbia Pictures at a time when that studio listed her among its top box-office stars of 1932. Directed by Frank Capra from Edward Paramore's adaptation of an exotic novel by Grace Zaring Stone, this was an unusual story of sexual attraction between East and West. Stanwyck plays Megan Davis, an American in war-torn Shanghai who insists on accompanying her fiancé, a missionary doctor, into the war zone to rescue orphans in peril. Their car is attacked by soldiers, and she's knocked unconscious, awakening to find herself traveling on the private train of the powerful, Oxford-educated warlord General Yen (Nils Asther). At his summer palace, she is kept a virtual prisoner, attended by Yen's beautiful mistress, Mah-Li (Toshia Mori), whose life Megan later saves by intervening with Yen when Mah-Li is caught betraying secrets to his enemies.

Later, admittedly attracted to the general but at the same time repelled by his (to her) barbaric

THE BITTER TEA OF GENERAL YEN: Barbara Stanwyck and Nils Asther.

THE BITTER TEA OF GENERAL YEN: Barbara Stanwyck and Nils Asther.

methods, Megan is overwhelmed by sympathy for him when Mah-Li's ultimate betrayal causes him to lose all his troops and his power. As she dresses in Oriental attire to please him, Megan is unaware that Yen is preparing to kill himself. It is as she falls on her knees to kiss his hand and, with tears in her eyes, confesses her love for him, that he drinks the fatal cup of poisoned tea. The film ends with Megan sailing back to her people with Yen's American former advisor (Walter Connolly), who remarks to her, "I'll bet your week in China seems like a lifetime." Megan can only gaze out across the water.

The Bitter Tea of General Yen is an offbeat film for Capra at this stage of his career, yet it frequently anticipates the exotic milieu and mysticism of his 1937 *Lost Horizon*. Nor can one ignore the obvious influence of Josef von Sternberg, whose *Shanghai Express* had appeared the year before.

In an extraordinary dream sequence, Capra underscores the latent sexual attraction Megan harbors for her attractive captor. Seated one balmy evening on the terrace outside her room, Megan dozes and fancies that a lust-filled Oriental villain resembling Yen is breaking down her door. As the panels splinter and the door flies open, she is confronted with a horrifying creature whose sharp, pointed ears and talon-like nails terrorize her. But she is saved from worse-than-death by a white-clad hero whose black mask falls away to reveal a *pleasant*-looking General Yen, who takes her into his arms. As they kiss, Megan is obviously in ecstacy. And she awakens quite shaken by the implications of her dream.

Joseph Walker's lighting and photography contribute enormously to the success of this lush melodrama. Stanwyck's often unattractive hairstyles (whether rumpled or over-marcelled) are considerably softened by his artistry, which gives Walter Wanger's fine production an air of beauty and opulence, despite the fact that we never actually see the *extent* of the magnificence that Yen's palace must surely contain.

If many of Stanwyck's fans balked at accepting the idea of her falling in love with an Oriental, at least suave, Swedish-born Nils Asther exuded sufficient sex appeal as General Yen to convince even the skeptical that it was possible. For Barbara Stanwyck in 1933, *The Bitter Tea of General Yen* offered a fascinating change of pace from the working-girl soap operas in which she usually toiled so steadily. It was also the first film to play New York City's famed Radio City Music Hall on January 11, 1933, following its initial life as a live presentation house. Frank

Capra has characterized this movie as "Art with a capital A;" but perhaps it was too arty for its own good, for it lost money. In Britain, it was banned completely, its interracial love affair apparently deemed to be beyond the pale.

THE SILVER CORD

1933

CREDITS

An RKO Radio Picture. Producer: Pandro S. Berman. Director: John Cromwell. Screenwriter: Jane Murfin. Based on the play by Sidney Howard. Cinematographer: Charles Rosher. Editor: George Nicholls, Jr. Sound: Clem Portman. Music: Max Steiner. Running Time: 75 minutes.

CAST

Irene Dunne (*Christina Phelps*); Joel McCrea (*David Phelps*); Frances Dee (*Hester*); Eric Linden (*Robert Phelps*); Laura Hope Crews (*Mrs. Phelps*); Helen Cromwell (*Delia*); Gustav von Seyffertitz (*German Doctor*); Perry Ivins (*Phelps Family Doctor*).

THE SILVER CORD: Irene Dunne and Joel McCrea.

THE SILVER CORD: Eric Linden, Frances Dee, Laura Hope Crews, Irene Dunne and Joel McCrea.

THE SILVER CORD: Irene Dunne and Frances Dee.

Sidney Howard's 1926 stage play of smother love with an unnatural flavor was, in its day, a strong and notable drama that shocked some with its considered attack on the sacred American institution of Motherhood. As directed on Broadway by John Cromwell three years before he began working in movies, Howard's play offered character actress Laura Hope Crews probably the juiciest role of her career as the devious, overprotective widow, Mrs. Phelps, who attempts to exercise total control over her two grown sons. Necessarily stronger in its women's roles, *The Silver Cord* offers its next-best part to Christina, the wife of the elder son David. She realizes she must wage battle with her newly-met mother-in-law to retain not only her marriage and career, but that of her husband as well, and the future of their unborn child. Elisabeth Risdon—best known later for her aunts and mothers in films— was the original Christina, with Margalo Gillmore as Hester, the unstable fiancée of Mrs. Phelps' younger, thin-spined son Robert. Dave and Rob, as they are frequently referred to in the text, were created, respectively, by a pair of actors whom time has obscured, Elliot Cabot and Earle Larimore.

RKO Radio Pictures was understandably slow about bringing *The Silver Cord* to the screen, for its subject matter was not what would usually be considered popular entertainment for a mass medium. That's why the emphasis is shifted away from the mother in the movie's casting, billing and advertising. Before Irene Dunne got the role of Christina, producer Pandro S. Berman had announced first Ann Harding and then the studio's newest sensation Katharine Hepburn. But Dunne had become the studio's most popular leading lady—equally at home in drama and comedy, and in *The Silver Cord*, her name alone stands in large, block letters as the selling factor. Berman wisely engaged Laura Hope Crews to repeat her stage performance as Mrs. Phelps, although she was relegated to billing *below* all four of the play's only other important roles. With Frances Dee as Hester, Joel McCrea as Dave and Eric Linden as Rob, Berman cannily hired the play's John Cromwell to direct.

Jane Murfin's well-wrought screenplay retained most of the Sidney Howard basics, while opening it up to begin with a scene in Germany establishing the promising career in biology of Christina, as well as Dave's bright future with an architectural firm in New York. Like the play, the film stays mostly within the confines of the Phelps' house, although it ventures outside twice—once when Hester hysterically runs off into the night and nearly drowns in an icy pond and, at the close, when those who have escaped from Mrs. Phelps' poisonous clutches are shown driving away from her home. And, rather

than remain confined to a living-room setting, the screenplay roams into bedrooms and kitchen, as well. Other than that, the filmed *Silver Cord* settles down to the business-at-hand, which is the emotional struggle between this monster-mother, her doting sons and the two women who may, or may not, be able to take the boys away from her.

Laura Hope Crews delivers an awe-inspiring performance in a long and verbose part which required effusive speech, subtle charm, thinly veiled self-pity, snobbism and cutting insults. Mrs. Phelps is often not what she seems, and it's the fascination of watching such an incredible monster in action that holds our interest, especially when the part is spun out with the wealth of detail Laura Hope Crews invests in it. For those who know her screen work solely by way of her flibbertigibbet Aunt Pittypat of *Gone With the Wind*, her all-the-stops-out work in *The Silver Cord* will be a revelation. The only reason why she was not nominated for a Best Supporting Actress Academy Award was simply that no such category then existed. As with the stage play, it is the characters of Christina and Hester with which we are most closely concerned here, and Irene Dunne and Frances Dee bring intelligence and emotional depth to these women who are not equally equipped to deal with someone like Mrs. Phelps. The action of the story covers only a day in this claustrophobic household, and yet it is more like a week in hell for all concerned. The film's one failing seems to be in having several decidedly private and crucial conversations conducted in a public manner that would surely have been overheard by the people being talked about. It is a minor complaint, for this is involving, meaty drama, directed and played to the hilt by a sterling cast.

THE SILVER CORD: Joel McCrea, Laura Hope Crews and Irene Dunne.

THE POWER AND THE GLORY

1 9 3 3

CREDITS

A Fox Film. Producer: Jesse L. Lasky. Director: William K. Howard. Screenwriter: Preston Sturges. Cinematographer: James Wong Howe. Editor: Paul Weatherwax. Art Director: Max Parker. Costumes: Rita Kaufman. Music: Louis De Francesco. Running Time: 76 minutes.

THE POWER AND THE GLORY: Colleen Moore and Spencer Tracy.

THE POWER AND THE GLORY: Spencer Tracy and Colleen Moore.

CAST

Spencer Tracy (*Tom Garner*); Colleen Moore (*Sally*); Ralph Morgan (*Henry*); Helen Vinson (*Eve*); Clifford Jones (*Tom Garner, Jr.*); Henry Kolker (*Mr. Borden*); Sarah Padden (*Henry's Wife*); Billy O'Brien (*Tom as a Boy*); Cullen Johnston (*Henry as a Boy*); J. Farrell MacDonald (*Mulligan*); Robert Warwick (*Edward*).

Though strong and downbeat in theme and execution, this little-remembered precursor of Orson Welles' masterpiece *Citizen Kane* tells the story of a ruthless business tycoon's life and death in nonconsecutive flashbacks. The movie owed everything to its imaginative young writer Preston Sturges, who devised the role specifically for Spencer Tracy. A seasoned stage actor before he began in movies, Tracy had been acting for three years in pictures of little lasting value, with the possible exception of *Up the River* and *20,000 Years in Sing Sing*. Producer Jesse L. Lasky was impressed enough with Sturges' script structure of onscreen flashbacks and offscreen commentary that he dubbed the style "narratage" and encouraged publicists to refer to it in the film's promotion. But "narratage" was not easily imitated by others, and was almost forgotten until it resurfaced, in more complex form eight years later in *Citizen Kane*.

In a great career, this is undoubtedly Spencer Tracy's first great performance. Sturges' screenplay afforded the actor a wonderful opportunity to exercise the talents he had built and developed in the theater, and Tracy dug deep within himself and rallied to the occasion. Although at first hesitant to take on a role he wasn't sure he could fulfill—because of its range, taking him from youth to old age—the actor secluded himself before production and memorized the screenplay as a stage actor would. The movie's director, William K. Howard, later reported his reaction to watching the evolution of Tracy's characterization, "I just gulped and said 'Roll.'"

The Power and the Glory begins with the funeral of railway magnate Tom Garner, with Henry (Ralph Morgan), the deceased's lifelong friend and secretary, serving as the movie's focal point as he reflects the negative feelings of his wife (Sarah Padden), and others speak nothing but ill of the dead man. Henry is driven to unload his inner feelings about Garner, and as he tells his wife about his ex-boss, the film moves into a jumble of flashbacks that reveal different aspects of Garner's reprehensible character. It seems that the man came from modest backwoods beginnings, marrying a young schoolteacher named Sally (silent star Colleen Moore in her finest talkie performance). It's she who's instrumental in driving him to advance from railway trackwalker to become company president, and she bears him a son, Tom Jr. (Clifford Jones). Eventually, Sally loses his affections to a rival magnate's daughter, the young and glamorous Eve (Helen Vinson). Garner's announcement that he intends to divorce Sally and marry Eve causes Sally to walk in the path of a bus and be killed. Garner weds Eve, only to discover that she and Tom Jr. have been having an affair. The elder Garner then commits suicide.

Sturges based his screenplay on ideas he derived from the stories his wife Eleanor Hutton recounted about her grandfather, cereal king C. W. Post, who ended *his* life a suicide. It occurred to Sturges that he could tell such a man's story in the manner in which it had reached his own ears—in fragments. And so *The Power and the Glory* was born. Seven years before its author would branch out to also *direct* his screenplays, his work already expressed the grasp of character and script structure that would so richly enhance his acclaimed later work.

FOOTLIGHT PARADE

1933

THE POWER AND THE GLORY: Spencer Tracy, Helen Vinson and Henry Kolker.

CREDITS

A Warner Bros. Picture. Producer: Darryl F. Zanuck. Directors: Lloyd Bacon and Busby Berkeley. Screenwriters: Manuel Seff and James Seymour. Cinematographer: George Barnes. Editor: George Amy. Art Directors: Anton Grot and Jack Okey. Dialogue Director: William Keighley. Costumes: Milo Anderson. Music Director: Leo F. Forbstein. Dances: created and staged by Busby Berkeley. Musical Numbers: "By a Waterfall," "Ah, the Moon Is Here" and "Sittin' on a Backyard Fence" by Sammy Fain and Irving Kahal; "Shanghai Lil" and "Honeymoon Hotel" by Harry Warren and Al Dubin. Running Time: 104 minutes.

CAST

James Cagney (*Chester Kent*); Joan Blondell (*Nan Prescott*); Ruby Keeler (*Bea Thorne*); Dick Powell (*Scotty Blair*); Guy Kibbee (*Silas Gould*); Ruth Donnelly (*Harriet Bowers Gould*); Claire Dodd (*Vivian Rich*); Hugh Herbert (*Charlie Bowers*); Frank McHugh (*Francis*); Arthur Hohl (*Al Frazer*); Gordon Westcott (*Harry Thompson*); Renée Whitney (*Cynthia Kent*); Philip Faversham (*Joe Farrington*); Juliet Ware (*Miss Smythe*); Herman Bing (*Fralick, the Music Director*); Paul Porcasi (*George Appolinaris*); William Granger (*Doorman*); Charles C. Wilson (*Cop*); Barbara Rogers (*Gracie*); Billy Taft (*Specialty Dancer*); Marjean Rogers, Pat Wing, Donna La Barr, Marlo Dwyer and Donna Mae Roberts (*Chorus Girls*); Dave O'Brien (*Chorus Boy*);

FOOTLIGHT PARADE: Dick Powell, Ruth Donnelly and James Cagney.

George Chandler (*Drugstore Clerk*); Hobart Cavanaugh (*Title Thinker-Upper*); William V. Mong (*Auditor*); Lee Moran (*Mac, the Dance Director*); Billy Barty (*Mouse in "Sittin' on a Backyard Fence" Number/Little Boy in "Honeymoon Hotel" Number*); Harry Seymour (*Joe, the Assistant Dance Director/Desk Clerk in "Honeymoon Hotel" Number*); Sam McDaniel (*Porter*); Fred Kelsey (*Hotel Detective*); Jimmy Conlin (*Uncle*); Roger Gray (*Sailor-Pal in*

FOOTLIGHT PARADE: Dick Powell and Ruby Keeler.

FOOTLIGHT PARADE: Ruby Keeler, Joan Blondell, James Cagney and bit players.

"*Shanghai Lil*" Number); John Garfield (*Sailor Behind Table in* "*Shanghai Lil*" *Number*); Duke York (*Sailor on Table in* "*Shanghai Lil*" *Number*).

After the colossal and unexpected success of *42nd Street* and *Gold Diggers of 1933*, Busby Berkeley, the 38-year-old creative genius of these films' groundbreaking, imaginative and spectacular musical segments, was given free rein in devising and directing the production numbers to be featured in *Footlight Parade*. The result, coming as the awe-inspiring finale of a fast-paced backstage musical, was a succession of three major numbers: "Honeymoon Hotel," "By a Waterfall" and "Shanghai Lil." And these multi-set, kaleidoscopic musical segments—taking place, totally unrealistically, on immense stages that no theater anywhere could have accommodated—are undoubtedly what audiences remember best about *Footlight Parade*. Not that its dialogue scenes are bad; quite the contrary, for its quick-moving plot was loaded with snappy talk, directed without a lag by Warner Bros. veteran

FOOTLIGHT PARADE: The "By a Waterfall" number.

Lloyd Bacon, and cast with a mass of Warners talent, topped by ex-*Public Enemy* James Cagney making his first song-and-dance appearance in films.

"By a Waterfall" alone runs more than 10 minutes, moving from the grassy woods knoll where Dick Powell sings romantically to Ruby Keeler, then into a forest pool fed by spectacular waterfalls, where bathing girls dive, frolic and swim in formations that hadn't previously been attempted on the screen. For this water ballet, Berkeley ordered a set that covered almost an entire sound stage, with the pool alone measuring 80 feet by 40, and into which technicians pumped 20,000 gallons of water per minute to keep a steady flow running down the falls and into the pool while the number was being shot. Berkeley reports that he even ordered plate-glass corridors built beneath the pool, so that he could light and photograph it from below.

There are many who consider *Footlight Parade* the best of all the Thirties musicals churned out each year by Warner Bros., and part of that enthusiasm can probably be attributed to the energy and talent of Cagney. In some of his dances, the viewer can detect those eccentric moves he later integrated so successfully into his Oscar-winning performance as George M. Cohan in *Yankee Doodle Dandy*. The plot of *Footlight Parade* is slight but utilitarian: Cagney plays a producer of stage musicals who finds himself challenged by the fact that talking pictures are taking audiences away from the live theater. And so he begins the mass production of musical "Prologues," which he books into movie palaces all over the country as companion pieces to the film features being shown there. He and his staff are constantly challenged to think up new gimmicks for these numbers, as they maintain steady rehearsals with a seemingly limitless supply of hoofing chorus girls.

Among the talents are tenor Dick Powell, tap dancer Ruby Keeler (once she decides to forsake her horn-rimmed glasses and behind-the-scenes job in Cagney's office). And, of course, there's the usual array of solid supporting actors that surround Cagney, topped by the solid professionalism of Joan Blondell as the sidekick who loves him from afar. Meanwhile, he's busy shedding his unpleasant first wife (Renée Whitney), after which flashy, money-grubbing Claire Dodd gets her hooks into him for awhile. But finally, Blondell tells off Dodd, booting her out of Cagney's place with the priceless quip, "As long as they've got sidewalks, *you've* got a job!"

Dick Powell is winning and pleasant-voiced with his sweet tenor rendering of several of the numbers, and Ruby Keeler makes up for what she lacks in

musical-comedy talent with a winning sweetness. This pert, pretty and eager-to-please performer always seemed to be singing slightly off-key, and her tap dancing bordered on the downright clumsy, as she made an exhaustive effort to keep up with the beat, her eyes watching her feet to make certain they were moving the way she wanted them to move. Years later, when Keeler returned to Broadway in the Sixties revival of *No, No, Nanette*, her marvelous dancing was a revelation to those who had winced at some of her efforts in those great old Warners musicals of 30 years earlier.

Of course, they don't make musicals like this anymore. Nor is it likely they could *afford* to! And, when one has the opportunity to rediscover them on TV or videocassette, silent tribute must be paid to the inventive master-director who made them special—Busby Berkeley.

I'M NO ANGEL

1933

CREDITS

A Paramount Picture. Producer: William LeBaron. Director: Wesley Ruggles. Screenwriter: Mae West. Based on *The Lady and the Lions* by Lowell Brentano. Continuity: Harlan Thompson. Cinematographer: Leo Tover. Art Directors: Hans Dreier and Bernard Herzbrun. Editor: Otho Lovering. Sound: F.E. Dine. Music: Harvey Brooks. Lyrics: Gladys du Boise and Ben Ellison. Songs: "Sister Honky-

I'M NO ANGEL: Mae West and Ralf Harolde.

I'M NO ANGEL: Cary Grant and Mae West.

I'M NO ANGEL: Edward Arnold and Mae West.

I'M NO ANGEL: Nat Pendleton, Mae West and Harry Schultz.

Tonk," "No One Loves Me Like That Dallas Man," "Goin' to Town," "I Want You, I Need You" and "I'm No Angel." Running Time: 87 minutes.

CAST

Mae West (*Tira*); Cary Grant (*Jack Clayton*); Gregory Ratoff (*Benny Pinkowitz*); Ralf Harolde (*Slick Wiley*); Edward Arnold (*Big Bill Barton*); Kent Taylor (*Kirk Lawrence*); Gertrude Michael (*Alicia Hatton*); Russell Hopton (*Flea Madigan, the Barker*); Dorothy Peterson (*Thelma*); William B. Davidson (*Ernest Brown, the Chump*); Gertrude Howard (*Beulah*); Libby Taylor and Hattie McDaniel (*Maids*); Nat Pendleton (*Harry, the Trapeze Artist*); Tom London (*Spectator*); Nigel de Brulier (*Rajah*); Irving Pichel (*Bob, the Attorney*); Morrie Cohen (*Chauffeur*); Walter Walker (*Judge*); George Bruggeman (*Omnes*); Monte Collins and Ray Cooke (*Sailors*); Dennis O'Keefe (*Reporter*); Edward Hearn (*Courtroom Spectator*).

Cary Grant is the only star of his caliber who enjoyed two major film appearances opposite Mae West. In 1933, he was her leading man in both the tongue-in-cheek Gay Nineties melodrama *She Done Him Wrong* and the rowdy contemporary comedy *I'm No Angel*. Quite possibly, the latter is the most entertaining of all Mae's films. As usual, Westian innuendos provide the comic strength of her vehicle, this time about the social progress of a midway carnival dancer and lion tamer named Tira (pronounced "TY-ra"), who goes through a succession of smitten males as she rises to a millionaire's gal. Grant plays Jack Clayton, a rich but elusive playboy and Mae's true love, whom she nevertheless sues for a million dollars, charging him with breach of promise. Serving as her own counsel, Tira wins her case by personally cross-examining her man (in a hilarious scene)—and winning him, as well. Mae, of course, was responsible for the leering script, a cleverly contrived bundle of wisecracks, good-natured sex and snatches of suggestive songs, which she sang herself.

I'm No Angel was directed by Wesley Ruggles, who had learned the craft of comedy as a Keystone Kop in the early 1900s and would later be responsible for some of the more inspired comedies of Claudette Colbert (*The Gilded Lily*), Carole Lombard (*True Confession*) and Jean Arthur (*Too Many Husbands*).

At the box-office, *I'm No Angel* outgrossed even *She Done Him Wrong*, and became one of the great comedy hits of the Thirties. In its review, *Variety* noted, "Mae West is today the biggest conversation-provoker, free-space-grabber and all-around box-office bet in the country," and they concluded, "She's as hot an issue as Hitler." Indeed, Mae and her two 1933 blockbusters have been credited with saving Paramount at a time when that studio was seriously considering selling out to Metro-Goldwyn-Mayer.

Again, as in *She Done Him Wrong*, Cary Grant served as a suave and handsome foil for the vulgarly funny West, whose inspired screenplay contributed to the language such catchphrases as "Beulah, peel me a grape," and "When I'm good, I'm very good. But when I'm bad, I'm better." Fortunately, *I'm No Angel* escaped unscathed just before the 1934 Motion Picture Production Code instituted rigid rules about displays or intimations of sexual matters.

LITTLE WOMEN

1933

CREDITS

An RKO Radio Picture. Executive Producer: Merian C. Cooper. Associate Producer: Kenneth MacGowan. Director: George Cukor. Screenwriters: Sarah Y. Mason and Victor Heerman. Based on the novel by Louisa May Alcott. Cinematographer: Henry Gerrard. Editor: Jack Kitchin. Art Director: Van Nest Polglase. Set Decorator: Hobe Erwin. Costumes: Walter Plunkett. Sound: Frank H. Harris. Music: Max Steiner. Special Effects: Harry Redmond. Assistant Director: Edward Killy. Production Associate: Del Andrews. Running Time: 115 minutes.

CAST

Katharine Hepburn (*Jo*); Joan Bennett (*Amy*); Paul Lukas (*Professor Bhaer*); Edna May Oliver (*Aunt March*); Jean Parker (*Beth*); Frances Dee (*Meg*); Henry Stephenson (*Mr. Laurence*); Douglass Montgomery (*Laurie*); John Davis Lodge (*Brooke*); Spring Byington (*Marmee*); Samuel S. Hinds (*Mr. Monk*); Mabel Colcord (*Hannah*); Marion Ballou (*Mrs. Kirke*); Nydia Westman (*Mamie*); Harry Beresford (*Dr. Bangs*); Marina Schubert (*Flo King*); Dorothy Gray and June Filmer (*Girls at Boarding House*); Olin Howland (*Mr. Davis*).

George Cukor's 1933 film version of Louisa May Alcott's *Little Women* is a classic adaptation of an American classic, in every sense of the word. Originally set up for RKO production by David O. Selznick just before he left that studio for MGM, the

LITTLE WOMEN: Katharine Hepburn.

LITTLE WOMEN: Frances Dee, Jean Parker, Katharine Hepburn and Joan Bennett.

movie was one of those fortuitous blends of astute casting and behind-the-scenes craftsmanship that leads to occasional greatness. George Cukor, who was assigned to direct the film, had never so much as read the book, having always dismissed it in his mind as a story for little girls. Years later, in a conversation with Gavin Lambert for the latter's book *On Cukor*, the director admitted, "When I came to read it, I was startled. It's not sentimental or saccharine, but very strong-minded, full of character and a wonderful picture of New England family life. It's full of that admirable New England sternness, about sacrifice and austerity."

Unlike Mervyn LeRoy's prettily Technicolored 1949 MGM remake, this *Little Women* adheres to the episodic, down-to-earth 19th-century realities of the novel, with a script so well written by the team of Victor Heerman and Sarah Y. Mason that it won them Academy Awards for Best Adaptation. It was also a relief to both the motion picture industry and the public (who paid to see it) that here was an honest-to-goodness family picture at a time when censorship groups everywhere were raising Cain about the amount of violence and sexual material so prevalent in many of the current Hollywood releases. A year later, the Production Code would change all that.

Walter Plunkett's authentic-looking period costumes have a lot to do with *Little Women*'s charm,

LITTLE WOMEN: Douglass Montgomery and Katharine Hepburn.

LITTLE WOMEN: Katharine Hepburn, Spring Byington, Jean Parker, Joan Bennett and Frances Dee.

and the detailed indoor and outdoor studio settings by Van Nest Polglase demonstrated why someone with such an unusual name was once so justly revered at RKO.

As the tomboyish Jo, budding writer and the eldest and most influential of the four March daughters, Katharine Hepburn offers one of her finest and most heart-felt performances (although she won 1933's Best Actress Academy Award, it wasn't for her work here, but for the slightly less impressive *Morning Glory*). And as her sisters, Joan Bennett, Jean Parker and Frances Dee afford just the right balance, with firm but gentle Spring Byington as their mother Marmee and vinegary, testy Edna Mae Oliver adding the appropriate acerbic note as their formidable Aunt March. Men are less important elements in the Alcott story, but Douglass Montgomery is well cast as the neighbor who admires Hepburn but wins Bennett, and (future Connecticut Governor and Ambassador to Spain) John Davis Lodge adds his handsome presence to the role of Dee's tutor suitor. All the atmospheric elements are just right here, from the falling snows of the cold season to the chill spring sunshine that finally brings promise of a long New England winter's passing. And, underscoring it all—both the funny moments and the sad—is Max Steiner's sentimental, but never too schmaltzy, background score in the years before his music became the mainstay of Warner Bros. melodramas.

Little Women was accorded Academy Award nominations for Best Picture and Best Director, but lost out to the excellent *Cavalcade* and *its* director, Frank Lloyd. However, *Little Women* turned up on everyone's Ten Best lists for 1933, and what it lacked in awards, it more than compensated for in box-office receipts, ending up one of the year's top money-makers for RKO.

COUNSELLOR AT LAW

1 9 3 3

CREDITS

A Universal Picture. Producer: Carl Laemmle, Jr. Director: William Wyler. Screenwriter: Elmer Rice, based on his stage play. Cinematographer: Norbert Brodine. Editor: Daniel Mandell. Art Director: Charles D. Hall. Sound: Gilbert Kurland. Running Time: 80 minutes.

COUNSELLOR AT LAW: Thelma Todd, Bebe Daniels and John Barrymore.

CAST

John Barrymore (*George Simon*); Bebe Daniels (*Regina Gordon*); Doris Kenyon (*Cora Simon*); Onslow Stevens (*John P. Tedesco*); Isabel Jewell (*Bessie Green*); Melvyn Douglas (*Roy Darwin*); Thelma Todd (*Lillian LaRue*); Marvin Kline (*Herbert Weinberg*); Conway Washburn (*Arthur Sandler*); John Qualen (*Johann Breitstein*); J. Hammond Dailey (*Charlie McFadden*); Clara Langsner (*Lena Simon*); Malka Kornstein (*Sarah Becker*); Angela Jacobs (*Goldie Rindskopf*); T.H. Manning (*Peter J. Malone*); Elmer Brown (*F.C. Baird*); Vincent Sherman (*Harry Becker*); Bobby Gordon (*Henry Susskind*); Barbara Perry (*Dorothy Dwight*); Richard Quine (*Richard Dwight, Jr.*); Victor Adams (*David Simon*); Mayo Methot (*Zedorah Chapman*); Frederick Burton (*Crayfield*); Ed Mortimer (*Man in Waiting Room*).

In a 1989 *Time* magazine article saluting the wealth of great motion pictures produced just 50 years earlier, Gerald Clarke wrote, ". . . a film from 1939 still looks modern, whereas one from 1933 looks like an antique." Quite likely, Mr. Clarke had never seen *Counsellor at Law*, not only one of 1933's finest movies, but one that still impresses 56 years later, thanks to a top-notch blend of script, acting and direction.

For William Wyler, this was an important dramatic breakthrough, after eight years of directing mostly minor Westerns and melodramas, for it paved the

COUNSELLOR AT LAW: Clara Langsner, John Barrymore and Doris Kenyon.

COUNSELLOR AT LAW: John Barrymore and Bebe Daniels.

way for the enduring classics (*Dodsworth, Dead End, Wuthering Heights,* etc.) he would begin directing for producer Samuel Goldwyn a couple of years later. And for John Barrymore, whose career (and health) had begun to decline, it was a rejuvenating shot-in-the-arm that temporarily restored his prestige as an actor.

On stage, Elmer Rice's study of the mounting crises in the hectic life of a successful New York City lawyer was the hit of the 1931–32 Broadway season and a great personal success for its star, Paul Muni. Universal Pictures snapped up the screen rights for a then-hefty $175,000, but whether they also wanted Muni is an issue made cloudy by time. In Jerome Lawrence's well-researched *Actor: The Life and Times of Paul Muni,* he states: "Muni was not even considered. Scared Hollywood took every Jewish element out of the work." Other sources claim that Muni was Universal's first choice for the movie, but that he turned it down for fear of being typecast in Jewish roles on the screen. Whatever the case, Lawrence's contention that all Jewish elements had been removed from Rice's screen adaptation isn't true; none of the play's ethnic character-names were al-

tered. Nor was the leading character's mother, who visits him in his office twice during the film, made to appear other than what she was: a stereotypical Jewish mama. Granted that religious references are non-existent and that there are no specific ethnic references in the dialogue, it isn't difficult to comprehend the background of any of the screenplay's various characters, be they named Weinberg or McFadden.

The action of the story is confined within the walls of the Empire State Building law offices of Simon and Tedesco, venturing out only into the adjacent marble hallways. Yet so involved is Rice's episodic plot and so interesting are his many interwoven characters that there is little time for the viewer to become restless. This is largely attributable to the breakneck pace with which William Wyler directs his excellent cast of players, eight of whom— in the supporting ranks—were recruited to repeat their stage roles. In a basically ensemble work that constantly reveals intriguing snatches of its inhabitants personalities, the primary focus is on George Simon (Barrymore).

Presented to us as one of the top attorneys in Manhattan, Simon is a middle-aged man who has pulled himself up out of a poor East Side Jewish background, and driven to reach the prominent position he now holds. He's married to an aristocratic Gentile divorcee named Cora (Doris Kenyon), a woman with two spoiled children (Barbara Perry and Richard Quine) from a previous union, who's obviously accustomed to a different social strata than George. Simon's chic wife and dowdy mother (Clara Langsner) meet with cool cordiality in his waiting room, as contrasted with the warmth expressed toward the senior Mrs. Simon by George's faithful secretary Regina Gordon (Bebe Daniels), who obviously cares about the older woman. Despite his apparent love for Cora, Simon allows his profession to consume most of his time, so when he and she discuss preparations to sail abroad, we know that something will manage to interfere with those plans.

An incipient crisis that threatens to ruin Simon's career tightens the plot and propels us to a fast conclusion, as evidence is brought forth that will provide Simon with the ammunition he needs to fight those who would see him fail. On top of that comes the realization that not only has his wife been unfaithful to him with a mutual friend (Melvyn Douglas), but—in Simon's enforced absence from that sea voyage—they are actually running away together. All this is too much for Simon. Emotionally distraught, he prepares to commit suicide by jumping from his office window—until the worried and adoring Regina suddenly returns and cries out to him. Brought abruptly to his senses, Simon is angered at having been stopped. But after a phone call brings a frantic request for his immediate help on a domestic murder case, Simon joyfully embraces Regina; the future now seems brighter for them both.

William Wyler's direction never flags as he propels a sizable cast through its paces. Only Isabel Jewell as the loud, *kvetching* office-switchboard operator, alternately phony-voiced (to the public) and sassy (to her fellow employees) seems a bit out of control. Less in her case would have been more. But all the others deliver memorable performances, and John Barrymore is absolutely brilliant in a role which must have required enormous personal discipline and energy. Driven by Wyler to employ an uncharacteristically rapid speech pattern, Barrymore offers a performance unlike any of his others. Wyler reportedly had to tone down the actor's tendency to employ markedly Jewish gestures and intonations in this role, but what remains establishes George Simon for what he is without leaving any doubts in the minds of the film's audience. His moods, his insecurities and his fears are all as evident in Barrymore's work as is his ultimate elation at the movie's close, when it's apparent that a new and more positive chapter is about to begin in his troubled life.

Counsellor at Law proved a great success for Universal, critically as well as comercially. Unfortunately, it has been little seen in recent years, a situation that cable-TV may help rectify. It's a movie well worth rediscovering.

GOING HOLLYWOOD

1933

CREDITS

A Metro-Goldwyn-Mayer Picture. A Cosmopolitan Production. Producer: Walter Wanger. Director: Raoul Walsh. Screenwriter: Donald Ogden Stewart. Based on an original story by Frances Marion. Cinematographer: George Folsey. Editor: Frank Sullivan. Music Director: Lennie Hayton. Songs: "Temptation," "We'll Make Hay While the Sun Shines," "Going Hollywood," "Our Big Love Scene," "After Sundown," "Cinderella's Fella" and "Beautiful Girl" by Nacio Herb Brown and Arthur Freed; "Just an Echo in the Valley" by Reginald Connelly, Jimmy Campbell and Harry Woods. Running Time: 80 minutes.

CAST

Marion Davies (*Sylvia Bruce*); Bing Crosby (*Bill Williams*); Fifi D'Orsay (*Lili Yvonne*); Stuart Erwin (*Ernest P. Baker*); Ned Sparks (*Conroy*); Patsy Kelly (*Jill*); Bobby Watson (*Thompson*); Lennie Hayton and his Orchestra, and The Three Radio Rogues (*Themselves*).

GOING HOLLYWOOD:
Marion Davies.

GOING HOLLYWOOD: Bing Crosby, Marion Davies and Fifi D'Orsay.

duction numbers hardly equalled the sort of all-out, expensive treatment that Metro accorded its own productions. But, in its unpretentious way, *Going Hollywood* was a highly entertaining diversion.

The foolish storyline has platinum-haired Davies as a teacher in a posh girls school who worships from afar crooning sensation Crosby. She gives up her job to follow him west when he heads to California to make a movie. Complications ensue involving his temperamental musical teammate, Fifi D'Orsay, who's got cause to be jealous of Davies' attentions to Crosby. With Stuart Erwin, Patsy Kelly (in her feature film bow) and Ned Sparks along for laughs, *Going Hollywood* weaves some pleasant songs—mostly by Nacio Herb Brown and Arthur Freed—into the proceedings. The film's one big hit is Bing's memorable rendition of "Temptation." And, of course, he and Davies wind up co-starring in that big movie-within-the-movie, after she manages to replace D'Orsay not only in Bing's heart but in his motion picture as well.

Going Hollywood not only proved a needed shot in the arm for Marion Davies' slumping film career, but it also pushed Bing Crosby into the Top Ten of movie stars. Six months after this movie's release, he was earning $500,000 a year, a staggering sum in Depression times.

Here was a case where *Variety*, the entertainment industry's so-called "bible," guessed wrong. Calling *Going Hollywood* a musical "with class in every department except one," it predicted that the weak plot would make public success elusive. But *Variety* underestimated, for one thing, the appeal of crooner Bing Crosby, then at the early peak of his fame as a popular radio singer and recording artist. And it also underestimated the cleverness of the movie's leading lady, Marion Davies, who had insisted on Crosby for the male lead opposite her. Her mentor, millionaire William Randolph Hearst whose Cosmopolitan Productions turned this one out under its ongoing arrangement with MGM, hadn't wanted Bing (he didn't appreciate his singing style). But Marion knew better and, as usual with her long-time "backer," she got her way.

In his autobiography, *Call Me Lucky*, Crosby later recalled *Going Hollywood* as "the most leisurely motion picture I ever had anything to do with." Davies' studio hours only began at 10:00 in the morning (two hours for make-up and costuming) and ended at 5:00 in the afternoon, with a luxurious three-hour lunch break. And so, in an era when many a film was in production only a matter of weeks, this one took a deliberate *six months* to reach completion. Nevertheless, an entertaining and well-made movie resulted, one that met with great success at the box-office. This despite the fact that its pro-

106   GOING HOLLYWOOD: Bing Crosby and
             Marion Davies.

GOING HOLLYWOOD: Bing Crosby and Marion Davies.

IT HAPPENED ONE NIGHT

1934

CREDITS

A Columbia Picture. A Frank Capra Production. Producer: Harry Cohn. Director: Frank Capra. Screenwriter: Robert Riskin. Based on the *Cosmopolitan* magazine short story *Night Bus* by Samuel Hopkins Adams. Cinematographer: Joseph Walker. Editor: Gene Havlick. Art Director: Stephen Gooson. Costumes: Robert Kalloch. Music: Louis Silvers. Sound: E.L. Bernds. Assistant Director: C.C. Coleman. Running Time: 105 minutes.

CAST

Clark Gable (*Peter Warne*); Claudette Colbert (*Ellie Andrews*); Walter Connolly (*Alexander Andrews*); Roscoe

107

IT HAPPENED ONE NIGHT: Claudette Colbert and Clark Gable.

Karns (*Mr. Shapeley*); Jameson Thomas (*King Westley*); Ward Bond and Eddy Chandler (*Bus Drivers*); Wallis Clark (*Lovington*); Arthur Hoyt (*Zeke*); Blanche Frederici (*Zeke's Wife*); Charles C. Wilson (*Joe Gordon*); Charles D. Brown (*Reporter*); Harry C. Bradley (*Henderson*); Harry Holman (*Auto Camp Manager*); Maidel Turner (*Manager's Wife*); Irving Bacon (*Station Attendant*); Harry Todd (*Flag Man*); Frank Yaconelli (*Tony*); Henry Wadsworth (*Drunken Boy*); Claire McDowell (*Mother*); Ky Robinson, Frank Holliday, James Burke and Joseph Crehan (*Detectives*); Milton Kibbee (*Drunk*); Mickey Daniels (*Vendor*); Oliver Eckhardt (*Dykes*); George Breakston (*Boy*); Bess Flowers (*Secretary*); Father Dodds (*Minister*); Edmund Burns (*Best Man*); Ethel Sykes (*Maid of Honor*); Tom Ricketts (*Old Man*); Eddie Kane (*Radio Announcer*); Eva Dennison (*Society Woman*); Fred Walton (*Butler*); Matty Rupert (*Newsboy*); Earl Pingree and Harry Hume (*Policemen*); Ernie Adams, Kit Guard, Billy Engle, Allen Fox, Marvin Loback, Dave Wengren, Bert Starkey and Rita Ross (*Bus Passengers*); Hal Price (*Reporter*).

As director Frank Capra describes it in his acclaimed autobiography, *The Name Above the Title*: "So quietly did the picture open, it failed to merit the usual second-week holdover at Radio City Music Hall—a black mark against future business. Then it happened. Happened all over the country—not in

one night, but within a month. People found the film longer than usual and, surprise, funnier, much funnier than the usual. The quietness burst into the proverbial prairie fire. Theaters sold out for weeks and weeks. Critics went back for a second look, a third, a fourth—and wondered how such excitement could be generated by such routine material. The picture was *It Happened One Night*."

Columbia was then still considered a Poverty Row studio, whose main creative asset was Capra. And Capra had developed for Columbia a script idea with writer Robert Riskin called *Night Bus*. But their every effort to interest an important star in playing either of the two leads met with frustration. Among the no-thank-you's: Myrna Loy, Constance Bennett, Margaret Sullavan, Miriam Hopkins and Robert Montgomery. However, things started looking up when MGM's Louis B. Mayer, seeking to punish his star Clark Gable for seeking a salary increase, packed him off to Columbia on loan-out. With a reluctant, grumbling male lead in place, Capra and Riskin approached Claudette Colbert, who was then enjoying a four-week vacation from Paramount. She wasn't interested, but they managed to badger her until she agreed, with the proviso that they double her Paramount salary and finish the picture within a month's time. And so it all began.

Colbert plays a willful, spoiled heiress who intends to wed a fortune-hunting flier (Jameson Thomas) against the wishes of her father (Walter Connolly),

IT HAPPENED ONE NIGHT: Clark Gable and Claudette Colbert.

IT HAPPENED ONE NIGHT: Clark Gable and Claudette Colbert.

then runs away when he forbids the match. On a bus trip from Miami to New York City, she loses her money and meets a reporter (Gable) who has just been fired from his newspaper. At first, they can't stand one another—until he discovers her identity and senses a story-in-the-making. He then pursues a relationship. When floods force the bus to stop for the night at an auto camp, Colbert and Gable share a cabin, posing as husband and wife, but erecting a makeshift wall with a blanket-on-a-rope between their beds for propriety.

When Colbert's father offers a well-publicized $10,000 reward for her safe return, their fellow passengers notice her picture in the newspapers, forcing the couple to leave the bus and hitchhike. By now they have grown fond of one another, but a misunderstanding ensues when, while Colbert sleeps, Gable steals off to sell his account of her fabricated adventures to his ex-editor for the $1,000 he hopes to use for the start of their marriage. Finding him gone, the disillusioned Colbert returns to

IT HAPPENED ONE NIGHT: Clark Gable, Claudette Colbert and Walter Connolly.

her father, who has by now agreed to her marriage to the aviator. However, he learns of his daughter's true feelings in time, and there is a last-minute change of partners, with Colbert marrying Gable. The final scene finds them again sharing a motel room, where they astound the management by asking for a rope and a blanket, so that they can once again erect—and this time tear down—those "walls of Jericho."

Much of *It Happened One Night* (the film's release title) was improvised as Capra and Riskin got into the picture, with the delighted cooperation of their originally disinterested stars. And, of course, the results struck a responsive spark in a Depression-weary populace. But who could guess *It Happened One Night* would also run off with five of the top Academy Awards for 1934: Best Picture, Director and Screenplay—as well as Actor Gable and Actress Colbert. The movie's success was instrumental in raising Columbia's prestige value from minor league to one of major importance. In 1956, the studio tried remaking this film as a musical with Jack Lemmon and June Allyson, but *You Can't Run Away From It* only proved the impossibility of duplicating 1934's "happy accident."

GAMBLING LADY

1934

CREDITS

A Warner Bros./First National Picture. Associate Producer: Robert Presnell. Director: Archie Mayo. Production Supervisor: Henry Blanke. Screenwriters: Ralph Block and Doris Malloy. Based on a story by Malloy. Cinematographer: George Barnes. Editor: Harold McLernon. Art Director: Anton Grot. Costumes: Orry-Kelly. Sound: Al Riggs. Music: Leo F. Forbstein. Running Time: 66 minutes.

CAST

Barbara Stanwyck (*Lady Lee*); Joel McCrea (*Garry Madison*); Pat O'Brien (*Charlie Lang*); C. Aubrey Smith (*Peter Madison*); Claire Dodd (*Sheila Aiken*); Philip Reed (*Steve*); Philip Faversham (*Don*); Robert Barrat (*Mike Lee*); Arthur Vinton (*Fallin*); Ferdinand Gottschalk (*Cornelius*); Robert Elliott (*Graves*); Arthur Treacher (*Pryor*); Margaret Morris (*Operator*); Willie Fung (*Ching*); Stanley Mack (*Secretary*); Renée Whitney (*Baby Doll*); Rev. Neal Dodd (*Minister*); Edward Keane (*Duke*); Wade Boteler (*Cop*); Willard Robertson (*District Attorney*); Bob Montgomery (*Crooked Gambler*); Milton Kibbee, Eddie Shubert and Ralph

Brooks (*Reporters*); Brooks Benedict (*Lou*); Leonard Carey (*Butler*); Frank Thornton (*Manservant*); Jay Eaton (*Clerk*); Charles C. Wilson and James Burke (*Detectives*); James Donlan (*Lawyer*); Ernie Alexander (*Bellboy*); Maurice Brierre (*Croupier*); Albert Conti (*French Lawyer*); Laura Treadwell (*Guest*); Edward Le Saint (*Sheila's Attorney*); Louis Natheaux (*Dope*).

Typical of the fast-paced, entertaining, program films that Warner Bros. was grinding out in the Thirties is *Gambling Lady*, a melodramatic soap opera that offered Barbara Stanwyck as a professional poker player with the curious monicker of "Lady Lee." She marries into society (Joel McCrea), but gets mixed up in the murder of an old bookie-friend (Pat O'Brien), and a blackmailing femme fatale (Claire Dodd), before the happy ending.

As he did in *Illicit* and *Ever in My Heart*, Archie Mayo again directed Stanwyck in some lively scenes with smart writing. "I'd like to play hearts with you sometime," remarks an enchanted Joel McCrea, soon after they've met. "I kinda' figured that!" retorts Stanwyck in that tough-but-not-unfriendly style she had nearly patented by this time. Flip dialogue aside, *Gambling Lady* offers Stanwyck little acting challenge—except for her climactic scene with Joel McCrea. Blackmailed by Claire Dodd into divorcing McCrea (it was the only way Stanwyck could help him get an alibi for his whereabouts on the night of O'Brien's murder), she faces him in the courtroom just after their divorce has been granted. He hands her her alimony check and she assures him that yes, that was all she wanted—his money. He's embittered; she's heartbroken, but forced to hide it with lies. In a speech designed to convince him that she cares nothing about him anymore, Stanwyck delivers, in one take, a beautifully controlled denunciation, through which she laughs, while her moist eyes provide the only sign of her inner heartbreak. The camera holds her in close-up as she tells McCrea off, then exits quickly to the next room, where she falls against the closed door in tears. As she rips up McCrea's check and walks away, she doesn't notice his wise old father (C. Aubrey Smith) taking it all in. This, of course, leads to an exposure of Claire Dodd's duplicity—and a happy ending.

Most notably, *Gambling Lady* marked the first teaming of Stanwyck and McCrea, resulting in a mutual-admiration alliance that would continue onscreen for 23 years, resulting in *Banjo on My Knee*, *Internes Can't Take Money*, *Union Pacific*, *The Great Man's Lady* and *Trooper Hook*. The movie is also enhanced by the beautiful "other woman" presence of Claire Dodd, a former Ziegfeld showgirl whose 12-year film career (1930–1942) customarily presented her in variations of the same role—the well-born second-female-lead who provides a romantic threat to the heroine. She also portrayed Della Street in a couple of Warners' Perry Mason mysteries of the mid-1930s.

GAMBLING LADY: Robert Barrat and Barbara Stanwyck.

GAMBLING LADY: Barbara Stanwyck, Joel McCrea and Pat O'Brien.

GAMBLING LADY: Claire Dodd and Barbara Stanwyck.

GAMBLING LADY: Barbara Stanwyck, Joel McCrea and Maurice Brierre.

111

VIVA VILLA!

1934

CREDITS

A Metro-Goldwyn-Mayer Picture. Producer: David O. Selznick. Directors: Jack Conway and (uncredited) Howard Hawks. Screenwriters: Ben Hecht and (uncredited) Howard Hawks. Suggested by the book by Edgcumb Pinchon and O.B. Stade. Cinematographers: James Wong Howe and Charles G. Clarke. Editor: Robert J. Kern. Art Director: Harry Oliver. Set Decorator: Edwin B. Willis. Costumes: Dolly Tree. Sound: Douglas Shearer. Music: Herbert Stothart. Music Consultant: Juan Aguilar. Assistant Directors: Art Rosson and John Waters. Technical Advisers: Carlos Novarro and Matias Santoyo. Running Time: 115 minutes.

CAST

Wallace Beery (*Pancho Villa*); Fay Wray (*Teresa*); Leo Carrillo (*Diego*); Donald Cook (*Don Felipe de Castillo*); Stuart Erwin (*Johnny Sykes*); George E. Stone (*Chavito*); Joseph Schildkraut (*General Pascal*); Henry B. Walthall (*Francisco Madero*); Katherine DeMille (*Rosita*); David Durand (*Bugle Boy*); Phillip Cooper (*Villa as a Boy*); Frank Puglia (*Pancho's Father*); Charles Stevens, Steve Clemento, Pedro Regas and John Merkel (*Pascal's Aides*); Harry Cording (*Majordomo*); Francis McDonald (*Villa's Man*); Clarence Hummel Wilson (*Jail Official*); Nigel DeBrulier (*Political Judge*); Sam Godfrey (*Prosecuting Attorney*); Julian Rivero (*Telegraph Operator*); Mischa Auer (*Military Attache*); Francis X. Bushman, Jr. (*Calloway*); Andre Cheron (*French Reporter*); William von Brincken (*German Reporter*); Chris-Pin Martin and Nick DeRuiz (*Peons*); Arthur Treacher (*British Reporter*); Carlos De Valdez (*Old Man*); Charles Requa and Tom Ricketts (*Grandees*); James Martin (*Mexican Officer*); Anita Giordana (*Dancer*); Harry Semels (*Soldier*); Bob McKenzie (*Bartender*); Dan Dix (*Drunkard*); Paul Stanton (*Newspaper Man*); Belle Mitchell (*Spanish Wife*); John Davidson, Brandon Hurst and Leonard Mudie (*Statesmen*); Herbert Prior and Emil Chautard (*Generals*); Adrian Rosley, Hector Sarno and Henry Armetta (*Mendoza Brothers*); Shirley Chambers (*Wrong Girl*); Arthur Thalasso (*Butcher*).

Variety called *Viva Villa!* "a corking good Western." And certainly the epic-sized movie has its share of exciting action scenes and sweeping vistas. As historical biography, however, this account of the life and death of Mexico's national hero, Francisco "Pancho" Villa (1877–1923) is pure Hollywood, as envisioned through the pen of screenwriter Ben

Hecht (with an assist from the film's original director, Howard Hawks). Hecht based his script on a book about Villa's escapades by Edgcumb Pinchon and O.B. Stade. As the film begins, we see Pancho as a boy witnessing his father's whipping-death at the hands of a soldier, because the elder Villa had protested the tyrannical methods of Mexican ruler Porfirio Diaz.

The movie's tone is set when young Pancho avenges his father's killing by stabbing the offending soldier and heading for the mountains, where he grows up as the Robin Hood of his native land, robbing the rich and helping the poor. On one of his forays, the now-adult Pancho (Wallace Beery) finds a lifelong friend in the American newspaper reporter Johnny Sykes (Stuart Erwin). He also finds unexpected allies to his cause in wealthy landowner Don Felipe de Castillo (Donald Cook) and his beautiful sister Teresa (Fay Wray), who introduce him to Francisco Madero (Henry B. Walthall), intellectual leader of the peon revolt that is threatening to erupt. With Villa's help, Madero succeeds in overthrowing Diaz, and is declared president. Madero urges Villa and his followers to disband, leaving military matters to his new advisor General Pascal (Joseph Schildkraut).

When Villa gets in trouble with his lawless ways, Madero grants him a pardon, on the condition that he leave Mexico—which is all that the treacherous Pascal needs. In short order, he kills Madero and takes command of the country himself. A vengeful Villa returns to stage a bloody revolution. However, this time Don Felipe and Teresa refuse Villa their cooperation. Villa captures Pascal, but rather than kill him outright, Villa has him tied to an anthill to face a slow and agonizing death. Teresa dies by a stray bullet from the gun of one of Villa's fighters, and Don Felipe shoots Villa to avenge her. Pancho dies in the arms of his friend Sykes, as the latter improvises the fallen leader's obituary.

Under Howard Hawks' direction, location footage and major action sequences of *Viva Villa!* were shot in Mexico—until an "incident" involving actor Lee Tracy (the movie's original Johnny Sykes) got the company ostracized. Reports differ, but it seems that Tracy, a notorious boozer, had awakened following a night of debauchery and relieved himself from his hotel's balcony while a parade of Mexican soldiers was passing beneath. With Tracy placed under temporary arrest and MGM publicly embarrassed, Louis B. Mayer feared a possible Mexican embargo on all Metro product. Accordingly, Tracy was sacked and replaced by comic actor Stuart Erwin, for whom the Sykes part had to be rewritten. Director Hawks refused to testify against Tracy, and walked out on

VIVA VILLA!: Katherine DeMille, Wallace Beery and bit players.

the project, to be replaced by Jack Conway, who directed the remaining footage that had to be shot in California.

Mexico, of course, also protested the casting of Wallace Beery, an actor better known for his oafish and comic character roles. As it turned out, his Pancho Villa was one of Beery's finest performances, drawing from the actor an unexpected range from vicious and egomaniacal outlaw leader to sheepish, overgrown child with an unexpected sense of humor and absolutely no moral recriminations for the outrageous path of destruction he had left in his wake. It's a performance for which Beery should have won at least an Academy Award *nomination*—especially in a year in which there were only *three* Best Actor nominees. He did, however, receive recognition elsewhere—the Best Actor prize at 1934's Venice Film Festival. As for the Academy of Motion Picture Arts and Sciences, it did accord *Viva Villa!* nominations for Best Picture, screenplay adaptation and sound, and a back-of-the-hand statuette—to John Waters in the now obsolete category of Best Assistant Director.

VIVA VILLA!: Wallace Beery and Fay Wray.

TWENTIETH CENTURY

1 9 3 4

CREDITS

A Columbia Picture. Producer-Director: Howard Hawks. Screenwriters: Charles MacArthur and Ben Hecht, based on their stage play, adapted from the unproduced play *The Napoleon of Broadway* by Charles Bruce Milholland. Cinematographer: Joseph August. Editor: Gene Havlick. Running Time: 91 minutes.

CAST

John Barrymore (*Oscar Jaffe*); Carole Lombard (*Mildred Plotka/Lily Garland*); Walter Connolly (*Oliver Webb*); Roscoe Karns (*Owen O'Malley*); Ralph Forbes (*George Smith*); Dale Fuller (*Sadie*); Etienne Girardot (*Matthew J. Clark*); Herman Bing and Lee Kohlmar (*Bearded Men*); James P. Burtis (*Train Conductor*); Billie Seward (*Anita*); Charles Lane (*Max Jacobs*); Mary Jo Mathews (*Emmy Lou*); Ed Gargan (*Sheriff*); Edgar Kennedy (*McGonigle*); Gigi Parrish (*Schultz*); Fred Kelsey (*Detective on Train*); Pat Flaherty (*Flannigan*); Ky Robinson (*Detective*); Cliff Thompson (*Lockwood*); Nick Copeland (*Treasurer*); Sherry Hall (*Reporter*); Howard Hickman (*Dr. Johnson*); James Burke (*Chicago Detective*); George Reed (*Uncle Remus*); Clarence Geldert (*Southern Colonel*); Lillian West (*Charwoman*); Fred "Snowflake" Toones (*Porter*); Steve Gaylord Pendleton (*Brother in Play*); King Mojave (*McGonigle's Assistant*); Eddy Chandler (*Cameraman*); Harry Semels (*Artist*); Lynton Brent (*Train Secretary*); Anita Brown (*Stage Show Girl*); Irene Thompson (*Stage Actress*); George Offerman, Jr. (*Stage Carpenter*); Buddy Williams (*Stage Actor*).

In a 1938 *New York Post* interview, Carole Lombard revealed some of her thoughts about what this, her 48th feature film, meant to her career: "My greatest opportunity came when I was cast with John Barrymore in *Twentieth Century*. I learned more about acting from that man in the six weeks it took to make the picture than I ever had before. I listened to him for the entire six weeks, and got a real course in dramatics. That was the beginning of knowing something."

Barrymore had requested her for the role in the first place, and was later to admit, "She is perhaps the greatest actress I ever worked with." By the same token, *Twentieth Century* is a wonderful example of

TWENTIETH CENTURY: Ralph Forbes, Carole Lombard and John Barrymore.

Thirties screwball comedy, and certainly the best movie comedy role—if not the best movie role—that the flamboyant actor ever had.

On the stage, *Twentieth Century* had confined its action aboard the Twentieth Century Limited during that train's journey from Chicago to New York, save for a final scene in Grand Central Station. But for the movie, playwrights Ben Hecht and Charles MacArthur opened up the action. They begin their story three years earlier and establish the relationships of its leading characters *before* they board the train. Thus we see egomaniacal Broadway impresario Oscar Jaffe (Barrymore) as he meets and makes a stage star out of former shopgirl Mildred Plotka (Lombard), whom he immediately rechristens "Lily Garland." Their partnership, both on and off the stage, leads to a succession of hit plays before Lily grows tired of Oscar's possessiveness—which includes having her tailed by a private eye named McGonigle (Edgar Kennedy)—and she walks out on him to accept a Hollywood contract. While Lily repeats her Broadway success in motion pictures, Oscar's stage productions without her are all flops.

Three years later, with his *Joan of Arc* a failure in Chicago, Jaffe is broke and forced to skip town in disguise. Traveling the Twentieth Century Limited, Jaffe learns that the important movie star Lily Gar-

TWENTIETH CENTURY: Carole Lombard, Roscoe Karns and Walter Connolly.

115

TWENTIETH CENTURY: Carole Lombard and Ralph Forbes.

land is, by coincidence, also on board. She is with her current fiancé, the football player George Smith (Ralph Forbes), to whom Jaffe takes an immediate dislike. Dead set on luring her back, Jaffe campaigns to convince Lily to play Mary Magdalene in his lavish, upcoming version of *The Passion Play*. But his plan goes up in smoke when it develops that Clark (Etienne Girardot), a fellow passenger who had promised to invest his wealth in Jaffe's play, is nothing more than a penniless, escaped lunatic. Lily is about to sign with Jaffe's rival, Max Jacobs (Charles Lane), when Jaffe feigns a mortal wound as a result of a struggle with Clark. He manages to win Lily's signature on a contract as her last gesture to a "dying" man. But too late Lily realizes his ruse and, at fadeout, the couple resume their embattled relationship of old.

As expected from Barrymore, he's in his actor's element as Oscar Jaffe. It's a marvel to watch him as he runs the gamut of inspired thespian tricks, impersonations, disguises and ploys to win his theatrical way with one and all. Barrymore based his characterization on a number of larger-than-life autocrats of the Broadway theater, and those of an earlier age would most certainly recognize elements attributable to the likes of David Belasco and Jed Harris. Carole Lombard, on the other hand, was at first somewhat awed by the role *and* her celebrated co-star, but director Howard Hawks painstakingly drew

from her the wonderful comedy performance that is now permanently preserved on celluloid. The movie was shot in three weeks, with Barrymore later recalling: "How Carole Lombard ever managed to stand the pace is more than I can imagine. But she took it in her stride, giving a whirlwind performance day after day, and always fresh as a daisy. Her terrific industry frightened me."

It was *Twentieth Century*, of course, that finally established the dramatically seasoned Lombard as the wonderful comedienne for which she is well and justly remembered. Unfortunately, the film, for all its madcap comedy scenes, and the great interacting of its stars and solid supporting cast, has the limitations of its eccentric subject matter—the theater— which has never been a subject of empathy for the general public, especially outside of big cities. And, as it was also the year of *It Happened One Night*, Columbia's Harry Cohn elected to have his publicists concentrate on *that* movie, which, of course, ran off with all the top Academy Awards for 1934. *Twentieth Century* failed even to win a nomination.

In 1978, a successful musical version of this work reached Broadway under the title *On the Twentieth Century*, with Madeline Kahn, John Cullum and Kevin Kline. But, thus far, no version has been able to erase the indelible 1934 creation of Barrymore, Lombard and Hawks.

TWENTIETH CENTURY: John Barrymore and Carole Lombard.

LITTLE MAN, WHAT NOW?: Margaret Sullavan.

LITTLE MAN, WHAT NOW?

1934

CREDITS

A Universal Picture. Producer: Carl Laemmle, Jr. Director: Frank Borzage. Screenwriter: William Anthony McGuire. Based on the novel *Kleine Man, Was Nun?* by Hans Fallada. Cinematographer: Norbert Brodine. Editor: Milton Carruth. Music: Arthur Kay. Art Director: Charles D. Hall. Running time: 95 minutes.

CAST

Margaret Sullavan (*Lämmchen*); Douglass Montgomery (*Johannes "Hans" Pinneberg*); Alan Hale (*Holger Jachman*); Catherine Doucet (*Mia Pinneberg*); Fred Kohler (*Karl Goebbler*); Mae Marsh (*Goebbler's Wife*); DeWitt Jennings (*Emil Kleinholtz*); Alan Mowbray (*Franz Schlüter*); Muriel Kirkland (*Marie Kleinholtz*); Hedda Hopper (*Nurse*); Sarah Padden (*Widow Scharrenhofer*); G.P. Huntley Jr. (*Heilbutt*); Christian Rub (*Puttbreese*); Frank Reicher (*Lehman*); Monroe Owsley (*Kessler*); Etienne Girardot (*Spannfuss*); Bodil Rosing (*Frau Kleinholtz*); Donald Haines (*Emil Kleinholtz*); Paul Fix (*Lauderback*); Tom Ricketts (*Mr. Sesam*); Carlos de Valdez (*Dr. Sesam*); Max Asher (*Chauffeur*); Earle Fox (*Frenchman*); George Meeker (*Schultz*).

With so many of the big-studio moguls harboring sentiments about their European roots, it was only natural that they should lean toward old-country source material for many of the movies that they produced during the Thirties. And the internationally best-selling 1933 German novel *Little Man, What Now?* by Hans Fallada (Rudolf Ditzen) caught the attention of producer Carl Laemmle, Jr., whose father had emigrated from Germany to found Universal Pictures. The book had already become a German film in 1933 under the title *Kleiner Man, Was Nun?* with Herta Thiele and Hermann Thiemig in the roles now cast with Margaret Sullavan (in only her second film) and Douglass Montgomery. The opinionated, stage-trained Sullavan had little use for most of her Hollywood motion pictures, but this was one she approved of, although there was little behind-the-scenes-rapport between her and her sensitive leading man. Fortunately for the movie, this is not evident on the screen, where they appear well matched and appropriate for the material.

LITTLE MAN, WHAT NOW?: Douglass Montgomery and Margaret Sullavan.

LITTLE MAN, WHAT NOW?: Alan Hale, Douglass Montgomery, Margaret Sullavan and Bill Morrison.

119

Little Man, What Now? bears some relationship to the silent D. W. Griffith classic *Isn't Life Wonderful*, in that both stories deal with young Germans coping with life in the Depression that followed World War I. But, while the Griffith film took a somewhat harsher, more realistic approach to its subject matter, Frank Borzage's 1934 drama reflected that director's penchant for romantic love stories in which the protagonists overcome adversity to face an optimistic future. And, indeed, the very-much-in-love young married couple here portrayed by Sullavan and Montgomery never waver in their mutual loyalty, despite his difficulty holding down jobs amid her pregnancy—a situation that they hadn't planned and can ill afford. At first, the husband is a clerk for a tyrant (DeWitt Jennings) who hires only bachelors in the hope one might become the husband of his ugly-duckling daughter (Muriel Kirkland). Unfortunately, the daughter has her sights set on Montgomery, who quits when his marital status is revealed. Next, he's a clothing salesman whose job is jeopardized by a selfish actor (Alan Mowbray), who takes up two hours of his time "doing research for a role" and refuses to buy anything. Montgomery justifiably berates the actor who cost him his job. The couple's situation changes when they go to live in an-other city with Montgomery's giddy stepmother (Catherine Doucet) and the good-hearted scoundrel (Alan Hale) who's her lover and partner in what amounts to a high-class bordello. The young couple next share a garret, where their child is born. And, in a fairytale ending, life suddenly looks incredibly bright for them as an old colleague of Montgomery's suddenly turns up to offer him a job in Amsterdam.

Aside from the movie's constant undercurrent of optimism amid all its peripheral political rumblings and incidental characters pointing toward the European rise of Communism and Fascism, its audience is seldom in doubt that the protagonists will come through it all unscathed. Borzage's ever-present sense of the romantic ideal in young love prevails throughout the story, and in case one has any doubts, there is always the lush romanticism of Arthur Kay's music. As so often has been the case in Hollywood movies, the background score tells us when not to worry as often as when to be concerned. But for the excellent performances by all concerned, especially Sullavan and Montgomery, *Little Man, What Now?* might lack the underlying tensions that would negate audience interest altogether. As it stands, the film remains an interesting relic of a less complex era.

CLEOPATRA

1934

CREDITS

A Paramount Picture. Producer-Director: Cecil B. De Mille. Screenwriters: Waldemar Young and Vincent Lawrence. Based on historical material by Bartlett Cormack, Jeanie McPherson and Finley Peter Dunne, Jr. Cinematographer: Victor Milner. Editor: Anne Bauchens. Music: Rudolph Kopp. Costumes: Travis Banton. Sound: Franklin Hansen. Assistant Director: Cullen Tate. Running Time: 102 minutes.

CAST

Claudette Colbert (*Cleopatra*); Warren William (*Julius Caesar*); Henry Wilcoxon (*Marc Antony*); Gertrude Michael (*Calpurnia*); Joseph Schildkraut (*Herod*); Ian Keith (*Octavian*); C. Aubrey Smith (*Enobarbus*); Ian MacLaren (*Cassius*); Arthur Hohl (*Brutus*); Leonard Mudie (*Pothinos*); Irving Pichel (*Apollodorus*); Claudia Dell (*Octavia*); Eleanor Phelps (*Chairman*); John Rutherford (*Drussus*); Grace Durkin (*Iras*); Robert Warwick (*Achilles*); Edwin Maxwell (*Casca*); Charles Morris (*Cicero*); Harry Beresford (*The Soothsayer*); Olga Celeste (*Slave Girl*); Ferdinand Gottschalk (*Glabrio*); William Farnum (*Senator*); Florence Roberts (*Flora*); Kenneth Gibson and Wedgwood Nowell (*Scribes*); John Carradine, Jane Regan, Celia Rylan and Robert Manning (*Romans*); Lionel Belmore (*Party Guest*); Dick Alexander (*Egyptian Messenger*); Jack Mulhall and Wilfred Lucas (*Romans Greeting Antony*); Hal Price (*Onlooker at Procession*); Edgar Dearing (*Murderer*).

CLEOPATRA: Claudette Colbert.

With his lavish but plodding 1932 costume spectacle *The Sign of the Cross*, master movie showman Cecil B. DeMille brought back to American audiences the sort of film not seen since the great days of silent pictures. He chose to follow that blockbuster with a pair of cheaper and less successful efforts, *This Day and Age* and *Four Frightened People*, that left his audiences somewhat confused as to what to expect from a DeMille picture. But with *Cleopatra*, grandiose and spectacular entertainment once again became the order of the day—with dashes of sexual suggestion in costuming, as well as situation. What DeMille would have done with the liberal attitudes of the Eighties will never be known. And while we now smile with amusement at the "camp" aspects of his big hits of yesteryear, one cannot deny that his public was entertained.

Variety's 1934 review of *Cleopatra* reveals that a sophisticated preview audience of that year was just as inclined to laugh at the movie's pretentious dialogue then as it would today. Did DeMille take his pictures seriously? By all reports of his colleagues and co-workers, he most certainly did. But the man was a complex figure not well known for his sense of humor, and he asked a lot from his casts. While taking a cavalier attitude toward historical facts, DeMille required much time, money and research be spent on authenticating what he *wished* to authenticate: sets, costumes and mores of the era being depicted. He wasn't above some clever manipulating to get his way. The climax of *Cleopatra* required that the actress portraying that famed Egyptian queen commit suicide by pressing an asp to her breast. But such was Claudette Colbert's fear of

CLEOPATRA: Warren Williams, Claudette Colbert, Leonard Mudie and players.

122

snakes that she refused to handle one. DeMille, having delayed that scene until all Colbert's earlier ones were completed, appeared on the set one day handling a large and intimidating boa constrictor. As he approached, his star screamed, "Oh, Mr. De Mille, don't come near me with that!" To which her director replied, "Well, how about this one?" And with that, he brought forth a little six-inch garden snake he had been hiding behind his back. Colbert accepted the snakelet with relief, and proceeded to shoot the scene.

Like most of DeMille's biggest pictures, *Cleopatra* did not please the critics. But the public devoured its lavish *kitsch* and marveled at its expensive excesses, the best example of which is the royal barge sequence in which Cleopatra seduces Marc Antony, played by the ruggedly handsome British actor Henry Wilcoxon. The barge itself required an immense set, from its banks of oars to the mass of cushions decorating the dais on which the lovers recline. To the cadenced beat of drums, near-naked slave girls dance about a garlanded ox. Writhing and dancing females are everywhere, with one contingent whipped into naked submission by a giant slave, while others, attired only in seaweed, are lifted up in a net to sprawl on the barge's deck with offerings of jewel-filled seashells. The signal that Antony has fallen under Cleopatra's spell occurs when veils swirl up around her couch while singing maidens scatter flower petals everywhere, and the barge begins moving out to sea. It is the grandest and gaudiest of grand DeMille set-pieces—the epitome of outrageously effective showmanship.

It's a great tribute to Claudette Colbert's artistry that her Cleopatra reached the screen in the same year that she displayed her versatility with both John M. Stahl's moving drama *Imitation of Life* and Frank Capra's delightful comedy *It Happened One Night,* for which she won her only Academy Award. In portraying the infamous Egyptian love goddess, Colbert models Travis Banton's lavish and daring costumes with panache and abandon, in the same manner that she delivers her sometimes risible dialogue with tongue-in-cheek flair. Colbert walks a cool middle line, on the one side letting her public know that she never takes this historic queen *too* seriously, while at the same time not insulting DeMille's serious-business approach to historical spectacle. Since this was her third picture for "C.B.," DeMille obviously respected her talent and liked her performance.

With Henry Wilcoxon as Antony and Warren William abandoning his customary business suits for the Roman togas of Julius Caesar, DeMille sur-

CLEOPATRA: Eleanor Phelps, Claudette Colbert, Grace Durkin and bit players.

CLEOPATRA: Henry Wilcoxon and Claudette Colbert.

rounded his Cleopatra with stalwart males to match the grandeur of the opulent sets and costumes. And although DeMille pictures did not then often impress the Academy of Motion Picture Arts and Sciences, *Cleopatra* did—to the extent that it brought Victor Milner an award for cinematography, as well as nominations for Best Picture, film editing, sound and Best Assistant Director.

Expensive though it obviously was, the 1934 *Cleopatra* did not threaten to ruin its producing studio, as did the 1963 Elizabeth Taylor-Richard Burton-Rex Harrison fiasco that cost 20th Century-Fox several fortunes—and bored everyone to tears.

OUR DAILY BREAD

1 9 3 4

CREDITS

A United Artists Picture. Producer-Director: King Vidor. Screenwriters: King Vidor, Elizabeth Hill and Joseph L. Mankiewicz. Cinematographer: Robert Planck. Editor: Lloyd Nosler. Music: Alfred Newman. Running Time: 74 minutes.

OUR DAILY BREAD:
Karen Morley.

OUR DAILY BREAD: Karen Morley.

OUR DAILY BREAD: Addison Richards and Barbara Pepper.

127

Karen Morley (*Mary Sims*); Tom Keene (*John Sims*); John Qualen (*Chris*); Barbara Pepper (*Sally*); Addison Richards (*Louie*); Lionel Baccus (*Barber*); Harris Gordon (*Cigar Salesman*); Bill Engel (*Jew*); Frank Minor (*Plumber*); Henry Hall (*Carpenter*); Frank Hammond (*Undertaker*); Lynton Brant (*Bully*); Henry Burroughs (*Politician*); Henry Bradley (*Professor*); Captain Anderson (*Blacksmith*); Si Clogg (*Lawyer*); Ray Spiker (*Ex-Convict*); Harry Semels (*Italian Shoemaker*); Sidney Miller (*Jewish Boy*); Alex Schumberg (*Violinist*); Bud Ray (*Stone Mason*); Bob Reeves (*Hannibal*); Ed Biel (*Powerhouse Man*).

King Vidor (1894–1982) was a truly eclectic film-maker whose raft of memorable movies range from timeless Twenties classics (*The Big Parade*), to camp Forties "classics" (*Beyond The Forest*), and from small-scale critics' favorites (*The Crowd*) to box-office epics (*Duel in the Sun* and *War and Peace*), as well as trenchant social commentary (*Street Scene* and *Our Daily Bread*). He was also the maverick director of such daringly uncommercial pictures as the all-black *Hallelujah*.

Prior to *Our Daily Bread*, Vidor had directed many of his movies for MGM. But this original Vidor story, whose screenplay was developed by Elizabeth Hill and Joseph L. Mankiewicz, met with strong resistance from Metro production chief Irving Thalberg, who told Vidor that he wanted no part of a motion picture dealing with communal farms and Socialist themes—which was most certainly the heart and soul of *Our Daily Bread*, no matter how innocently intended in 1934.

And so a dedicated Vidor was forced to do without the well-heeled production facilities of MGM and, using his own money, became both the film's producer and director. Forming Viking Pictures, for release through United Artists, he worked resourcefully on a shoestring budget with only one professional "name" among his cast—that of Karen Morley (who, significantly, would later abbreviate her own career through controversial political affiliations). In Vidor's simplistic, but naïvely effective story, Morley plays Mary, the strong and steadfast wife of John Sims (Tom Keene, a star of minor Westerns who sometimes used the pseudonym of George Duryea). This downtrodden young couple inherit a largely rundown old farm, which they subsequently attempt to save by rounding up homeless workers to join them in a communal enterprise.

While this collective tills the soil and Mary uses her wits to keep them fed, John begins to grow restless and loses heart in the project. And when a city tramp named Sally (Barbara Pepper, made up as a carbon copy Jean Harlow) turns up at the farm and seduces him, John abandons wife and friends to run off with her when they need his support most—amid a crop-threatening drought.

But the discovery of a hidden stream brings John to his senses, and he returns in time to organize the farm workers in a massive ditch-digging effort that ultimately saves both their wheat crops—and his marriage. This sequence—justly celebrated as a landmark of American Thirties cinema—shows director Vidor at his inventive best, working in obvious homage to the great Russian moviemakers of the silent screen as he offers an unforgettable montage of men, women and children united in carting rocks, felling trees and literally moving earth until that precious water is free to flow down into their valley and irrigate the parched crops.

Unfortunately, *Our Daily Bread*'s whole is not as great as its parts, due to a low budget and some undernourished performances. But the movie remains an engrossingly well intentioned human drama—almost Capra-esque in its optimistic faith in the survival of the human spirit. On the occasion of its first national TV showing on PBS in 1972, critic Judith Crist called *Our Daily Bread*, "a piece of Americana to revel in."

OUR DAILY BREAD: John Qualen, Karen Morley and Tom Keene.

MENACE: Berton Churchill, Gertrude Michael, Raymond Milland and Paul Cavanagh.

MENACE

1934

CREDITS

A Paramount Picture. Director: Ralph Murphy. Screenwriters: Anthony Veiller and Chandler Sprague. Based on a story by Philip MacDonald. Cinematographer: Benjamin Reynolds. Running Time: 58 minutes.

CAST

Gertrude Michael (*Helen Chalmers*); Paul Cavanagh (*Colonel Crecy*); Henrietta Crosman (*Mrs. Thornton*); John Lodge (*Ronald Cavendish*); Robert Allen (*Andrew Forsythe*); Raymond Milland (*Freddie Bastion*); Berton Churchill (*Norman Bellamy*); Desmond Roberts (*Underwood*); Halliwell Hobbes (*Skinner*); Arletta Duncan (*Gloria Chalmers*); Doris Llewellyn (*Cynthia Bastion*); Gwenllian

Gill (*Alison Bastion*); Forrester Harvey (*Wilcox*); Montagu Love (*Police Inspector*); Arthur Clayton (*Police Officer*); Rita Carlyle (*English Landlady*); A.S. Byron (*English Police Sergeant*).

In the Thirties, every Hollywood studio turned out many a B-picture, along with the more costly, big star movies that were the main attraction. These smaller-scaled motion pictures were often a training ground for studio contract players. Frequently, these actors would have leads in the programmers and small roles in the big, important A-films, while their studios groomed them for whatever future their talent and/or sex appeal might promise them. At Paramount in the mid-Thirties, blonde contract star Carole Lombard justifiably balked at some of the assignments she was handed by her superiors, and so blonde contract *starlet* Gertrude Michael—with her aristocratic profile and Alabama accent—was given some of those roles. And that's how Michael came by her first leading part, in Paramount's 1934 *The Notorious Sophie Lang*, the first of three movies in which she portrayed a glamorous jewel thief by that name. Michael also got the glamour treatment in

MENACE: Halliwell Hobbes and Gertrude Michael.

Paramount's portrait gallery, and it's interesting to note that their make-up artists tried to make her look as much like Carole Lombard as possible. And so they also did in the 1934 melodrama entitled *Menace.*

In a tight 58 minutes, *Menace* does little but entertain. For this is a compact and fast moving mystery melodrama that wastes no time setting up its plot, and then proceeds to throw its various protagonists together in an isolated house for an evening of tensions and terrors perpetrated by persons unknown—until the last few minutes. *Menace* covers a lot of territory for a murder mystery that runs less than an hour (not an unusual length for a Thirties "B"). And even the conservative *New York Times* remarked that "It ranks several notches higher than the average murder film."

The story opens in British East Africa, where Gertrude Michael, Paul Cavanagh and Berton Churchill, in search of a fourth person to join them

for bridge, persuade mining engineer Raymond (before he became "Ray") Milland to leave his dam for the evening and join them. This he does, flying over from the construction camp where he shares a cottage with his two sisters. But a violent rainstorm erupts during the evening and, despite his friends' pleas for him to stay for the night, Milland takes off in his plane, only to witness from high above the destruction of the dam and a flood which wipes out his home and family. Distraught, he crashes to his death. Michael, Cavanagh and Churchill soon begin receiving mailed death threats from Milland's insane brother, who blames them for his family tragedy and swears vengeance.

Two years later, the narrative finds its three protagonists living at Michael's remote but lavish house in Santa Barbara, California, where no time is lost in setting them all up for murder. We learn that Milland's mad brother has escaped from the asylum where he's been held and is headed their way. After

130

MENACE: Gertrude Michael, Arletta Duncan and Henrietta Crosman.

which, several male strangers arrive on the scene to provide the story with its necessary suspects: a rather sinister looking butler (Halliwell Hobbes) is sent them by an employment agency; their eccentric, elderly neighbor (Henrietta Crosman) comes visiting unannounced and accompanied by a suavely handsome professional actor (John Lodge) whom she admits to having only recently befriended; and Michael's younger sister (Arletta Duncan) turns up with a new "fiancé" (Robert Allan) in tow. Lights go off, the phone line is cut and Churchill is stabbed to death with an ornamental knife that disappears. But murder mysteries should be kept secret; the killer won't be divulged in these pages.

Credit for *Menace*'s effectiveness can be directed toward its unsung, and nearly forgotten, director Ralph Murphy (1895–1967), who remained a Paramount "house fixture" from the early Thirties to the mid-Forties. A list of his movie titles won't mean much to most readers of this book, and there's not

MENACE: Paul Cavanagh, Halliwell Hobbes and Gertrude Michael.

even a near-classic among them. But Murphy obviously possessed the knowledge and the efficiency of a competent craftsman and, for what it sets out to accomplish, *Menace* entirely succeeds.

THE BARRETTS OF WIMPOLE STREET

(THE FORBIDDEN ALLIANCE)

1934

CREDITS

A Metro-Goldwyn-Mayer Picture. Producer: Irving Thalberg. Director: Sidney Franklin. Screenwriters: Ernst Vajda, Claudine West and Donald Ogden Stewart. Based on the play by Rudolf Besier. Cinematographer: William Daniels. Editor: Margaret Booth. Art Directors: Cedric Gibbons and Harry McAfee. Set Decorator: Edwin B. Willis. Costumes: Adrian. Music: Herbert Stothart. Sound: Douglas Shearer. Assistant Director: Hugh Boswell. Running Time: 110 minutes.

CAST

Norma Shearer (*Elizabeth Barrett*); Fredric March (*Robert Browning*); Charles Laughton (*Edward Moulton Barrett*); Maureen O'Sullivan (*Henrietta Barrett*); Katherine Alexander (*Arabel Barrett*); Ralph Forbes (*Capt. Surtees Cook*); Una O'Connor (*Wilson*); Marion Clayton (*Bella Hedley*); Ian Wolfe (*Harry Bevan*); Ferdinand Munier (*Dr. Chambers*); Leo G. Carroll (*Dr. Ford-Waterlow*); Vernon Downing (*Octavius Barrett*); Neville Clark (*Charles Barrett*); Matthew Smith (*George Barrett*); Robert Carleton (*Alfred Barrett*); Alan Conrad (*Henry Barrett*); Peter Hobbes (*Septimus Barrett*); George Kirby (*Coachman*); Winter Hall (*Clergyman*); Lowden Adams (*Butler*); Margaret Seddon (*Woman*); Robert Bolder (*Old Man*).

Seldom in Hollywood history have stage stars been invited to re-create the roles of their triumphs in motion pictures. Instead, film producers have always considered Broadway fair pickings for the movies, constantly shopping New York theaters for plays that might make good pictures, while ignoring the actors who helped make those plays a success. Such was the case with *The Barretts of Wimpole Street*, perhaps the greatest triumph of that first lady of the theatre, Katharine Cornell, who racked up over 700 performances of that play. Later she toured it for the GIs overseas during World War II, and made her television debut in a 90-minute adaptation in 1956.

But for motion pictures, a medium in which Miss Cornell was not interested, a genuine movie star would be needed to promote this costume drama about a 19th century invalid-poetess. And so MGM executive-producer Irving Thalberg acquired it for his wife, Norma Shearer, who at first resisted the role, not wanting to play a part that would confine her as an invalid to a chair or bed throughout. Star rivalry, however, changed her mind. When Shearer learned that Marion Davies coveted the part as a possible comeback vehicle, she set about convincing Davies that she would be hopelessly miscast.

Delighted with the role now, Norma Shearer went on to give a performance of charm and pathos that earned her a Best Actress Academy Award nomination. Unfortunately, it was the year of *It Happened One Night*, and Claudette Colbert was the victor for that. In similar fashion, Frank Capra's acclaimed movie also beat out *Barretts* for Best Picture recognition.

Victorian London provides the handsome settings for this true story of the romance of Elizabeth Barrett (Shearer) and Robert Browning (Fredric March). A frail invalid, she is a virtual prisoner of her health in the home of her father, the tyrannical Edward Moulton Barrett (masterfully portrayed by 35-year-old Charles Laughton, himself only one year Shearer's senior!). Indeed, Barrett's three daughters all live confining lives because of their possessive father. Elizabeth, who is the eldest, has, in fact, only two reasons for living—her verse and her spaniel Flush. It was the little-known writer Browning who discovered her poetry and began to secretly correspond with her. Even before their eventual meeting (he manages to avoid her formidable father and pay her visits), the two establish an unusual love affair. But when Robert proposes taking her away and marrying her, Elizabeth hesitates, fearing that her poor health would ruin such a union.

Eventually, Robert meets Elizabeth's father and becomes aware of the unnaturally close feelings Barrett harbors for his daughter. Elizabeth's love gives her the strength to leave her prison, and agree to marry Robert and go with him to Italy. A subsequent confrontation with her father opens her eyes to his incestuous emotions before she leaves his house forever. Her sisters exult in Elizabeth's escape; Arabel (Katherine Alexander) finds her farewell letter to their father, which Henrietta (Maureen O'Sullivan) triumphantly presents to him.

The Barretts of Wimpole Street scored an immedi-

THE BARRETTS OF WIMPOLE STREET: Fredric March and Norma Shearer.

THE BARRETTS OF WIMPOLE STREET: Maureen O'Sullivan, Norma Shearer and Charles Laughton.

THE BARRETTS OF WIMPOLE STREET: Charles Laughton and Norma Shearer.

THE BARRETTS OF WIMPOLE STREET: Fredric March and Norma Shearer.

134

ate and well deserved success with critics and audiences alike, ending on most of the year's Ten Best lists. Norma Shearer won ·a Best Actress award at the Venice Film Festival for this performance, and *Photoplay* magazine handed the film its Gold Medal as 1934's Best Picture.

In 1957, MGM released a handsome, British-made remake of *The Barretts of Wimpole Street*, starring Jennifer Jones, Bill Travers and John Gielgud, and once again under the direction of Sidney Franklin. But it wasn't very successful, and only underscored the excellence of the 1934 production. To avoid confusion between two versions, Metro renamed the earlier film *The Forbidden Alliance* for its TV showings.

FOLIES BERGÈRE

1935

CREDITS

A United Artists Picture. A 20th Century Production. Executive Producer: Darryl F. Zanuck. Associate Producers: William Goetz and Raymond Griffith. Director: Roy Del Ruth. Screenwriters: Bess Meredyth and Hal

FOLIES BERGERE: Ann Sothern.

FOLIES BERGERE: Maurice Chevalier, Walter Byron, Lumsden Hare, Merle Oberon and Robert Greig.

Long. Based on the play *The Red Cat* by Rudolph Lothar and Hans Adler. Cinematographers: Barney McGill and Peverell Marley. Editors: Allen McNeil and Sherman Todd. Art Director: William Darling. Costumes: Albert M. Levy. Miss Oberon's Gowns: Omar Kiam. Choreographer: Dave Gould. Sound: E.H. Hansen. Music Arranger-Conductor: Alfred Newman. Songs: "Singing a Happy Song," "I Was Lucky," "Au Revoir l'Amour" and "Rhythm in the Rain" by Jack Meskill and Jack Stern; "You Took the Words Right Out of My Mouth" by Harold Adamson and Burton Lane; "I Don't Stand a Ghost of a Chance With You" by Victor Young, Ned Washington and Bing Crosby; and "Valentine" by Andre Christien and Albert Willemetz, with English lyrics by Herbert Reynolds (M.E. Rourke). Running Time: 83 minutes.

CAST

Maurice Chevalier (*Eugene Charlier* and *Fernand, the Baron Cassini*); Merle Oberon (*Baroness Genevieve Cassini*); Ann Sothern (*Mimi*); Eric Blore (*Francois*); Ferdinand Munier (*Monsieur Morrisot*); Walter Byron (*Rene*); Lumsden Hare (*Gustave*); Robert Greig (*Henri*); Halliwell

136

Hobbes (*Monsieur Paulet*); Philip Dare (*Victor*); Frank McGlynn Sr. (*Joseph*); Ferdinand Gottschalk (*Ferdinand*); Barbara Leonard (*Toinette*); Georges Renavent (*Premiere of France*); Olin Howland (*Stage Manager*); Albert Pollet (*Secretary*); Sailor Vincent (*Rubber*); Robert Graves and Paul Kruger (*Doormen*); Olga Borget, Irene Bentley, Vivian Martin, Jenny Gray and Doris Morton (*Usherettes*); Joseph E. Bernard (*Butler*); Perry Ivins (*Airport Official*); Mario Dominici (*Doctor*); Paul Toien (*Page Boy*); Lew Hicks and Leon Baron (*Attendants*); Nam Dibot (*Ticket Man*); Harry Holman (*Cafe Waiter*); Leonard Walker (*Assistant Stage Manager*); Albert Pollet and Max Barwyn (*Waiters in Box*).

At 47, Maurice Chevalier was nearing the end of his first Hollywood career when he took on the dual lead in *Folies Bergère*. This followed on the heels of his appearance opposite his frequent co-star Jeanette MacDonald in Ernst Lubitsch's *The Merry Widow* at MGM, a studio with which he parted company when it was suggested that he take second billing to soprano Grace Moore. *Folies Bergère* was produced by 20th Century Pictures, a firm that had been formed by Darryl F. Zanuck in partnership with Joseph Schenck—and which would, in May 1935, merge with Fox Films to become 20th Century-Fox. Zanuck had originally wanted Charles Boyer for this picture, but Boyer declined, suggesting his friend Chevalier, who accepted. Much of the old Chevalier *boulevardier* charm is present here in his impersonation of cabaret performer Eugene Charlier, while his alternate scenes as the less zestful financier Baron Cassini display a more restrained side of the actor which is almost a relief from the cutesy personality that some find hard to take in the younger Chevalier.

The durable mistaken-identity plot derives from a stage farce called *The Red Cat*, with the customary Hollywood "improvements" made, in this case by screenwriters Bess Meredyth and Hal Long, with the addition of lavish musical production numbers that often bear an uncanny resemblance to the work of Busby Berkeley. Zanuck was the Warner Bros. producer behind Berkeley's initial success with *42nd Street*—after which he (Zanuck) parted company with Warners. So it's easy to see why, in the absence of Berkeley, *Folies Bergère* nevertheless offers such derivative production numbers with hordes of chorus beauties and overhead shots of girls forming kaleidoscopic patterns far below. Nowadays, this would be termed an *homage*; then, it was blatantly a steal.

Folies Bergère's musical numbers serve as the bread slices sandwiching the storyline about look-alike men whose paths intertwine, much to the con-

fusion of the women in their lives—and the audience watching this film. It's all very light and trivial, and after awhile the viewer loses track of who knows what about whom, and merely waits for the next song and the final clinches. Ann Sothern plays the temperamental and effervescent performing partner (and lover) of the song-and-dance Chevalier and gets to share the spectacular "Rhythm in the Rain" number with him; Merle Oberon (in her first American movie) has little to do other than look gorgeous and glamorous in her Omar Kiam gowns as the titled wife of financial-whiz Chevalier. As the critics remarked at the time, it was hardly worth her while to cross the Atlantic from England.

In 1941, 20th Century-Fox recycled this film's plot to produce the Technicolored *That Night in Rio*, with Don Ameche, Alice Faye and Carmen Miranda in the Chevalier, Oberon and Sothern roles. And in 1952 it served as a Danny Kaye vehicle, in the company of Gene Tierney and Corinne Calvet under the title *On the Riviera*. All have their merits, depending on one's appreciation for the talents involved.

FOLIES BERGERE: Merle Oberon and Maurice Chevalier.

FOLIES BERGERE: Ann Sothern, Maurice Chevalier and chorus girls.

Folies Bergère copped an Academy Award for its dance director, Dave Gould, for his "Straw Hat" number, the same year that Gould also picked up a second statuette for choreographing "I've Got a Feeling You're Fooling" from MGM's *Broadway Melody of 1936.*

THE WHOLE TOWN'S TALKING

1935

CREDITS

A Columbia Picture. Producer: Lester Cowan. Director: John Ford. Screenwriters: Jo Swerling and Robert Riskin. Based on the novel by William R. Burnett. Assistant Director: Wilbur McGaugh. Cinematographer: Joseph August. Editor: Viola Lawrence. Running Time: 95 minutes.

CAST

Edward G. Robinson (*Arthur Ferguson Jones/Killer Mannion*); Jean Arthur (*Wilhelmina "Bill" Clark*); Arthur Hohl (*Detective Sgt. Mike Boyle*); Wallace Ford (*Healy*); Arthur Byron (*District Attorney Spencer*); Donald Meek (*Hoyt*); Paul Harvey (*J.G. Carpenter*); Edward Brophy (*Bugs Martin*); Etienne Girardot (*Seaver*); James Donlan (*Detective Sgt. Pat Howe*); J. Farrell MacDonald (*Warden*); Effie Ellsler (*Aunt Agatha*); Robert Emmett O'Connor (*Police Lt. Mac*); John Wray and Joe Sauers/Sawyer (*Mannion's Henchmen*); Frank Sheridan (*Russell*); Clarence Hummel Wilson (*President of the Chamber of Commerce*); Ralph M. Remley (*Ribber*); Virginia Pine (*Seaver's Private Secretary*); Ferdinand Munier (*Mayor*); Cornelius Keefe (*Radio Man*); Francis Ford (*Reporter at Dock*); Lucille Ball (*Girl*); Ben Taggart (*Traffic Cop*); Walter Long (*Convict*); Mary Gordon (*Landlady*); Bess Flowers (*Secretary*); Charles King and Gordon DeMain (*Men*); Robert E. Homans (*Detective*); Grace Hayle (*Sob Sister*); Al Hill (*Gangster*); Sam Flint (*City Official*); Emmett Vogan (*Reporter*); Tom London (*Guard*).

If ever a movie was totally uncharacteristic of its director, this one was, for John Ford's mid-Thirties output is more closely associated with historical Americana (*Steamboat 'Round the Bend*), military strife (*The Lost Patrol*) and Irish morality (*The Informer*). With its comically clever screenplay by Jo Swerling and Robert Riskin (*It Happened One Night*), its use of leading lady Jean Arthur, and its potshots at establishment institutions, anyone com-

THE WHOLE TOWN'S TALKING: Edward G. Robinson and Jean Arthur.

ing in late and missing the credits might likely think of Frank Capra, for whose studio—Columbia—this delightful film was made.

Years later, when interviewed for a study of his work by Peter Bogdanovich, Ford could only comment of *The Whole Town's Talking:* "It was all right; I never saw it." The movie was much *more* than "all right" for its star, Edward G. Robinson, who enjoyed an actor's field day portraying both a notorious gangster and his innocent lookalike.

A conscientious mild-mannered clerk, Arthur Ferguson Jones (Robinson) spends his leisure hours writing romantic fiction and anonymously sending poems to colleague Wilhelmina "Bill" Clark (Arthur), whom he secretly admires. After teasing him about his likeness to the imprisoned public enemy called Killer Mannion, Bill finds herself taken into police custody with Jones when he's mistaken for Mannion, who has just broken out of prison. With the mistake discovered, they're released, and Jones is given a police "passport" to prevent further misunderstandings. The experience so unnerves Jones he gets drunk for the first time in his life, and returns home to find Mannion awaiting him. Mannion proposes that he borrow Jones' passport for his nocturnal escapades. Jones, who has been commissioned by newspaperman Healy (Wallace Ford) to write a series of anti-Mannion articles, is fearful for his life. When the gangster coerces Jones into reporting the inside story of his prison break, the police become suspicious.

After Bill mistakes Mannion for Jones and responds to his romantic flirtations, she's kidnapped by his gang. And then the authorities decide temporarily to imprison Jones for his own safety, while Mannion cleverly takes his place, the better to settle an old feud with prisoner Bugs Martin (Edward Brophy). And, although Mannion escapes, his plot to have Jones killed in his place goes awry, and Mannion's own gang, mistaking him for Jones, shoots down their own boss! No longer in danger of being mistaken for a public menace, Jones marries Bill.

After a succession of impressive pictures, Edward G. Robinson won both critical and public acclaim for this brilliant virtuoso performance. *Little Caesar* had made him a star as that unforgettable bantam mobster named Rico; and *Little Giant* had offered him in a comic variation on the genre. But *The Whole Town's Talking* elicited yet another facet of Robinson's stage-honed versatility—the ability to put over a sweet-mannered, cultured law-abider who gets the girl, not by force, but by winning her admiration. Contrasted with his comic-gangster Mannion, it's a true tour de force that stands the test of time.

The movie also marked a milestone for Jean Arthur, who had recently taken refuge from too many B-movies by honing her skills on the Broadway stage. *Variety* was the first publication to note a new, "more individualistic" and "sassy" Jean Arthur. And it predicted a brighter future for her—which soon came true with the first of her three great Capra films, *Mr. Deeds Goes to Town.*

THE WHOLE TOWN'S TALKING: Edward G. Robinson beside himself.

THE WHOLE TOWN'S TALKING: Jean Arthur and Edward G. Robinson.

MISSISSIPPI

1935

CREDITS

A Paramount Picture. Producer: Arthur Hornblow, Jr. Director: A. Edward Sutherland. Screenwriters: Francis Martin, Jack Cunningham, Claude Binyon and Herbert Fields. Based on the play *Magnolia* by Booth Tarkington. Cinematographer: Charles Lang. Editor: Chandler House. Art Directors: Hans Dreier, Bernard Herzbrun. Songs: "Down by the River," "Soon" and "It's Easy to Remember" by Richard Rodgers and Lorenz Hart; and "Swanee River" by Stephen Foster. Running Time: 73 minutes.

CAST

Bing Crosby (*Tom Grayson/Col. Steele*); W. C. Fields (*Commodore Orlando Jackson*); Joan Bennett (*Lucy Rumford*); Queenie Smith (*Alabam*); Gail Patrick (*Elvira Rum-*

ford); Claude Gillingwater (*Gen. Rumford*); John Miljan (*Maj. Patterson*); Edward Pawley (*Joe Patterson*); Fred Kohler, Sr. (*Capt. Blackie*); John Larkin (*Rumbo*); Libby Taylor (*Lavinia Washington*); Harry Myers (*Joe, Stage Manager*); Paul Hurst (*Hefty*); Theresa Maxwell Conover (*Miss Markham*); Al Richmond, Francis McDonald, Stanley Andrews, Eddie Sturgis and George Lloyd (*Gamblers*); Bruce Covington (*Colonel*); Jules Cowles (*Bartender*); Harry Cody (*Abner, Bartender*); Lew Kelly and Matthew Betz (*Men at Bar*); Jack Mulhall (*Duelist*); Victor Potel (*Guest*); Bill Howard (*Man in Auditorium*); Jack Carlyle (*Referee*); Richard Scott (*Second*); Jan Duggan (*Passenger on Boat*); James Burke (*Passenger in Pilot House*); Helene Chadwick and Jerome Storm (*Extras at Opening*); The Cabin Kids, Molasses and January (*Themselves*); King Baggott (*1st Gambler*); Mahlon Hamilton (*2nd Gambler*); Charles L. King (*Desk Clerk*); Jean Rouverol (*Friend of Lucy*); Mildred Stone, Mary Ellen Brown, Mabel Van Buren and Bill Harwood (*Party Guests*); J. P. McGowan (*Dealer*); Clarence Geldert (*Hotel Proprietor*); Fred "Snowflake" Toones (*Valet*); Forrest Taylor (*Man at Bar Who Orders Sarsaparilla*); Warner Richmond (*Man at Bar Who Pulls a Gun*); Oscar Smith (*Valet*); Robert McKenzie (*Show Patron*); Ann Sheridan (*Girl at Engagement Party and Girls' School*).

Booth Tarkington's 1923 play *Magnolia* was a work that Paramount got much wear out of: first as a 1924 comedy-drama retitled *The Fighting Coward*, with Ernest Torrence, Cullen Landis and Mary Astor; next as a screenplay opting for romantic drama over comedy and called *River of Romance*, a 1929 movie starring Charles "Buddy" Rogers, Mary Brian and Henry B. Walthall; and finally, in 1935, reshaped as what could best be termed a "musical comedy" to suit the oddly matched talents of Bing Crosby, W.C. Fields and Joan Bennett, entitled *Mississippi*.

Little of Tarkington seems left in *Mississippi*, save for the charming atmosphere of the old 19th-century riverboat era. Fields, of course, performs some of his usual comedy *shtick*, although there is perhaps more *dialogue* humor than *pantomime* humor assigned to him, for a change. And then there's Bing Crosby, the popular crooner, whose mellow, contemporary style was hardly suited to costume films. Not that this bothered his Hollywood producers. Crosby looks good with Joan Bennett, then still a natural blonde (she wouldn't turn brunette until 1939's *Trade Winds*, attempting a deliberate take-off on Hedy Lamarr that met with unexpected audience approval). And, although the movie provides an entertaining package, it's nevertheless an unusual stew of comedy, music and melodrama that sometimes blends uneasily. However, *Mississippi* turned out to be one of the crowd-pleasers of 1935, enhanced by Fields' hilarious poker game (in

MISSISSIPPI: Joan Bennett.

MISSISSIPPI: W.C. Fields, Queenie Smith and bit players.

MISSISSIPPI: Bing Crosby and W.C. Fields.

which he ends up with *five aces!*), and Bing's rendering of several pleasing Rodgers and Hart songs ("It's Easy to Remember," "Soon" and "Down by the River"), as well as the Stephen Foster standard, "Swanee River."

A. Edward Sutherland (1895–1973), who had already worked well with W.C. Fields (*It's the Old Army Game, International House*) and Crosby (*Too Much Harmony*), directed in his customarily smooth fashion, allowing the comedian free rein with the sort of material that had made him popular, and showcasing the Crosby musical interludes to their best advantage. And in between there was the decorative Miss Bennett—and the plot.

Sporting an uncharacteristic moustache, Crosby attends a party held to announce his engagement to Gail Patrick. That evening, a misunderstanding on the part of Southern major John Miljan ends in his demanding "satisfaction" from Crosby in the form

144

Bing replaced the originally-cast Lanny Ross, a pleasant-voiced singing actor who was deemed too bland. Following this career setback, Ross found his niche as a popular radio singer.

W.C. Fields' scenes seem interpolated into the narrative, almost as "comedy relief" from Crosby's romantic episodes with Bennett. But they contain some classic humor: introducing his familiar expletive, "Mother of Pearl!" or delivering nonsense dialogue along the lines of—"How long have you been navigating the river?" "Ever since I took it away from the Indians."

Those who look closely will spot one of the many brief early appearances of Ann Sheridan, as a schoolgirl. Before the year's end, she would graduate to leading roles in Paramount programmers like *Car 99* and *Rocky Mountain Mystery*.

MISSISSIPPI: Joan Bennett and Bing Crosby.

of a duel. But Bing's refusal to fight brands him a coward in the eyes of his future wife and in-laws, and he retreats from the community to join Commodore Fields on the showboat that the latter plies up and down the Mississippi. Crosby's pacifism, however, appeals to Patrick's younger sister, Bennett, to whom he later switches his affections. But not before becoming a major singing sensation on the showboat—especially after he's billed as "The Singing Killer," following the accidental shooting of bully Fred Kohler, for which Crosby becomes a hero.

ALICE ADAMS

1935

CREDITS

An RKO Radio Picture. Producer: Pandro S. Berman. Director: George Stevens. Screenwriters: Dorothy Yost and Mortimer Offner. Adaptation: Jane Murfin. Based on

ALICE ADAMS: Fred MacMurray and Katharine Hepburn.

the novel by Booth Tarkington. Cinematographer: Robert De Grasse. Editor: Jane Loring. Art Director: Van Nest Polglase. Sound: Denzil A. Cutler. Costumes: Walter Plunkett. Music: Max Steiner. Song: "I Can't Waltz Alone" by Max Steiner and Dorothy Fields. Music Director: Roy Webb. Assistant Director: Edward Killy. Running Time: 99 minutes.

CAST

Katharine Hepburn (*Alice Adams*); Fred MacMurray (*Arthur Russell*); Fred Stone (*Mr. Adams*); Evelyn Venable (*Mildred Palmer*); Frank Albertson (*Walter Adams*); Ann Shoemaker (*Mrs. Adams*); Charles Grapewin (*Mr. Lamb*); Grady Sutton (*Frank Dowling*); Hedda Hopper (*Mrs. Palmer*); Jonathan Hale (*Mr. Palmer*); Janet McLeod (*Henrietta Lamb*); Virginia Howell (*Mrs. Dowling*); Zeffie Tilbury (*Mrs. Dresser*); Ella McKenzie (*Ella Dowling*); Hattie McDaniel (*Malena*);

After the failure of RKO's 1934 *Break Of Hearts*, Katharine Hepburn had talked with the studio about starring in an adaptation of Booth Tarkington's *Seventeen*. But producer Pandro S. Berman preferred her in a remake of the writer's Pulitzer Prize win-

ning *Alice Adams* (Tarkington's realistic 1921 novel on small-town social values and pretensions had previously been filmed as a silent in 1923 with Florence Vidor). For her director, Hepburn elected to take a chance on 30-year-old George Stevens, whose background had previously been limited to slapstick shorts and the comedies of Wheeler and Woolsey.

All those choices were fortunate ones, for *Alice Adams* turned out to be not only Hepburn's best Thirties movie next to *Little Women*, but also one of the decade's enduring classics. Nominated for a Best Actress Academy Award, Hepburn lost the statuette to Bette Davis (for *Dangerous*), who later admitted that Hepburn was the more deserving nominee.

In the small midwestern town of South Renford, Alice Adams (Hepburn) dreams romantically of a future life among the smart set, despite her lower-middle-class family, of whom she is ashamed. Her father (Fred Stone) has remained a clerk after 20 years with the same employer, and her worthless brother Walter (Frank Albertson) grumbles about escorting Alice to the social event of the season—a

ALICE ADAMS: Katharine Hepburn and Fred Stone.

ALICE ADAMS: Katharine Hepburn and Fred MacMurray.

dance given by wealthy and beautiful Mildred Palmer (Evelyn Venable). At the soirée, Alice is an awkward wallflower, sporting her own hand-picked corsage of wilting violets. Only effete, unpopular Frank Dowling (Grady Sutton) offers to dance with her—until Alice finally manages a whirl with Arthur Russell (Fred MacMurray), a handsome and charming newcomer who, unfortunately for Alice, turns out to be "practically engaged" to Mildred.

The rest of the film details Arthur's unusual friendship with Alice, who puts on airs of affluence and creates an imaginary social background. When she is finally forced to invite him to her home for dinner, it's an unforgettable evening—but for all the wrong reasons. Alice's pretentious plans unravel, spearheaded by the slovenly serving of a gum-chewing hired maid (Hattie McDaniel, in a hilarious delineation of sullen incompetence). By the end of the evening, the humiliated, pathetic Alice is certain she's seen the last of the embarrassed Arthur.

In the Tarkington novel—and in the 1923 film—Arthur retreats, recoiling from her snobbish affecta-

tions, and leaving Alice with her romantic delusions in ruins. But Alice matures from this misguided experience and puts her dreams aside to face practical reality: she enrolls in a secretarial school. But now the film and the novel part company, for such a conclusion was out of the question for moviegoers in the mid-Thirties. Correctly reasoning that Depression-era audiences wanted an emotional lift—and not the "downer" of Tarkington's social realism—RKO demanded a more upbeat denouement. And so, not only does the cinematic Cinderella Alice win her Prince Charming, but her father also enjoys a miraculous business opportunity, as he and his former boss reconcile their differences to join in a glue-factory enterprise. Sunshine cuts through tears, and Alice's world turns happy.

As a result of this "compromise" with Tarkington's novel, RKO enjoyed the prestige of a box-office hit and George Stevens, despite his directorial problems with the opinionated Hepburn, established his reputation as a major new feature-film director.

148

NAUGHTY MARIETTA

1935

CREDITS

A Metro-Goldwyn-Mayer Picture. Producer: Hunt Stromberg. Director: W.S. Van Dyke. Screenwriters: John Lee Mahin, Frances Goodrich and Albert Hackett. Based on the operetta by Victor Herbert and Rida Johnson Young. Cinematographer: William Daniels. Editor: Blanche Sewell. Art Director: Cedric Gibbons. Costumes: Adrian. Sound: Douglas Shearer. Music Adapter: Herbert Stothart. Songs by Herbert, Young and Gus Kahn: "Italian Street Song," "Chansonette," "Antoinette and Anatole," "Prayer," "Tramp, Tramp, Tramp," "The Owl and the Bobcat," "'Neath the Southern Moon," "Mon Ami Pierrot," "Ship Ahoy," "I'm Falling in Love With Someone" and "Ah, Sweet Mystery of Life." Assistant Director: Eddie Woehler. Running Time: 106 minutes.

CAST

Jeanette MacDonald (*Princess Marie de la Bonfain/ "Marietta Franini"*); Nelson Eddy (*Capt. Richard Warrington*); Frank Morgan (*Governor Gaspard d'Annard*); Elsa Lanchester (*Madame d'Annard*); Douglass Dumbrille (*Prince de la Bonfain*); Joseph Cawthorn (*Herr Schuman*); Cecilia Parker (*Julie*); Walter Kingsford (*Don Carlos de Braganza*); Greta Meyer (*Frau Schuman*); Akim Tamiroff (*Rudolpho*); Harold Huber (*Abe*); Edward Brophy (*Zeke*); Mary Doran, Jean Chatburn, Pat Farley, Jane Barnes, Kay English, Linda Parker and Jane Mercer (*Casquette Girls*); Olive Carey (*Madame Renavant*); Dr. Edouard Lippé (*Lackey*); Walter Long (*Pirate Leader*); Cora Sue Collins (*Felice*); Guy Usher (*Ship's Captain*); Harry Tenbrook (*Prospective Groom*); Edward Keane (*Major Bonnell*); Edward Norris and Ralph Brooks (*Marie's Suitors*); Richard Powell (*Messenger*); Wilfred Lucas (*Announcer*); Arthur Belasco, Frank Hagney, Edmund Cobb, Edward Hearn, Tex Driscoll, Ed Brady and Charles Dunbar (*Scouts*); William Des-

149

NAUGHTY MARIETTA: Douglass Dumbrille and Jeanette MacDonald.

mond (*Havre Gendarme Chief*); Helen Shipman (*Marietta Franini*); William Burress (*Bouget, the Petshop Keeper*); Catherine Griffith (*Prunella, Marie's Maid*); Billy Dooley (*Drunk, Marietta's "Brother"*); Harry Cording and Constantine Romanoff (*Pirates*); Henry Roquemore (*Herald*); Mary Foy (*Duenna*); James C. Morton (*Barber*); Louis Mercier (*Dueler*); Robert McKenzie (*Town Crier*); Delos Jewkes (*Priest on Dock*); William Moore (*Jacques, the Suitor*); Harry Tenbrook (*Suitor*); Ben Hall (*Mama's Boy*); Ed Keane (*Major Cornell*); Roger Gray (*Sergeant*); Jack Mower (*Nobleman*); Zarubi Elmassian (*Soprano*).

If MGM's Louis B. Mayer had had his way, the top movie singing team of the Thirties might have been Jeanette MacDonald and Allan Jones. Jones was his first choice to co-star with Mayer's favorite Metro singer. Unfortunately for Jones, a previously-contracted concert tour for the Shuberts made him unavailable to Hollywood. Two years later, Mayer

got his wish, and the two were successfully co-starred in *The Firefly*. But that ponderous though handsome movie wasn't successful enough to shake the by-then great popularity of soprano MacDonald's professional partnership with baritone Nelson Eddy. After their first joint vehicle, *Naughty Marietta*, public response was so enthusiastic that between 1935 and 1942, MGM turned out seven additional vehicles to fit their musical talents.

Today, public attitudes toward the MacDonald-Eddy movies range from the reverence of a staunch group of fans to those who ridicule their talents and dismiss their vehicles as purest "camp." MacDonald came to talkies in 1929 from a succession of Broadway musical comedies, and her early-Thirties movies at Paramount proved (arguably) not only that she could sing (she certainly wasn't the finest soprano ever to have her voice captured on a soundtrack), but that this beauty could also act—especially in comedy scenes. Eddy was another matter. Prior to *Naughty Marietta*, his musical experience had been limited to specialty bits in three movies, *Broadway to Hollywood, Dancing Lady* and *Student Tour*. And his acting experience consisted of the rudimentary requirements then attached to the grand-opera stage. Consequently, Eddy's stiffness as an actor and fear of teaming with the vivacious and experienced MacDonald presented their director, W.S. Van Dyke II, with a tremendous challenge. That Eddy's attractive, masculine performance charmed distaff audiences and seemed very well matched with his costar is a tribute to Van Dyke. A good-looking couple, Jeanette and Nelson also offered a congenial vocal blend and a winning, tongue-in-cheek humor that helped tremendously in putting over this hoary old operetta that had first seen the lights of Broadway in 1910.

Some consider *Naughty Marietta* worthless, except for its timeless Victor Herbert melodies like "Italian Street Song," "Tramp, Tramp, Tramp," "I'm Falling in Love With Someone" and, of course, "Ah, Sweet Mystery of Life." However, MGM did well by engaging the resourceful team of John Lee Mahin, Frances Goodrich and Albert Hackett to update the operetta's Rida Johnson Young libretto. And fast-shooting director Van Dyke pulled it all together in short order in an expensive production that eventually became one of Hollywood's hundred best-grossing movies of all time.

NAUGHTY MARIETTA: Jeanette MacDonald and Nelson Eddy.

NAUGHTY MARIETTA: Elsa Lanchester, Frank Morgan and Nelson Eddy.

151

NAUGHTY MARIETTA: Nelson Eddy and Jeanette MacDonald.

Naughty Marietta has its slow sections, and at 106 minutes, it's longer than necessary (re-release versions have been cut to 80 minutes!), but audiences with a taste for schmaltz and old-fashioned operetta won't likely complain. Even the somewhat corny character actors, like blustery Frank Morgan and hammy Elsa Lanchester, are just right for this sort of show.

Critics have singled out other, later MacDonald-Eddy vehicles (*Rose Marie*, *Maytime*) as their best films, but *Naughty Marietta* was the first. And for countless fans, it remains a memorable cinema landmark.

LET 'EM HAVE IT

1935

CREDITS

A United Artists Picture. A Reliance Production. Producer: Edward Small. Director: Sam Wood. Screenwriters: Joseph Moncure March and Elmer Harris. Cinematographers: J. Peverell Marley and Robert Planck. Editor: Grant Whytock. Sound: Frank Maher. Running Time: 90 minutes.

CAST

Richard Arlen (*Mal Stevens*); Virginia Bruce (*Eleanor Spencer*); Alice Brady (*Aunt Ethel*); Bruce Cabot (*Joe Keefer*); Harvey Stephens (*Van Rensseler*); Eric Linden (*Buddy Spencer*); Joyce Compton (*Barbara*); Gordon Jones (*Tex Logan*); J. Farrell MacDonald (*Mr. Keefer*); Bodil Rosing (*Mrs. Keefer*); Paul Stanton (*Department Chief*); Robert Emmett O'Connor (*Police Captain*); Hale Hamilton (*Ex-Senator Reilly*); Dorothy Appleby (*Lola*); Barbara Pepper (*Milly*); Matthew Betz (*Thompson*); Harry Woods (*Big Bill*); Clyde Dillson (*Pete*); Matty Fain (*Brooklyn*); Paul Fix (*Sam*); Donald Kirke (*Curley*); Eugene Strong (*Dude*); Christian Rub (*Henkel*); Eleanor Wesselhoeff (*Mrs. Henkel*); Wesley Barry (*Walton*); Ian MacLaren (*Reconstructionist*); George Pauncefort (*Dr. Hoffman*); Landers Stevens (*Parole Chairman*); Katharine Clare Ward (*Ma Harrison*); Sidney Bracy (*Butler*); Dennis O'Keefe (*Trainee*); Tom London (*Guard*); Jed Prouty, Joseph Crehan and Hooper Atchley (*Bits*).

Following close on the heels of Warner Bros.' *G-Men*, this independently produced variation on the same theme—the lawless criminal career of John Dillinger—has nearly disappeared into obscurity

LET 'EM HAVE IT: Richard Arlen, Harvey Stephens and Virginia Bruce.

now. But it's still remembered by a small hardcore of film buffs, most of whom saw it in the early days of television, when independent features were the mainstay of feature film programming.

Directed with professional flair by Sam Wood, in between regular assignments for MGM, *Let 'em Have It* remains highly effective filmmaking, its story divided between exploring FBI investigative methods with some fairly uninteresting protagonists (Richard Arlen, Eric Linden and Virginia Bruce) and following the far more exciting underworld exploits of mobster Bruce Cabot and his gang, with their gun battles and car chases. The movie's basic storyline is thin: Bruce plays a society girl who's advised that her mysterious chauffeur (Cabot) will attempt to kidnap her. And when he's sent to jail, she gets him freed, only to have him rejoin his old gang and embark on a Midwestern reign of terror. Bruce's brother, Linden, then joins the G-Men, only to be killed by Cabot's gang—which sends Arlen and his men off to smash the mob, once and for all.

No one who has seen *Let 'em Have It* will forget the film's most memorable sequence, in which Cabot submits to plastic surgery to gain a new face and avoid recognition by the authorities. After the

LET 'EM HAVE IT: Barbara Pepper and Bruce Cabot.

operation, he orders the killing of the surgeon, only to find that, after later removing his bandages, his own initials have been indelibly carved into his cheeks. Now he's literally a marked man.

Like this part of the movie, *Let 'em Have It* is at its best when the Joseph Moncure March-Elmer Harris script abandons words for action, and Wood's direction of these scenes is tough and relentless, making the movie one of the best—if least known—gangster epics from an era remembered for producing some of the best of the genre.

PETER IBBETSON

1935

CREDITS

A Paramount Picture. Producer: Louis D. Lighton. Director: Henry Hathaway. Screenwriters: Vincent Lawrence, Waldemar Young, John Meehan, Edwin Justis Mayer and

LET 'EM HAVE IT: G-men close in on the gang.

PETER IBBETSON: Ann Harding and Gary Cooper.

Constance Collier. Based on the novel by George du Maurier and the play by John Nathaniel Raphael. Cinematographer: Charles Lang. Editor: Stuart Heisler. Art Directors: Hans Drier and Robert Usher. Sound: Harry D. Mills. Special Effects: Gordon Jennings. Music: Ernst Toch. Music Supervisor: Nat W. Finston. Running Time: 88 minutes.

CAST

Gary Cooper (*Peter Ibbetson*); Ann Harding (*Mary, Duchess of Towers*); John Halliday (*Duke of Towers*); Ida Lupino (*Agnes*); Douglass Dumbrille (*Col. Forsythe*); Virginia Weidler (*Mimsey*); Dickie Moore (*Gogo*); Doris Lloyd (*Mrs. Dorian*); Elsa Buchanan (*Mme. Pasquier*); Christian Rub (*Maj. Duquesnoit*); Donald Meek (*Mr. Slade*); Gilbert Emery (*Wilkins*); Marguerite Namara (*Mme. Ginghi*); Elsa Prescott (*Katherine*); Marcelle Corday (*Maid*); Adrienne D'Ambricourt (*Nun*); Theresa Maxwell Conover (*Sister of Mercy*); Colin Tapley, Ambrose Barker, Clive Morgan and Thomas Monk (*Clerks*); Blanche Craig (*The Countess*); Stanley Andrews (*Judge*).

Novelist George du Maurier, author of the popular *Trilby*, enjoyed an even greater success with his

PETER IBBETSON: Gary Cooper and Ida Lupino.

PETER IBBETSON: John Halliday, Gary Cooper and Ann Harding.

PETER IBBETSON: Ann Harding and Gary Cooper.

157

subsequent *Peter Ibbetson* (1891), which was adapted for the stage by John Nathaniel Raphael in a 1917 production that teamed Constance Collier with John and Lionel Barrymore. In 1921, it was brought to the screen as the silent *Forever* with Elsie Ferguson, Wallace Reid and Montagu Love. But *Peter Ibbetson*'s only talkie remake to date is the handsome 1935 film that Henry Hathaway directed with Ann Harding, Gary Cooper and John Halliday. Hathaway appeared at first to be as odd a choice for this picture, as was Cooper. Both had worked together earlier that same year on the excellent action yarn *The Lives of a Bengal Lancer*, as well as previously, in the romantic comedy-drama *Now and Forever*. But both were far more closely associated with the more rugged type of movie, and Hathaway's basic background was as the director of Zane Grey Westerns. All of which was a far cry from the metaphysical costume romance that is *Peter Ibbetson*.

For some reason, the film was a greater success overseas than in the U.S. But its production values are exquisite, and its dedicated artists and craftsmen created a motion picture that many found impressive. Ann Harding, whose patrician beauty had found a wider audience earlier in the decade, here enjoyed one of her most congenial roles, and looked particularly attractive in the 19th-century costumes and hairstyles. Some thought Gary Cooper ill at ease in these surroundings, although others were impressed by his sensitivity, well aware that romantic drama (*A Farewell to Arms*) was nothing new to his career. But everything about this admirable production stands out today as an example of a time in which a studio like Paramount took enormous pains with production details. It seems doubtful that anything approaching the look of 1935's *Peter Ibbetson* would be possible today.

Perhaps the movie takes too much time establishing Mary and Peter as children (portrayed by Virginia Weidler and Dickie Moore). But it's important that we realize the childhood bond of affection that exists between them as they play in a beautiful garden to which the story will return in their adulthood. Years pass and the beautiful garden has become a sea of weeds. By then, Mary is the Duchess of Towers, and Peter is an architect hired by her husband the Duke (John Halliday) to build new stables for his horses on the property. Unaware of each other's identity, Mary disagrees with Peter's architectural ideas and has him dismissed, only to reverse her decision after a unique mannerism of Peter's reveals his identity to her. They then become such close—but platonic—friends that the Duke harbors unjustified jealous suspicions. Later, in celebration of his work's completion, Peter is seen by the Duke in a farewell embrace with the Duchess that results in a struggle over a gun—and the Duke's accidental death. Peter is sentenced to life in prison and, as the years pass, he and Mary visit one another in their dreams. Physically they grow older, but their dream selves remain young. After death, they are reunited forever.

Aside from the graceful performances of the film's co-stars, there is excellent work from Halliday as the envious Duke, and an especially energetic contribution by young Ida Lupino in her first prestige film. As a lower-class girl, she sets her sights on Peter, only to lose him to the Duchess. Although production stills indicate that Lupino's original role was larger, in the release print of *Peter Ibbetson*, she has only a couple of scenes with Cooper before she disappears from the story. But she really makes them count, and it isn't difficult to realize that this is an actress to be reckoned with.

HANDS ACROSS THE TABLE

1935

CREDITS

A Paramount Picture. Production Supervisor: Ernst Lubitsch. Producer: E. Lloyd Sheldon. Director: Mitchell Leisen. Screenwriters: Norman Krasna, Vincent Lawrence and Herbert Fields. Based on the story *Bracelets* by Viña Delmar. Cinematographer: Ted Tetzlaff. Editor: William Shea. Music and Lyrics: Sam Coslow, Frederick Hollander, Mitchell Parish and Jean Delettre. Costumes: Travis Banton. Running Time: 80 minutes.

CAST

Carole Lombard (*Regi Allen*); Fred MacMurray (*Theodore Drew III*); Ralph Bellamy (*Allen Macklyn*); Astrid Allwyn (*Vivian Snowden*); Ruth Donnelly (*Laura*); Marie Prevost (*Nona*); Joseph Tozer (*Peter*); William Demarest (*Matty*); Edward Gargan (*Pinky Kelly*); Ferdinand Munier (*Miles, the Butler*); Harold Minjir (*Couturier at Valentine's*); Marcelle Corday (*Celeste, the French Maid*); Bess Flowers (*Diner*); Harold Miller (*Barber Customer*); Nell Craig (*Saleslady*); Jerry Mandy (*Headwaiter*); Phil Kramer (*Supper Club Waiter*); Murray Alper (*Cab Driver*); Nelson McDowell (*Man in Nightshirt*); Sam Ash (*Maitre D'Hotel*); Edward Peil Sr., Jerry Storm, Francis Sayles, Chauncey M. Drake,

S. H. Young, Rafael Gavilan, Harry Williams and Sterling Campbell (*Barbers*); Mary MacLaren (*Chambermaid*); Rod Wilson (*Piano Player*); Albert Conti (*Maitre d'Hotel in Speakeasy*); John Buettner (*Shoe Clerk*); Pat Sweeney (*Manicurist*); Alla Mentone (*Saleslady*); Fred "Snowflake" Toones (*Porter*); James Adamson (*Porter*); Peter Allen (*Jewelry Clerk*); Ira Reed and Dutch Hendrian (*Taxi Drivers*).

Beautiful, talented and popular though she was, by 1935 Carole Lombard had only had one motion picture, *Twentieth Century*, that matched her talent for comedy—until *Hands Across the Table*. Under contract to Paramount since 1930, not only was this Lombard's first actual starring vehicle, but it was also the first film expressly written for her and would be produced under the guidance of Paramount's newly appointed comedy specialist, Ernst Lubitsch. Viña Delmar's story *Bracelets* was the basis for the clever screenplay whipped up by Norman Krasna, Vincent Lawrence and Herbert Fields, and it was at Lombard's request that Mitchell Leisen was assigned to direct her.

At first, the casting of her leading man offered problems. Leisen wanted Ray Milland, whom he had recently worked with in *Four Hours to Kill*. But, difficult to believe in hindsight, Milland doubted his ability to play comedy, so Leisen took a chance with Fred MacMurray, a novice Paramount contract player who had only made two previous pictures, one of which was the delightful 1935 comedy, *The Gilded Lily*, opposite Claudette Colbert. Colbert had apparently helped ex-saxophone player MacMurray solidify the basis of his unique and charming penchant for comic acting, and although Lombard at first found him stiff and sexless, she went out of her way to help the young actor relax, and drew out his natural ability. As MacMurray later told Leisen biographer David Chierichetti, "She worked with me on every scene. I owe so much of that performance and my subsequent career to her."

Hands Across the Table's humor springs from a situation of basic male-female role-reversal. Lombard plays the aggressor here, a disillusioned hotel manicurist named Regi Allen who no longer believes

159

HANDS ACROSS THE TABLE: Edward Gargan, Marie Prevost and Carole Lombard.

HANDS ACROSS THE TABLE: Carole Lombard, Ralph Bellamy and Joseph Tozer.

in marrying for love. Instead, she plans to find herself a rich husband and improve her social lot. At first, Regi's best prospect appears to be wealthy and attractive Allen Macklyn (Ralph Bellamy), a former flier now confined by accident to a wheelchair. But then she finds herself giving a manicure to the handsome and supposedly well-heeled Theodore Drew III (MacMurray) whose family, she later is chagrined to learn, lost everything in the stock-market crash. It seems that Ted is little more than a charming wastrel who, like Regi, aspires to marry wealth—in his case, fiancée Vivian Snowden (Astrid Allwyn, who forged a brief Thirties career out of playing the unexciting "other woman").

But Ted is as reluctantly attracted to Regi as she is to him, and he impulsively treats her to a costly evening with the money Vivian's given him for a Bermuda vacation. At the end of the evening, he's too intoxicated to get home and spends the night (innocently, of course; this was the Code-restricted mid-Thirties) and eventually *the week* at Regi's apartment. This occasions one of the movie's best scenes, an inspired comedy turn in which, over the telephone, Lombard poses as a nasal-voiced Bermuda phone operator, and MacMurray attempts to convince Allwyn he's enjoying a week of rest on that

island. As Mitchell Leisen describes it: "When they finished the take, Carole and Fred collapsed on the floor in laughter; they laughed until they couldn't laugh any more. It wasn't in the script, but I made sure the cameras kept turning and I used it in the picture. It is so hard to make actors laugh naturally, I wasn't about to throw that bit out."

160

ball Thirties comedy. The characters of Regi and Ted in particular are far from cut-and-paste cardboard. Indeed, their complexities are as well suggested in Leisen's direction as they are in the serio-comic playing of Lombard and MacMurray, whose cinematic chemistry worked so well that they were re-teamed in three subsequent movies. None, however, equalled the quality of *Hands Across the Table*, one of 1935's surprise box-office hits.

MUTINY ON THE BOUNTY

1935

CREDITS

A Metro-Goldwyn-Mayer Picture. Producer: Irving Thalberg. Director: Frank Lloyd. Screenwriters: Talbot Jennings, Jules Furthman and Carey Wilson. Based on the novels *Mutiny on the Bounty* and *Men Against the Sea* by Charles Nordhoff and James Norman Hall. Cinematographer: Arthur Edeson. Editor: Margaret Booth. Art Directors: Cedric Gibbons and A. Arnold Gillespie. Music: Herbert Stothart. Song: "Love Song of Tahiti" by Gus Kahn, Bronislau Kaper and Walter Jurmann. Running Time: 132 minutes.

By the film's end, Regi and Ted have reasoned that their old mercenary values be damned, they're meant for each other. They'll marry as soon as he finds himself a job, thus leaving Allen and Vivian to fend for themselves—or each other?

As the above description scarcely makes clear, *Hands Across the Table* is much more than a screw-

MUTINY ON THE BOUNTY: Clark Gable and Charles Laughton.

CAST

Charles Laughton (*Capt. William Bligh*); Clark Gable (*Fletcher Christian*); Franchot Tone (*Roger Byam*); Dudley Digges (*Dr. Bachus*); Henry Stephenson (*Sir Joseph Banks*); Donald Crisp (*Burkitt*); Eddie Quillan (*Ellison*); Francis Lister (*Captain Nelson*); Spring Byington (*Mrs. Byam*); Movita Castenada (*Tehani*); Mamo Clark (*Maimiti*); Robert Livingston (*Young*); Douglas Walton (*Stewart*); Ian Wolfe (*Samuel*); DeWitt Jennings (*Fryer*); Ivan Simpson (*Morgan*); Vernon Downing (*Hayward*); Stanley Fields (*Muspratt*); Wallis Clark (*Morrison*); Dick Winslow (*Tinkler*); Byron Russell (*Quintal*); Percy Waram (*Coleman*); David Torrence (*Lord Hood*); John Harrington (*Mr. Purcell*); Marion Clayton (*Mary Ellison*); Hal LeSueur (*Millard*); Crauford Kent (*Lieutenant Edwards*); David Thursby (*McIntosh*); King Mojave (*Richard Skinner*); Doris Lloyd (*Cockney Moll*); Lionel Belmore (*Innkeeper*); Harry Cording (*Soldier*); Mary Gordon (*Peddler*); Herbert Mundin (*Smith*); Eric Wilton (*Captain of Board*).

Frank Lloyd (1888–1960) was twice the winner of Academy Awards for his direction of *The Divine Lady* (1929) and *Cavalcade* (1933). His name was also among the six nominations for 1935's *Mutiny on the*

Bounty. It has been written that Lloyd's forte was spectacle, and that he was not good with actors. However, this is immediately contradicted by a study of this movie—all three leading men, Charles Laughton, Clark Gable and Franchot Tone, won Best Actor nominations. *Mutiny on the Bounty* was also a nominee for its screenplay, editing and score. And, while all of the above were losers in the final votes, *Mutiny on the Bounty* managed to bypass all of its 11 (rules were different then) fellow-nominees to win the coveted award for Best Picture of 1935. That prize was well deserved, for this is a rousing

adventure tale of men at odds with one another and the elements, and its production details so well worked out, its casting so astute, that the end result is one of the decade's finest films.

The fact-based story begins in 1787, when the *HMS Bounty* sets sail from Portsmouth, England for the South Seas, its mission to transport breadfruit trees from Polynesia to the West Indies, as an inexpensive food for slave labor. In the command of the *Bounty* is the justly feared Capt. William Bligh (Charles Laughton), a sadistic skipper whose first order to his new first mate Fletcher Christian (Clark

MUTINY ON THE BOUNTY: Clark Gable, Dudley Digges and Charles Laughton.

Gable) is the memorably uttered "Mr. Christian, clear the decks of this rabble!" Things don't improve after that start, and Bligh's cruelty surfaces time and again in floggings, keel haulings and restricting of the sailor's rations. But, just before a mutiny breaks out, Tahiti is sighted. Immediately, the peaceful atmosphere of island life offsets the brutality of the *Bounty*, with the crew enjoying the female and scenic beauties of Polynesia. But, finally, the trees are ready for shipment and the ship's mission there is completed.

Back at sea, Bligh resumes his inhumane treatment of the crew—until, creating a final break with Christian, he orders his elderly, ailing ship's surgeon (Dudley Digges) on deck, where the latter dies. Christian responds, "Bligh, you've given your last

MUTINY ON THE BOUNTY: Eddie Quillan, Clark Gable, Movita Castenada and players.

MUTINY ON THE BOUNTY: Franchot Tone and Charles Laughton.

order on this ship!" And the *Bounty* erupts with the mutiny that has been waiting to happen, with Bligh and his faithful followers cast off to drift in an open boat. Undefeated, Bligh vows, "I'll live to see you—all of you—hanging from the highest yardarm in the fleet!" We're shown the memorable sight of the breadfruit plants, dumped and floating in the Bounty's wake as it returns to Tahiti.

Captain Bligh survives his ordeal by water; a year later he takes command of another ship, the *Pandora*, determined to track down the mutineers, some

An expensive production, *Mutiny on the Bounty* was not filmed without difficulty. To begin with, Louis B. Mayer had turned thumbs down on the project, reasoning that the public would not be interested in a romance-less story about 18th-century mutineers. But production chief Irving Thalberg argued successfully in its favor. And, in fact, a romance is depicted in the movie—between Fletcher Christian and the native girl Tehani (Movita Castenada)—a deciding factor in Thalberg's convincing a reluctant Clark Gable to accept his first costume role, and one that required his shaving off his trademark mustache. Wallace Beery had been the first choice for Captain Bligh—until it was thought that he'd be "too American," and Laughton was sought. Franchot Tone was a replacement for Robert Montgomery, who refused to cancel vacation plans to take the third male lead.

Laughton and Gable did not get along well during production, and it has been reported that their behind-the-scenes squabbles surpassed the onscreen strife between Bligh and Christian. Nor was director Lloyd left out of the disagreements, and producer Thalberg is said to have been a frequent visitor to the embattled Catalina Island location, where there were numerous arguments among stars, director and producer—often in front of the entire company. Fortunately for the film, it only benefited from whatever problems arose in the midst of filming, leaving us with one of the Thirties' finest adventure films.

In 1962, Metro released a Tahiti-filmed color remake that starred Marlon Brando and Trevor Howard, and cost the company an unbelievable $18,500,000 that was never recouped at the box-office. It met with widespread critical dissatisfaction, and nearly bankrupted MGM. Nor did a 1984 version, entitled *The Bounty* win much favor, even with Mel Gibson and Anthony Hopkins as, respectively, Christian and Bligh. *Bounty*-interested parties would do best to turn to the black-and-white videocassette of 1935's *Mutiny on the Bounty*.

of whom have retreated to uninhabited Pitcairn Island. Bligh arrests those he finds on Tahiti, including the loyal Roger Byam (Franchot Tone), but he's stopped from locating the others when the *Pandora* is shipwrecked. Back in England, a mutiny trial uncovers Bligh's inhumanity, and although Byam's sentenced to death, he wins a reprieve from George III. Bligh is left an outcast from maritime society, while, back on Pitcairn, Christian has found a permanent home, having burned the *Bounty* and, with it, his link to a life he's pleased to forget.

DANGEROUS

1935

CREDITS

A Warner Bros.-Vitaphone Picture. Director: Alfred E. Green. Producer: Harry Joe Brown. Screenwriter: Laird Doyle. Cinematographer: Ernest Haller. Editor: Thomas

DANGEROUS: Franchot Tone and Bette Davis.

166

Richards. Art Director: Hugh Reticker. Gowns: Orry-Kelly. Music: Leo F. Forbstein and Bernhard Kaun. Running Time: 78 minutes.

CAST

Bette Davis (*Joyce Heath*); Franchot Tone (*Don Bellows*); Margaret Lindsay (*Gail Armitage*); Alison Skipworth (*Mrs. Williams*); John Eldredge (*Gordon Heath*); Richard "Dick" Foran (*Teddy*); Pierre Watkin (*George Sheffield*); Walter Walker (*Roger Farnsworth*); George Irving (*Charles Melton*); William B. Davidson (*Reed Walsh*); Douglas Wood (*Elmont*); Richard Carle (*Pitt Hanly*); Milton Kibbee (*Williams, Roger's Chauffeur*); George Andre Beranger and Larry McGrath (*Waiters*); Frank O'Connor (*Bartender*); Miki Morita (*Cato*); Eddie Shubert (*Foreman*); Florence Fair (*Secretary*); Pauline Garon (*Betty, Gail's Maid*); Gordon "Bill" Elliott (*Male Lead in Play*); Libby Taylor (*Beulah*); Craig Reynolds (*Reporter*); Mary Treen (*Nurse*); Edward Keane (*Doctor*); Eddie Foster (*Passerby*); Billy Wayne (*Teddy's Chauffeur*).

Bette Davis reports that she was "punch-drunk" from overwork when Warner Bros. gave her Laird Doyle's screenplay for *Dangerous* (or, as it was then known, *Hard Luck Dame*), loosely based on the life of stage star Jeanne Eagels, who had died in 1929 at the age of 35 from a drug overdose. In the Doyle dramatization, Davis plays Joyce Heath, a bottle-swigging, once famous stage actress hell-bent on her own destruction—until an admiring architect (Franchot Tone) befriends her and sponsors her theatrical comeback. Unfortunately, the star has a weakling secret husband (John Eldredge), and when he refuses her a divorce so she can marry the architect, Joyce attempts to kill them both by driving into a tree. As in Edith Wharton's *Ethan Frome*, they both survive, though the husband is crippled for life. Joyce returns to the stage in triumph, sacrificing love (Tone) for duty (Eldredge). Returning to his forgiving fiancée (Margaret Lindsay), the architect marries her.

Alfred E. Green directed this uneven soap opera, and Davis gave a performance of extraordinary intensity. In fact, Davis's Joyce Heath is so highly charged, so kinetic and mannered as to be, at times, almost laughable. Yet in other scenes she is quite moving, as in her first encounter with Tone in which she tells him about her ill-starred past and her belief that she jinxes everyone who knows her. She also has some effective scenes of harsh comedy with Alison Skipworth, playing a housekeeper who is righteously disgusted by Joyce's drinking.

Davis says she considered the *Dangerous* screenplay "maudlin and mawkish, with a pretense at quality," and that she "worked like ten men" to

DANGEROUS: Bette Davis.

DANGEROUS: Franchot Tone and Bette Davis.

167

DANGEROUS: Bette Davis and John Eldredge.

make something of it. She also later admitted, "I fell in love with Franchot Tone, professionally and personally—alas—Joan Crawford had him!"

That year Bette Davis was among the six Best Actress nominees for an Academy Award. Her competition was Elisabeth Bergner in the British-made *Escape Me Never*; Claudette Colbert in *Private Worlds*; Katharine Hepburn in *Alice Adams*; Miriam Hopkins in *Becky Sharp*, and Merle Oberon in *The Dark Angel*. And she still believes that the Oscar she won for *Dangerous* was a consolation prize for losing out the previous year with *Of Human Bondage*. In her opinion, Hepburn gave the best performance of 1935 and *she* deserved the statuette. This was the first of what came to be known as the "Holdover" awards—a belated prize for work unrewarded the previous year.

Typical of Warner Bros. resourcefulness, *Dangerous* was remade six years later, resurfacing as a forgettable programmer entitled *Singapore Woman* with Brenda Marshall. With a South Seas rubber plantation setting, little remained except for its leading lady's personal "jinx."

CAPTAIN BLOOD

1935

CREDITS

A Warner Bros./First National Picture. A Cosmopolitan Production. Executive Producer: Hal B. Wallis. Associate Producers: Harry Joe Brown and Gordon Hollingshead. Director: Michael Curtiz. Screenwriter: Casey Robinson. Based on the novel by Rafael Sabatini. Cinematographers: Hal Mohr and Ernest Haller. Editor: George Amy. Music: Erich Wolfgang Korngold. Orchestration: Hugo Friedhofer and Ray Heindorf. Art Director: Anton Grot. Costumes: Milo Anderson. Special Effects: Fred Jackman. Sound: Nathan Levinson. Assistant Director: Sherry Shrouds. Fencing Master: Fred Cavens. Running Time: 119 minutes.

CAST

Errol Flynn (*Dr. Peter Blood*); Olivia de Havilland (*Arabella Bishop*); Lionel Atwill (*Colonel Bishop*); Basil Rathbone (*Captain Levasseur*); Ross Alexander (*Jeremy Pitt*); Guy Kibbee (*Hagthorpe*); Henry Stephenson (*Lord Willoughby*); George Hassell (*Governor Steed*); Forrester Harvey (*Honesty Nuttall*); Frank McGlynn, Sr. (*Reverend Ogle*); Robert Barrat (*Wolverstone*); Hobart Cavanaugh (*Dr. Bronson*); Donald Meek (*Dr. Wacker*); David Torrence (*Andrew Baynes*); J. Carrol Naish (*Cahusac*); Pedro de Cordoba (*Don Diego*); Leonard Mudie (*Lord Jeffries*); Jessie Ralph (*Mrs. Barlowe*); Stuart Casey (*Captain Hobart*); Halliwell Hobbes (*Lord Sunderland*); Colin Kenny (*Lord Dyke*); E.E. Clive (*Court Clerk*); Holmes Herbert (*Captain Gardiner*); Mary Forbes (*Mrs. Steed*); Reginald Barlow (*Dixon*); Ivan F. Simpson (*Prosecutor*); Denis d'Auburn (*Lord Gildoy*); Vernon Steel (*King James*); Georges Renavent (*French Captain*); Murray Kinnell (*Clerk in Gov. Steed's Court*); Harry Cording (*Kent*); Maude Leslie (*Baynes' Wife*); Chris-Pin Martin (*Sentry*); Tom Wilson and Henry Otho (*Pirates*); David Thursby (*Lookout*); Yola D'Avril, Renee Terres, Lucille Porcett and Tina Minard (*Tavern Girls*); Alphonse Martell, Andre Cheron and Frank Puglia (*French Officers*).

The great success of United Artists' 1934 swashbuckler, *The Count of Monte Cristo*, prompted Warner Bros. to plan a remake of their 1924 adventure epic, *Captain Blood*, which had starred J. Warren Kerrigan and Jean Paige. Warners contracted to use the services of UA's excellent "Count," English-born Robert Donat, about whom there was such enthusiasm that no less than three productions were planned for him: *Captain Blood, Anthony Adverse* and *The Adventures of Robin Hood*. But Donat, a life-long asthma sufferer, had to bow out for health reasons, and litigation followed. Warners thus needed an immediate replacement for Dr. Peter

CAPTAIN BLOOD: Olivia de Havilland and Errol Flynn.

Blood, which they found in Australian import Errol Flynn, who had come from England and at this point had played only a silent bit in *The Case of the Curious Bride* (directed by Michael Curtiz) and a five-minute, two-scene role in *Don't Bet on Blondes*—both unimportant programmers. Neither experience did much to prepare him for the title role in Curtiz' *Captain Blood*. Nor did the lady cast opposite Flynn yet hold much prestige, although her leading-ingenue roles in *Alibi Ike, The Irish in Us* and *A Midsummer Night's Dream* had certainly given her excellent experience for a teen-ager. When they first teamed, Olivia de Havilland was 19 and Flynn 26, and although she fell in love with her roguish, married co-star, the young lady kept it to herself until many years later. But their on-screen magic made these two beautiful people ideal co-stars, and resulted in their appearing in seven subse-

169

quent teamings, under the direction of either Curtiz or Raoul Walsh. Curtiz was an egotistical tyrant on the set, but his demanding direction time and again produced impressive results for Warner Bros., where he became the top director on the lot. *Captain Blood* did much to make him so, as by the same token, it was equally instrumental in making major movie stars of de Havilland and Flynn.

The film's plot put Flynn into long hair and 17th-century clothing as Dr. Peter Blood, a doctor caught treating a rebel in King James II's England. Con-victed of treason, he's banished to the English colony of Port Royal, Jamaica, as a slave. There he ingratiates himself with the governor, whom he treats for gout, and gains special privileges. He also falls in love with Arabella Bishop (de Havilland), the high-spirited daughter of a sadistic plantation owner (Lionel Atwill). When Spanish pirates attack the is-land and capture the town, Blood and a number of other slaves escape, commandeer the pirates' ship and commence their *own* Caribbean reign as free-booting pirates. Later, Blood engages in an exciting

CAPTAIN BLOOD: Errol Flynn, Henry Stephenson, Ross Alexander, Guy Kibbee, David Torrance and players.

170

CAPTAIN BLOOD: J. Carrol Naish, Errol
Flynn and Basil Rathbone.

CAPTAIN BLOOD: J. Carrol Naish, Errol Flynn and Basil Rathbone.

CAPTAIN BLOOD: Olivia de Havilland and Errol Flynn.

duel with a rival for Arabella's hand, the French buccaneer Captain Levasseur (Basil Rathbone), whom Blood kills.

When the reign of James II ends in his being dethroned by William of Orange, Blood is given a naval commission and defeats a pair of French galleys. King William and Queen Mary pardon Blood and make him the new governor of Port Royal, where Arabella waits for him.

Released at Christmastime of 1935, directly in the wake of *Mutiny on the Bounty*, Warners' *Captain Blood* found immediate favor with critics and audiences alike. Not only did it promise swashbuckling action and excitement, but with reviewers like *The New York Times'* Andre Sennwald calling Flynn "spirited and criminally good-looking" and de Havilland, "a lady of rapturous loveliness," *Captain Blood* thus launched two of Hollywood's major movie-star careers. In the year-end Academy Award nominations, *Captain Blood* was up for Best Picture, but the statuette went to its seagoing predecessor, *Mutiny on the Bounty*.

THE PETRIFIED FOREST

1936

CREDITS

A Warner Bros. Picture. Associate Producer: Henry Blanke. Director: Archie Mayo. Screenwriters: Charles Kenyon and Delmer Daves. Based on the play by Robert E. Sherwood. Cinematographer: Sol Polito. Editor: Owen Marks. Sound: Charles Lang. Music: Bernhard Kaun. Art Director: John Hughes. Gowns: Orry-Kelly. Special Effects: Warren E. Lynch, Fred Jackman and Willard Van Enger. Running Time: 83 minutes.

CAST

Leslie Howard (*Alan Squier*); Bette Davis (*Gabrielle Maple*); Genevieve Tobin (*Mrs. Chisholm*); Dick Foran (*Boze Hertzlinger*); Humphrey Bogart (*Duke Mantee*); Joseph Sawyer (*Jackie*); Porter Hall (*Jason Maple*); Charley Grapewin (*Gramp Maple*); Paul Harvey (*Mr. Chisholm*); Eddie Acuff (*Lineman*); Adrian Morris (*Ruby*); Nina Campana (*Paula*); Slim Thompson (*Slim*); John Alexander (*Joseph*); Arthur Aylesworth (*Commander of Black Horse Troopers*); George Guhl (*Trooper*); James Farley (*Sheriff*); Jack Cheatham (*Deputy*); Addison Richards (*Radio Announcer*).

In the Warner Bros. screen adaptation of Robert E. Sherwood's stage melodrama *The Petrified Forest*, Leslie Howard was engaged to repeat his stage performance, and insisted that the studio hire Humphrey Bogart to re-create *his* stage role of the psychopathic gangster, Duke Mantee. Warners, which already had Edward G. Robinson and James Cagney under contract, agreed reluctantly. And Bette Davis got the role Peggy Conklin had created on Broadway—Gaby Maple, a romantic minded girl who longs to escape her arid life in the Arizona desert cafe run by her father. Onto the scene comes Alan Squier (Howard), a burned-out intellectual with a death wish. Gaby falls in love with him, but her idyll is short lived when the murderous Duke Mantee and his henchmen, fleeing from the police, arrive on the scene and keep everyone prisoners in the cafe. At the climax, Alan forces Mantee to shoot him, and Gaby is left with Alan's insurance policy—money that will enable her to study art in Paris.

Though largely a photographed stage play in which the Sherwood symbolism (intellectual and killer both die in barren desert) is somewhat too obvious, the film benefits from fine performances and the restrained direction of Archie Mayo. As Squier, Leslie Howard is sensitive and moving, delicately conveying the sadness and resignation of the character. And Davis took full advantage of the unusual opportunity to play a simple romantic girl, plainly dressed and free of neurotic tics and quirks. She is genuinely touching as she yearns for Paris or

THE PETRIFIED FOREST: Bette Davis and Genevieve Tobin.

THE PETRIFIED FOREST: Leslie Howard and Bette Davis.

THE PETRIFIED FOREST: Leslie Howard, Bette Davis, Charley Grapewin and Dick Foran.

reacts with awe to Alan Squier's tenderness and concern.

As Mantee, Bogart proved a sensation, revitalizing his previously unmemorable screen career, which he had abandoned two years earlier to return to the Broadway stage, where he had begun. And, although Warners gave in to Howard's casting demands, they paid Bogart a mere $400 per week and relegated his billing to fifth, under the supporting-role names of Genevieve Tobin and Dick Foran, both of whom were studio contract players. Bogart subsequently went on to play a succession of secondary roles at that studio—mostly of the gangster variety—but it wasn't until 1941 and *High Sierra* that he finally achieved the superstardom for which he is remembered.

Characteristic of Warner Bros., *The Petrified Forest*'s plot was recycled in 1945 as *Escape in the Desert*, when its villains were changed to escaped Nazis. Ten years later, Humphrey Bogart made a rare TV appearance, repeating his Duke Mantee role in an adaptation of *The Petrified Forest* that featured Henry Fonda and Lauren Bacall in the respective Howard and Davis roles. Bogart is one of the few major stars who've played on screen, in radio and on television the role created on the Broadway stage.

THE GREAT ZIEGFELD

1936

CREDITS

A Metro-Goldwyn-Mayer Picture. Producer: Hunt Stromberg. Director: Robert Z. Leonard. Screenwriter: William Anthony McGuire. Cinematographers: Ray June, Oliver T. Marsh, Karl Freund, Merritt B. Gerstad and George

THE PETRIFIED FOREST: Bette Davis, Leslie Howard and Humphrey Bogart.

Folsey. Editor: William S. Gray. Art Director: Cedric Gibbons. Costumes: Adrian. Music Director: Arthur Lange. Sound: Douglas Shearer. Songs by Irving Berlin, Walter Donaldson and Harold Adamson. Running Time: 180 minutes.

CAST

William Powell (*Florenz Ziegfeld*); Luise Rainer (*Anna Held*); Myrna Loy (*Billie Burke*); Frank Morgan (*Billings*); Reginald Owen (*Sampston*); Nat Pendleton (*Sandow*); Virginia Bruce (*Audrey Lane*); Ernest Cossart (*Sidney*); Robert Greig (*Joe*); Raymond Walburn (*Sage*); Fannie Brice (*Herself*); Jean Chatburn (*Mary Lou*); Ann Pennington (*Herself*); Ray Bolger (*Himself*); Harriet Hoctor (*Herself*);

Charles Trowbridge (*Julian Mitchell*); Gilda Gray (*Herself*); A.A. Trimble (*Will Rogers*); Joan Holland (*Patricia Ziegfeld*); Buddy Doyle (*Eddie Cantor*); Charles Judels (*Pierre*); Leon Errol (*Himself*); Marcelle Corday (*Marie*); Esther Muir (*Prima Donna*); Herman Bing (*Customer*); Joseph Cawthorn (*Dr. Ziegfeld*); Paul Irving (*Erlanger*); William Demarest (*Gene Buck*); Alfred P. James (*Stage Doorman*); Miss Morocco (*Little Egypt*); Suzanne Kaaren (*Miss Blair*); Sarah Edwards (*Wardrobe Woman*); James P. Burtis (*Bill*); Mickey Daniel (*Telegraph Boy*); William Griffith (*Husband*); Grace Hayle (*Wife*); Richard Tucker, Clay Clement, Lawrence Wheat and Selmer Jackson (*Customers*); Alice Keating (*Alice*); Rosina Lawrence (*Marilyn Miller*); Jack Baxley (*Detective*); Charles Coleman (*Carriage Starter*); Eric Wilton (*Desk Clerk*); Mary Howard (*Miss Carlisle*); Bert Hanlon (*Jim*); Evelyn Dockson (*Fat Woman*); Franklyn Ardell (*Allen*); John Larkin (*Sam*); David Burns (*Clarence*); Phil Tead (*Press Agent*); Susan Fleming (*Girl with Sage*); Adrienne D'Ambricourt (*Wife of French Ambassador*); Charles Fallon (*French Ambassador*); Boothe Howard (*Willie Zimmerman*); Edwin Maxwell (*Charles Frohman*); Ruth Gillette (*Lillian Russell*); John Hyams (*Dave Stamper*); Wallis Clark (*Broker*); Ray Brown (*Inspector Doyle*); Stanley Morner/Dennis Morgan (*"Pretty Girl" Singer*); Virginia Grey (*Chorus Girl*).

After the initial rash of musicals reached the screen with the coming of sound, oversatiated audiences began to stay away from them—until the imaginative innovations of Busby Berkeley and the fortuitous pairing of Fred Astaire with Ginger Rogers renewed public interest in the genre. MGM cannily decided to combine the idea of a spectacular screen musical with another genre that had recently enjoyed popularity—the movie biography. The result was *The Great Ziegfeld*, a three-hour film marathon that cost $1.5 million, then an astronomical sum—more than Metro had spent on any one project outside of the trouble-ridden $4-million *Ben-Hur* of 1925.

A motion picture that spaced out its musical numbers in patches between the chunks of biography, *The Great Ziegfeld* takes Florenz Ziegfeld (William Powell) through most of his life, beginning with the enterprising young novice showman who exploits strongman Sandow the Great (Nat Pendleton) at the Chicago Fair of 1893. After amassing a small fortune, Ziegfeld goes on to lose it gambling in Monte Carlo, but while in Europe, he is charmed by the temperamental musical-comedy actress Anna Held (Luise Rainer), whom he puts under personal contract, at the expense of his rival Billings (Frank Morgan). The showman later marries his delightful star, but their union is less than tranquil, due to her jealousy and his extravagance. Their marriage fails, but Ziegfeld's career soars and his reputation as a master showman continues, while he marries again, this time actress Billie Burke (Myrna Loy). But his

THE GREAT ZIEGFELD: William Powell and Luise Rainer.

wastefulness brings financial reversals to Ziegfeld, and Billie helps him out by insisting on selling her jewels. Ziegfeld once more regains his reputation with a string of Broadway musical hits, including *Rio Rita* and *Show Boat*. It is the Depression that finally undermines Ziegfeld's fortunes and his health. He dies nearly bankrupt.

Originally, it was Universal that had planned a major film production on the life of Flo Ziegfeld (1869–1932), but it became obvious that that studio was not financially equipped to deal with an expensive production, especially one that required extravagant musical numbers the public would expect in a screen depiction of the showman whose extrava-

176

ganzas were legendary. Thus it was that MGM acquired the rights for $250,000, including a screenplay that had been written for Universal by former Ziegfeld confidant William Anthony McGuire.

Movie biographies of real people have always been a touchy area, especially with regard to what facts to gloss over, since there is always the possibility of scandalous subject matter and the potential of libel suits arising from the protests of living associates of the person portrayed. In the case of the Ziegfeld project, Metro need not have worried, for McGuire's script portrayed the life of a known compulsive womanizer in a positive light, of course aided and abetted by the dapper charm and skill of actor William Powell, whose performance might have earned him an Academy Award nomination, had he not already impressed the 1936 voters even more with his work in *My Man Godfrey*—a film that *did* bring him a nomination. But *The Great Ziegfeld* took home Oscars for Best Picture and for Best Actress Luise Rainer's expressive performance as his first wife (especially the famed telephone scene in

which she emotionally congratulates her ex-husband on his forthcoming second marriage). And it also drew nominations for director Robert Z. Leonard, McGuire's original screenplay, art direction and film editing.

MGM need not have worried about their expenditure on *The Great Ziegfeld*, for it not only impressed the critics, but also proved a major box office attraction of 1936, more than doubling its expenditure in terms of box office receipts.

Today, *The Great Ziegfeld* seems overlong and in need of tighter editing. Yet one cannot help but marvel at the production of a movie in a Hollywood filmmaking style that no longer exists. Powell's performance holds up better than Rainer's, for the whininess of her character becomes trying, and relief arrives almost too late when the always-charming Myrna Loy finally appears in the latter half of the movie. Those who watch carefully will see a future star, Dennis Morgan, then known by his real name, Stanley Morner. Although later to use his own pleasing tenor voice in *The Desert Song* (1944), he was dubbed here by another singer, Allan Jones, in the

THE GREAT ZIEGFELD: "A Pretty Girl Is Like a Melody" number.

THE GREAT ZIEGFELD: Frank Morgan and William Powell.

song "A Pretty Girl Is Like a Melody," one of *The Great Ziegfeld*'s most awe-inspiring production numbers. It's sequences like this one that help make this mid-Thirties movie marathon still worth watching.

DESIRE

1936

CREDITS

A Paramount Picture. Producer: Ernst Lubitsch. Director: Frank Borzage. Screenwriters: Edwin Justus Mayer, Waldemar Young and Samuel Hoffenstein. Based on the play *Die schönen Tage von Aranjuez* by Hans Szekeley and R.A. Stemmle. Cinematographers: Charles Lang and Victor Milner. Editor: William Shea. Art Directors: Hans Dreier and Robert Usher. Costumes: Travis Banton. Sound: Harry D. Mills. Music: Frederick Hollander. Song: "Awake in a Dream" by Frederick Hollander and Leo Robin. Special Effects: Farciot Edouart and Harry Perry. Running Time: 89 minutes.

180

CAST

Marlene Dietrich (*Madeleine de Beaupré*); Gary Cooper (*Tom Bradley*); John Halliday (*Carlos Margoli*); William Frawley (*Mr. Gibson*); Ernest Cossart (*Aristide Duval*); Akim Tamiroff (*Police Official*); Alan Mowbray (*Dr. Edouart Pauquet*); Zeffie Tilbury (*Aunt Olga*); Harry Depp (*Clerk*); Marc Lawrence (*Valet*); Henry Antrim (*Chauffeur*); Armand Kaliz and Gaston Glass (*Jewelry Clerks*); Albert Pollet (*French Policeman*); George Davis (*Garage Man*); Constant Franke (*Border Official*); Robert O'Connor (*Customs Official*); Stanley Andrews (*Customs Inspector*); Rafael Blanco (*Haywagon Driver*); Alden [Stephen] Chase (*Hotel Clerk*); Tony Merlo (*Waiter*); Anna Delinsky (*Servant*); Alice Feliz (*Pepi*); Enrique Acosta (*Pedro*); George MacQuarrie (*Clerk with Gun*); Isabel La Mal (*Nurse*); Oliver Eckhardt and Blanche Craig (*Couple*); Rollo Lloyd (*Clerk in Mayor's Office*); Alfonso Pedrosa (*Oxcart Driver*).

Marlene Dietrich and Gary Cooper had been teamed to chemical advantage in 1930's *Morocco*, in the days when the lady made all of her movies under the tutelage of her mentor Josef von Sternberg. For his part, Cooper had vowed never again to work with Sternberg, due to the director's all-consuming attention to Dietrich. But 1935's *The Devil Is a Woman* ended the Dietrich/Sternberg association, and she was now sufficiently freed from the constraints of Sternbergian exotica to try comedy again, a movie genre she had not essayed since her German silent films of the Twenties. Of course, there were elements of ironic humor in films like *Morocco* and *Shanghai Express*, but out-and-out comedy was not exactly Sternberg's cinematic cup of tea. As a result, his obsession with Dietrich's glamorous appearance had nearly robbed her screen persona of life itself and almost made her little more than a beautiful mannequin on an exquisitely photographed pedestal. *Desire*, a deliciously sophisticated comedy, changed all that.

Although directed by that supreme romanticist Frank Borzage, the movie owes everything to the sly, comedic sensibilities of Ernst Lubitsch, a celebrated director here-turned-producer. Although its romantic scenes bear the Borzage charm, there is always the pervasive yet subtle sophistication of Lubitsch, especially when Production Code requirements tended to hamper the screenplay's more suggestive aspects.

Dietrich is well cast as a glamorous jewel thief who perpetrates the clever heist of a valuable pearl necklace in Paris, and then sets out by car for a fast drive to the Spanish border, near where she encounters a vacationing American (Cooper). To avoid a problem

DESIRE: Marlene Dietrich.

DESIRE: Gary Cooper, John Halliday and Marlene Dietrich.

with customs, she manages to slip the pearls into Cooper's coat pocket. But then he drives off, and she must catch up with him to retrieve her necklace, using whatever flirtatious means she can muster to distract him from her true purpose. Of course they fall in love before Dietrich meets up with her confederate (John Halliday), after which Cooper discovers what she has been after. Additional romantic misunderstandings follow before an upbeat finale in which she returns the necklace to Paris, marries Cooper and accompanies him back to what one can only anticipate as unlikely domesticity as . . . a Detroit housewife!

Between the traditional sly wit of Lubitsch and the characteristic romanticism of Borzage, *Desire* evokes the essence of perfect Thirties escapism. Everyday cares take a holiday as fanciful plot machinations throw two beautiful strangers together over the device of stolen pearls, in an exotic setting, yet one so different from the atmosphere of their earlier teaming in *Morocco*. Free of the Sternberg influence, Dietrich evidences much more looseness in her acting, and her scenes with Cooper show the ease which both of them had attained in the intervening years. As for her physical appearance, Dietrich need not have worried about not having her former mentor present to "protect" her; hairstyles, make-up and Travis Banton's wardrobe all set her off

DESIRE: John Halliday and Marlene Dietrich.

to best advantage. And the careful photography of Charles Lang and Victor Milner combine to put the icing on the cake. *Desire* remains a supreme example of sophisticated style in Hollywood filmmaking.

FURY

1936

CREDITS

A Metro-Goldwyn-Mayer Picture. Producer: Joseph L. Mankiewics. Director: Fritz Lang. Screenwriters: Bartlett Cormack and Fritz Lang. Based on the story *Mob Rule* by Norman Krasna. Cinematographer: Joseph Ruttenberg. Editor: Frank Sullivan. Art Directors: Cedric Gibbons and William A. Horning. Set Decorator: Edwin B. Willis. Costumes: Dolly Tree. Sound: Douglas Shearer. Music: Franz Waxman. Assistant Director: Horace Hough. Running Time: 90 minutes.

CAST

Sylvia Sidney (*Katherine Grant*); Spencer Tracy (*Joe Wilson*); Walter Abel (*District Attorney*); Bruce Cabot (*Kirby Dawson*); Edward Ellis (*Sheriff*); Walter Brennan (*Bugs Meyers*); George Walcott (*Tom*); Frank Albertson (*Charlie*); Arthur Stone (*Durkin*); Morgan Wallace (*Fred Garrett*); George Chandler (*Milton Jackson*); Roger Gray (*Stranger*); Edwin Maxwell (*Vickery*); Howard Hickman (*Governor*); Jonathan Hale (*Defense Attorney*); Leila Bennett (*Edna Hooper*); Esther Dale (*Mrs. Whipple*); Helen Flint (*Franchette*); Edward Le Saint (*Doctor*); Everett Sullivan (*New Deputy*); Murdock MacQuarrie (*Dawson's Friend*); Ben Hall (*Goofy*); Janet Young, Jane Corcoran, Mira McKinney, Mary Foy and Edna Mae Harris (*Women*); Edwin J. Brady, James Quinn, Al Herman and Frank Mills (*Dawson's Friends*); George Offerman, Jr. (*Defendant*); Frank Sully (*Dynamiter*); Dutch Hendrian (*Miner*); Albert Taylor (*Old Man*); Ray Brown (*Farmer*); Guy Usher (*Assistant Defense Attorney*); Nora Cecil (*Albert's Mother*); Frederick Burton (*Judge Hopkins*); Tom Mahoney (*Bailiff*); Tommy Tomlinson (*Reporter*); Sherry Hall (*Court Clerk*); Carlos Martin (*Donelli*); Jack Daley (*Factory Foreman*); Duke York (*Taxi Driver*); Charles Coleman (*Innkeeper*); Will Stanton (*Drunk*); Esther Muir (*Girl in Nightclub*); Bert Roach (*Waiter*); Raymond Hatton (*Hector*); Victor Potel (*Jorgenson*); Clara Blandick (*Judge's Wife*); Erville Alderson (*Plumber*); Herbert Ashley (*Oscar*); Harry Hayden (*Lock-up Keeper*); Si Jenks (*Hillbilly*); Christian Rub (*Ahem*); Carl Stockdale (*Hardware Man*); Elsa Newell (*Hot-Dog Stand Owner*); Alexander Cross and Robert E. Homans (*Guards*); Arthur Hoydt (*Grouch*); Ward Bond (*Objector*); Franklin Parker, Wally Maher and Huey White (*Men*); Gertrude Sutton (*Mrs. Tuttle*); Minerva Urecal (*Fanny*); Daniel

DESIRE: John Halliday, Marlene Dietrich and Gary Cooper.

Haynes (*Taxi Driver*); Sam Hayes (*Announcer*); Harvey Clark (*Pippen*); Clarence Kolb (*Mayor*).

Fury, a hard-hitting drama about mob violence, was not the sort of movie usually associated with MGM, that star-laden studio of glossy entertainment. Warner Bros. was the expected source of social-commentary films in the Thirties, and *Fury* made Metro's executives extremely uneasy prior to its release. First, the studio planned to distribute it without any fanfare, as part of a double-bill. But that idea was abandoned after W.R. Wilkerson, publisher of *The Hollywood Reporter*, caught the picture at a sneak-preview and began to spread favorable word-of-mouth within the industry. MGM was then forced to release this film in which they had no faith in a first-run New York theatre, where the press reaction was quite positive. *Fury*'s box-office take wasn't exactly one for the record books, but it more than compensated in the prestige value it garnered for Metro; and it brought accolades for its leading actor, Spencer Tracy, as well as its German-born director, Fritz Lang.

This was Lang's first American movie after a distinguished career in Germany, where *Metropolis* and

FURY: Spencer Tracy.

a notable string of silents had led to *M* (that classic study of a child murderer) and an eventual break with the German film industry. Lang was brought to Metro in 1934 after signing a contract in Europe with David O. Selznick before the latter's departure from that studio. But MGM didn't know what to do with Lang, and he was given several scripts to "prepare," just to keep him busy. Finally, he was at-tracted to a screen story entitled *Mob Rule* that Norman Krasna was working on. Its inspiration was the real-life incident of two kidnap-killers who fell victim to vigilante justice in San Jose, California in 1933. Lang and Bartlett Cormack took Krasna's four-page outline and proceeded to flesh out a screenplay. The project was assigned to producer Joseph L. Mankiewicz, a former contract writer from

FURY: Sylvia Sidney.

Paramount who was newly arrived at MGM. Nobody seemed to care if Lang flopped with his first production.

Fury begins by detailing the relationship of garageman Joe Wilson (Spencer Tracy) and his teacher fiancée Katherine Grant (Sylvia Sidney). Anxious to marry, they must live apart until Joe can save enough to make their union feasible. That accomplished, Joe drives south to meet Katherine. But on the way, he's picked up and taken into police custody, and it develops that Joe's been mistaken for the kidnapper of a little girl. From that point on what seems like a simple case of mistaken identity snowballs into Joe's arrest on circumstantial evidence that gets him jailed in a small-town courthouse, where the citizenry stirs itself into a lynching mood. Storming the building where Joe's imprisoned, they set fire to it, while Katherine—who has learned of his arrest and rushed to the scene—looks on in horror.

FURY: Sylvia Sidney and Walter Abel.

FURY: Spencer Tracy, Bruce Cabot and players.

Later, it turns out that Joe was able to escape by sliding down a drainpipe, and he hides out with his brothers (Frank Albertson and George Walcott) while the 22 townspeople actively responsible for the violence are put on trial. At first, the embittered Joe wants only to see the culpable punished. But after the real kidnapper is apprehended, he "returns from the dead" to make a surprise appearance in the courtroom. Addressing the judge, Joe makes an impassioned statement: "I know that by coming here I've saved these people. But that isn't why I'm here. I don't care anything about saving them. The law doesn't know that a lot of things that were important to me, silly things maybe, like a belief in justice, and an idea that men were civilized, and a feeling of pride that this country of mine was different from all others . . . the law doesn't know that these things were burned to death within me that night." The movie closes with Joe and Katherine happily reunited.

Many were disappointed at the Hollywood-type ending to this otherwise strong and important story. But Louis B. Mayer had stated that his family-oriented studio was not in business to produce social commentary (he had also excised footage showing blacks victimized by the all-white mob).

In 1937, Warner Bros. characteristically produced the highly regarded lynch-mob drama *They Won't Forget*, based on the celebrated Leo Frank case of an innocent man who was murdered. But there are those who prefer *Fury* for the intensity of its performances and the power of Fritz Lang's direction. Spencer Tracy's fine acting only served to strengthen his new-found position among Metro's prestigious galaxy of stars. As if in backhanded compliment, *Fury* was accorded a sole Academy Award nomination—to Norman Krasna's original story.

SWING TIME

1936

CREDITS

An RKO Radio Picture. Producer: Pandro S. Berman. Director: George Stevens. Screenwriters: Howard Lindsay and Allan Scott. Based on a story by Erwin Gelsey. Cinematographer: David Abel. Editor: Henry Berman. Songs by Jerome Kern and Dorothy Fields: "The Way You Look Tonight," "Bojangles of Harlem," "Waltz in Swing Time," "Pick Yourself Up," "A Fine Romance" and "Never Gonna Dance." Musical Director: Nathaniel Shilkret. Dance Director: Hermes Pan. Photographic Effects: Vernon Walker. Art Directors: Van Nest Polglase and Carroll Clark. Set Decorator: Darrell Silvera. Costumes: Bernard Newman. Sets and Costumes for "Bojangles": John Harkrider. Sound: George Marsh and Hugh McDowell Jr. Running Time: 105 minutes.

SWING TIME: Ginger Rogers and Fred Astaire.

SWING TIME: Victor Moore, Fred Astaire and Ginger Rogers.

SWING TIME: Fred Astaire and Betty Furness.

CAST

Fred Astaire (*John "Lucky" Garnett*); Ginger Rogers (*Penelope "Penny" Carroll*); Victor Moore (*Dr. Everett "Pop" Cardetti*); Helen Broderick (*Mabel Anderson*); Eric Blore (*Mr. Gordon*); Georges Metaxa (*Ricardo Romero*); Betty Furness (*Margaret Watson*); Landers Stevens (*Judge Watson*); John Harrington (*Dice Raymond*); Pierre Watkin (*Al Simpson*); Abe Reynolds (*Schmidt, the Tailor*); Gerald Hamer (*Eric Facannistrom*); Edgar Dearing (*Policeman*); Harry Bowen and Harry Bernard (*Stagehands*); Frank Jenks (*Red*); Donald Kerr, Ted O'Shea, Frank Edmunds and Bill Brand (*Dancers*); Ralph Byrd (*Hotel Clerk*); Charles Hall (*Chauffeur*); Jean Perry (*Roulette Dealer*); Olin Francis (*Muggsy*); Floyd Shackleford (*Butler*); Fern Emmett (*Watson's Maid*); Dale Van Sickel (*Diner*); Dennis O'Keefe, Bess Flowers and Ralph Brooks (*Dance Extras in "The Way You Look Tonight"*); Howard Hickman (*First Minister*); Ferdinand Munier (*Second Minister*); Joey Ray (*Announcer*); Jack Rice (*Wedding Guest*).

For all the many other motion pictures in which they individually performed during their long and successful careers, Fred Astaire and Ginger Rogers will doubtless always be best remembered for the 10 films they made together as a team. Except for their Technicolored 1949 MGM reunion movie, *The Barkleys of Broadway*, all were black-and-white musicals, produced at RKO in the Thirties. *Swing Time*, filmed in 1936 was the sixth, and certainly among their best—in the minds of certain fans and critics, *the* best. As usual, it's the dance numbers—not the flimsy plot—that are the main attraction. And the fact that Jerome Kern wrote the music and Dorothy Fields supplied the lyrics, means it's a vintage score. On Academy Award night, their now-timeless standard "The Way You Look Tonight" deservedly took the Oscar for Best Song. Choreographer Hermes Pan had received a nomination for his inventive "Bojangles of Harlem" number, which Astaire performs in blackface. That still leaves for consideration the sounds and visions of Fred and Ginger tuned in to the likes of "Pick Yourself Up," "A Fine Ro-

mance," "Never Gonna Dance" and the exquisite "Waltz in Swing Time." But those who only read *The New York Times* would hardly know what they missed, judging by critic Frank S. Nugent, who termed *Swing Time*'s Kern-Fields score "merely adequate," and further admitted, "Right now we could not even whistle a bar of "A Fine Romance." In summation, Nugent dismissed the film's music as "Neither good Kern nor good swing." So much for *The New York Times*!

Admittedly, the plot is foolish and slight. Astaire plays a professional hoofer who's addicted to gambling and also engaged to marry Betty Furness, much to the disapproval of her father, who considers

SWING TIME: Fred Astaire in the "Bojangles of Harlem" number.

189

the dancer a ne'er-do-well. When Astaire fails to turn up for his own wedding (he arrives after all the guests and the minister have departed), he's packed off until he's able to prove he can support a wife; only *then* can he come back for Furness. Soon thereafter, Astaire spies pretty Ginger Rogers on the street, and follows her to a dance studio where she teaches. His ploy, of course, is to feign clumsiness on the dance floor. She begins to get wise to his strategy and it all unfolds in the exhilarating "Pick Yourself Up," which ends as a dazzling Astaire-Rogers dance number.

But Ginger's engaged to jealous bandleader Georges Metaxa, and for awhile it looks like she and Fred won't have his necessary accompaniment for their subsequent routines. However, that's all ironed out in some plot complications involving more gambling, with a few underworld types mixed in for good measure. There are also the obligatory comic sidekicks for the stars, here amusingly played by sarcastic Helen Broderick and vague Victor Moore (who never quite equals the addled fussiness of Edward Everett Horton in some of the previous Fred-and-Ginger vehicles). Our stars, of course, get to dance their stuff, both indoors and out, and on a Manhattan nightclub floor as well as in a snowy country setting before everything's conveniently—if unbelievably—resolved, with Furness showing up to admit she's not in love with Astaire after all, and Rogers breaking off with Metaxa in time to join her dancing partner for what can only be a happily-ever-after ending.

Until just before its release, *Swing Time* was in production as *Never Gonna Dance*—a title which might have unnecessarily alarmed the fans of Fred Astaire and Ginger Rogers.

THE GAY DESPERADO

1 9 3 6

CREDITS

A United Artists Picture. Producers: Mary Pickford and Jesse L. Lasky. Director: Rouben Mamoulian. Screenwriter: Wallace Smith. Based on a story by Leo Birinski. Cinematographer: Lucien Andriot. Editor: Margaret Clancey. Art Director: Richard Day. Music Director: Al-

fred Newman. Sound: Paul Neal. Costumes: Omar Kiam. Songs: "The World Is Mine Tonight" by Holt Marvell (Eric Maschwitz) and George Posford; "Cielito Lindo" by Neil Wilson, Carlo Fernandez and Sebastian Yradier; "Estrellita" by Frank LaForge and Manuel Ponce; "Adios Mi Terra" by Miguel Sandoval; "Lamento Gitano" by Walter Samuels and Leonard Whitcup; "Mamacita Mia" (Anon.); and "Celeste Aida" from the opera *Aida* by Giuseppe Verdi. Running Time: 86 minutes.

CAST

Nino Martini (*Chico*); Ida Lupino (*Jane*); Leo Carrillo (*Pablo Braganza*); Harold Huber (*Campo*); James Blakely (*Bill*); Harold Huber (*Butch*); Mischa Auer (*Diego*); Adrian Rosley (*Radio Station Manager*); Paul Hurst (*American Detective*); Alan Garcia (*Police Captain*); Frank Puglia (*Lopez*); Michael Visaroff (*Theatre Manager*); Chris-Pin Martin (*Pancho*); Harry Semels (*Manuel*); George Du Count (*Salvador*); Alphonso Pedroza (*Coloso*); Len Brixton (*Nick*); Trovadores Chinacos (*Guitar Trio*); M. Alvarez Maciste (*Guitar Soloist*).

The Thirties was a decade when serious singers like Grace Moore, Lawrence Tibbett, Lily Pons and Gladys Swarthout were taking leaves of absence from The Metropolitan Opera for occasional cinema forays, and moviemakers were kept busy digging for stories that would accomodate these special talents, as typified by this vehicle for Met tenor Nino Martini. In this second and last of the independent productions turned out by retired actress Mary Pickford in partnership with Jesse L. Lasky, Rouben Mamoulian directed an offbeat musical Western that satirized Hollywood gangsters of the Cagney-Robinson-Raft variety, as seen through the eyes of some comic Mexican bandits, led by the small-time Pancho Villa portrayed by Leo Carrillo.

Essentially, *The Gay Desperado* is an operetta in which Carrillo is sufficiently impressed with American gangster films to reorganize his band of outlaws à la a Chicago mob, south of the border. Because he's also a music lover, Carrillo kidnaps singer Martini, as well as (for ransom) a spoiled heiress (Ida Lupino) and the cowardly young man (James Blakely) with whom she's eloping. Most of the film's humor stems from the American gangland influence on the bandito chief, who's given to movie-mobster posturing and slang expressions like "Give 'em the woiks!"

Already highly respected as a motion picture stylist, Mamoulian skillfully employs his customary directorial inventiveness to keep this satirical material fresh and sparkling, and to this end he's helped immeasurably by Lucien Andriot's brilliant black-and-white, sunlight-and-shadow photography of the picturesque Mexican locations. But it was necessary

THE GAY DESPERADO: Harold Huber, Leo Carrillo, James Blakely, Ida Lupino and Nino Martini.

THE GAY DESPERADO: Nino Martini and Ida Lupino.

THE GAY DESPERADO: Leo Carrillo, Stanley Fields and Ida Lupino.

also to allow sufficient musical interludes for Martini, and his songs and arias ("Cielito Lindo," "Estrellita" and Verdi's "Celeste Aida" among them) undoubtedly slow the picture's pace and lessen the comic thrust of the material. It also presented Mamoulian with a challenge that some felt he failed to meet completely.

British-born Ida Lupino is comically effective as the rich and spirited American girl who engages in a crockery-smashing battle with Martini before eventually falling in love with him (somehow one knew she'd never remain with a stiff like Blakely). With her physical appearance now softened from the pencil-eyebrowed platinum blonde of her previous Ameri-

191

can films, Lupino more closely resembles, in *The Gay Desperado*, the image recognizable to those who associate her with her Forties heyday at Warner Bros.

Of course, *The Gay Desperado* is only as "gay" as its light-hearted Thirties connotation of that word allowed; a present-day remake would require an immediate change of title. *Webster's New World Dictionary* initially defines that word as "joyous and lively," a term that's most applicable here to Leo Carrillo as he plays cupid to that tenor-heiress romance. And not far behind him are those veteran character actors Harold Huber and Mischa Auer, obviously having the time of their lives as his comic henchmen. Today, *The Gay Desperado* may be difficult to locate, but its rediscovery should offer a pleasant surprise.

THE GAY DESPERADO: Ida Lupino and Nino Martini.

COME AND GET IT

(ROARING TIMBER)

1936

CREDITS

A United Artists Picture. A Samuel Goldwyn Production. Directors: Howard Hawks, William Wyler and (logging scenes) Richard Rosson. Screenwriters: Jules Furthman and Jane Murfin. Based on the novel by Edna Ferber. Cinematographers: Gregg Toland and Rudolph Maté. Editor: Edward Curtiss. Art Director: Richard Day. Set Decorator: Julia Heron. Costumes: Omar Kiam. Special Effects: Ray Binger. Assistant Director: Walter Mayo. Music: Alfred Newman. Running Time: 99 minutes.

CAST

Edward Arnold (*Barney Glasgow*); Joel McCrea (*Richard Glasgow*); Frances Farmer (*Lotta Morgan/Lotta Bostrom*); Walter Brennan (*Swan Bostrom*); Andrea Leeds (*Evvie Glasgow*); Frank Shields (*Tony Schwerke*); Mady Christians (*Karie Linbeck*); Mary Nash (*Emma Louise Glasgow*); Clem Bevans (*Gunner Gallagher*); Edwin Maxwell (*Sid LeMaire*); Cecil Cunningham (*Josie*); Harry Bradley (*Gubbins*); Rollo Lloyd (*Steward*); Charles Halton (*Hewitt*); Phillip Cooper (*Chore Boy*); Al K. Hall (*Goodnow*); Robert Lowery (*Young Man*); Stanley Blystone, Constantine Romanoff and Harry Tenbrook (*Lumberjacks*); Max Wagner (*Scalded Lumberjack*); Jack Pennick (*Foreman*); Russell Simpson (*Hewitt's Secretary*); Earle Hodgins (*Shell-Game Operator*); Lee Shumway (*Diner*); George Humbert (*Headwaiter*); Fred Toones (*Snowflake*); Gino Corrado (*Waiter*); Egon Brecher (*Schwerke*); William Wagner (*Wine Steward*); Bud Jamison (*Man in Saloon*); Fred Warren (*Pianist*).

In the Thirties, most actors were either handsome leading men or else they were supporting "character" actors. But there were a few exceptional "character leading men"—usually larger-than-life performers like Wallace Beery, Charles Laughton, Victor McLaglen and Edward Arnold.

Edward Arnold was most often cast in supporting roles—with the exception of three mid-Thirties biodramas in which he portrayed some of the builders and shakers of America: *Sutter's Gold* (as John Sutter, on whose land the 1848 California Gold Rush began); *Diamond Jim* (as Diamond Jim Brady, the

COME AND GET IT: Joel McCrea and Frances Farmer.

Barney's Swedish pal, Swan Bostrom (Walter Brennan). Barney's ambitions require that he "make a good marriage," which means the homely but wealthy girl (Mary Nash) who's waiting for him back home. All of this raises the question "Is Lotta Bostrom actually Barney's daughter, made legitimate by Lotta Morgan's quick marriage to Swan?" It's an issue carefully side-stepped in *Come and Get It*, but remains an especially good reason why Barney never gets to first base with the younger Lotta who, of course, is the softer and sweeter mirror-image of her mother. Instead, young Lotta wisely elects to team up with Barney's handsome son Richard (Joel McCrea), thus leaving the older man alone with his wife—and his memories.

Frances Farmer portrays the two Lottas beautifully, making them similar in some ways but individual in others—important reasons why Barney is

great financier and philanthropist); and *Come and Get It* (as Barney Glasgow, American lumber tycoon). Of course, while Sutter and Brady were actual historical figures, Glasgow was merely a figment of novelist Edna Ferber's fertile imagination; he only *seemed* like a real person. And that's a sound tribute to Barney Glasgow's motion-picture creator, Edward Arnold. In a career encompassing some 150-odd pictures, Arnold was always a good, solid actor—and sometimes a great one. Some consider *Come and Get It* the film that offers his single finest performance.

Barney Glasgow is a long and demanding role as he ambitiously brawls his way up from a lumber camp in 1880s Wisconsin to become the wealthiest of the early 20th century timber tycoons. Barney ends up having everything, except the women he loved—first the spirited, tough but sweet Lotta Morgan (Frances Farmer in her finest screen work), the beauty he loved and left back in that lumber camp long ago; and then Morgan's daughter, Lotta Bostrom (also portrayed by Farmer). The young Lotta was born following her mother's marriage to

COME AND GET IT: Edward Arnold and Andrea Leeds.

193

attracted to both of them. Walter Brennan's excellent character work as Swan earned him the very first Academy Award ever given in the category of Best Supporting Actor.

Come and Get It has the high-gloss craftsmanship that stamps it a Sam Goldwyn production, despite the behind-the-scenes upset resulting in two directors (Howard Hawks and William Wyler) sharing credit for the film. Apparently Hawks, who had been assigned *Come and Get It* from the start, had taken advantage of the fact that producer Goldwyn was hospitalized for a gall bladder/appendix operation to rewrite a few scenes from the Jules Furthman-Jane Murfin screenplay and proceed to shoot those scenes. Upon his recovery, Goldwyn screened the new footage, raised his objections and battled with Hawks, asserting, "Directors are supposed to direct, not write!" The confrontation resulted in Hawks walking off the nearly-completed picture, thus forcing Goldwyn to find someone else to finish the job. Because William Wyler was then under contract to Goldwyn and working on a neighboring sound stage shooting *Dodsworth*, he became the logical choice. Wyler was not at all happy about it, and only his contractual obligations to Goldwyn made Wyler re-shoot the Hawks scenes that Goldwyn disliked. As Wyler explained the situation to his biographer, Axel Madsen: "At the end, I had to do it. I don't think it helped much. The best parts—the first half hour—were done by Hawks, and the magnificent logger-operations footage by second-unit director Richard

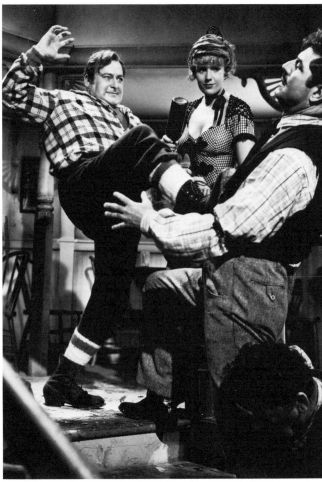

COME AND GET IT: Edward Arnold, Frances Farmer and player.

COME AND GET IT: Joel McCrea, Frances Farmer, Walter Brennan and Mady Christians.

Rosson. When I finished, Goldwyn was still sore at Hawks and wanted to take his name off the picture altogether and give me credit alone. I said, 'Absolutely no,' and we had another blowup. Goldwyn finally agreed on a half measure—putting both our names on the screen, and I insisted that Hawks' name come first, and that's how it appears—directed by Howard Hawks and William Wyler. Needless to say, I don't count *Come and Get It* as one of my pictures."

THEODORA GOES WILD

1936

CREDITS

A Columbia Picture. Associate Producer: Everett Riskin. Director: Richard Boleslawski. Screenwriter: Sidney Buchman. Based on the story by Mary McCarthy. Cinematographer: Joseph Walker. Editor: Otto Meyer. Art Director: Stephen Goosson. Costumes: Bernard Newman. Sound: George Cooper. Music Director: Morris Stoloff. Assistant Director: William E. Muel. Running Time: 94 minutes.

CAST

Irene Dunne (*Theodora Lynn*); Melvyn Douglas (*Michael Grant*); Thomas Mitchell (*Jed Waterbury*); Thurston Hall (*Arthur Stevenson*); Rosalind Keith (*Adelaide Perry*); Spring Byington (*Rebecca Perry*); Elizabeth Risdon (*Aunt Mary*); Margaret McWade (*Aunt Elsie*); Nana Bryant (*Ethel Stevenson*); Henry Kolker (*Jonathan Grant*); Leona Maricle (*Agnes Grant*); Robert Greig (*Uncle John*); Frederick Burton (*Governor Wyatt*); Mary Forbes (*Mrs. Wyatt*); Grace Hayle (*Mrs. Cobb*); Sarah Edwards (*Mrs. Moffat*); Mary MacLaren (*Mrs. Wilson*); Wilfred Hari (*Toki*); Laura Treadwell (*Mrs. Grant*); Corbet Morris (*Artist*); Ben F. Hendricks (*Taxi Driver*); Frank Sully (*Clarence*); James T. Mack (*Minister*); William Benedict (*Henry*); Carolyn Lee Bourland (*Baby*); Paul Barrett (*Adelaide's Husband*); Leora Thatcher (*Miss Baldwin*); Billy Wayne, Harold Goodwin and Jack Hatfield (*Photographers*); Harry Harvey, Don Brodie, Eddie Fetherstone, Ed Hart, Lee Phelps, Sherry Hall, Ralph Malone and Beatrice Curtis (*Reporters*); Maurice Brierre (*Waiter*); Sven Borg (*Bartender*); Dennis O'Keefe (*Man*); Rex Moore (*Newsboy*); Georgia Cooper, Jane Keckley, Jessie Perry, Noel Bates, Betty Farrington, Stella Adams, Isabelle LaMal, Georgia O'Dell and Dorothy Vernon (*Townswomen*).

THEODORA GOES WILD: Nana Bryant, Thurston Hall, Irene Dunne and Melvyn Douglas.

THEODORA GOES WILD: Melvyn Douglas and Irene Dunne.

THEODORA GOES WILD: Irene Dunne.

At 37, Irene Dunne had established a solid career in motion pictures as a dramatic actress—mostly in soap operas, with occasional forays into musicals. But, after 20 films, she wasn't well known for comedy, and when she signed a contract with Columbia Pictures in mid-1935, there was an understanding that her initial project at the studio would be a comedy. Apparently, this gave the actress considerable pause, for she suddenly packed herself off for a lengthy European vacation with her husband, returning to find herself on salary suspension until she settled on that agreed-upon vehicle.

If Sidney Buchman's amusing script for the screwball comedy *Theodora Goes Wild* made Dunne uncertain of her ability to portray the lead, then she was all the more skeptical of working with Richard Boleslawski, the Polish-born director of such non-amusing movies as *Rasputin and the Empress*, *Men in White*, *The Painted Veil* and *Les Miserables*. To his credit, Columbia's Harry Cohn granted his new star the right to replace her director, were she not satisfied with him after the first week's shooting. No such replacement was requested; Boleslawski proved entirely congenial with the material, and the unexpected result was one of the best comedies of the Thirties.

Predating the real-life story of Grace Metalious, the smalltown New Englander who shocked her neighbors by writing a sensational novel (*Peyton Place*) that became a best seller, *Theodora Goes Wild* begins in Lynnfield, Connecticut, where demure Theodora Lynn (Dunne) shares a house with her two maiden aunts (Elizabeth Risdon and Margaret McWade). Unknown to anyone but her New York publisher, Theodora is the secret author of a much-talked-about new novel called *The Sinner*, published under the pseudonym of Caroline Adams. In fact, the local newspaper has been running the book in serial form—until the local people rise in protest and demand that *Lynnfield Bugle* editor Jed Waterbury (Thomas Mitchell) cease and desist.

Theodora finally meets her publisher and his wife (Thurston Hall and Nana Bryant) on a rare trip to Manhattan, where she also encounters Michael Grant (Melvyn Douglas), the artist who designed her book jacket. None is prepared for the prim and drably-attired young lady who claims to have written *The Sinner*, but during a luncheon with the threesome, Theodora is challenged to have a drink—and before long she's the life of the party. Indeed, Michael later tries to duplicate the big seduction scene from her novel at his apartment, only to be be met with a sound rebuff. He doesn't know what to make of her.

Back home in the self-righteous atmosphere of Lynnfield, Theodora's surprised to find Michael on her doorstep, posing as a job seeker, and he persuades her aunts to take him on as a gardener. By the time the wary Theodora is ready to admit she's in love with Michael—and lets him know it—he gets cold feet and departs, leaving a note indicating that she's got a big future and, freed of the restrictions of her small-town background, she'll "travel faster alone." But Theodora follows Michael to the big city, and really begins to cut loose, dressing more fashionably and getting herself into all manner of innocent but eyebrow-raising situations (including two divorce actions) until the amusing denouement where she makes a triumphant return to Lynnfield, carrying a newborn baby. Of course, the child isn't Theodora's; it's the legitimate infant of a secretly wed local girl. But Buchman's script employs the device as one more guffaw at the expense of the hypocritical mores of small-minded small-town America.

The real pleasure of *Theodora Goes Wild* lies in the enthusiastic abandon with which Irene Dunne tackles this delightful role, and not a few 1936 critics were pleasantly surprised at witnessing her transformation from soap heroine to comedienne. New York's *Daily News* saluted her "spirited gift for clowning," and *Variety* thought she took "the hurdle into comedy . . . with versatile grace." But Dunne was in good company, playing opposite the suave and witty Melvyn Douglas, and surrounded by a wonderful roster of familiar charactor actors of the sort that every Hollywood studio then seemed to have on ready call. Perhaps most surprising of all is the smooth and knowing way in which director Boleslawski handled this Capra-esque material, so different not only from his Eastern European background but also from the mainstream of his previous movies. Unfortunately, this was to be Boleslawski's last completed picture, for he died suddenly at 47 during production of 1937's *The Last of Mrs. Cheyney*, which was finished by an uncredited Dorothy Arzner.

Theodora Goes Wild gathered up two Academy Award nominations, including Otto Meyer's Film Editing and Best Actress Irene Dunne—who lost the ultimate honor to Luise Rainer for *The Great Ziegfeld.*

THEODORA GOES WILD: Sarah Edwards, Spring Byington, Grace Hayle, Irene Dunne and Melvyn Douglas.

PIGSKIN PARADE

1 9 3 6

CREDITS

A 20th Century-Fox Picture. A Darryl F. Zanuck Production. Director: David Butler. Associate Producer: Bogart Rogers. Screenwriters: Harry Tugend, Jack Yellen and William Conselman. Based on a story by Arthur Sheekman, Nat Perrin and Mark Kelly. Cinematographer: Arthur Miller. Editor: Irene Morra. Costumes: Gwen Wakeling. Music Director: David Buttolph. Songs: "The Balboa," "The Texas Tornado," "It's Love I'm After," "You're Simply Terrific," "You Do the Darndest Things, Baby," "T.S.U. Alma Mater" and "Hold That Bulldog" by Lew Pollack and Sidney Mitchell; and "Down With Everything," "We'd Rather Be in College" and "Woo! Woo!" by The Yacht Club Boys. Running Time: 93 minutes.

CAST

Stuart Erwin (*Amos Dodd*); Patsy Kelly (*Bessie Winters*); Jack Haley ("*Slug*" *Winston Winters*); Johnny Downs (*Chip Carson*); Betty Grable (*Laura Watson*); Arline Judge (*Sally Saxon*); Dixie Dunbar (*Ginger Jones*); Judy Garland (*Sairy Dodd*); Anthony "Tony" Martin (*Tommy Barker*); Fred Kohler, Jr. (*Biff Bentley*); Elisha Cook, Jr. (*Herbert Terwilliger Van Dyck*); Eddie Nugent (*Sparks*); Grady Sutton (*Mortimer Higgins*); Julius Tannen (*Dr. Burke*); Sam Hayes (*Radio Announcer, Himself*); Robert McClung (*Country*

Boy); George Herbert (*Professor*); Jack Murphy (*Usher*); Pat Flaherty (*Referee*); Dave Sharpe (*Messenger Boy*); Si Jenks (*Baggage Master*); John Dilson (*Doctor*); Jack Stoney (*Policemen*); George Y. Harvey (*Brakeman*); Ben Hall (*Boy in Stadium*); Lynn Bari (*Girl in Stadium*); Charles Wilson (*Yale Coach*); George Offerman, Jr. (*Freddy, Yale Reporter*); Maurice Cass (*Prof. Tutweiler*); Jack Best (*Prof. McCormick*); Douglas Wood (*Prof. Dutton*); Charles Croker King (*Prof. Pillsbury*); Alan Ladd (*Student*); Edward Le Saint (*Judge*); Jed Prouty (*Mr. Van Dyke*); Emma Dunn (*Mrs. Van Dyke*); The Yacht Club Boys (*Themselves*).

In the mid-Thirties, nearly every American movie studio produced light comedy-musical entertainments, often with a backstage or college setting. While Paramount turned out titles like *Rose Bowl* and *College Swing*, and Warner Bros. offered *Flirtation Walk*, 20th Century-Fox released *Pigskin Parade*—which *Variety* appropriately dubbed ". . . a marathon of comedy, songs and undergraduate nonsense . . ."

Efficiently assembled by Fox "house director" David Butler, *Pigskin Parade*'s premise is both silly and slight: an administrative error causes the unimpressive football team from mythical Texas State University to receive an invitation to play against Yale in New Haven, Connecticut. But before they can do so, they must shape up their team. That task is assigned to a new coach (Jack Haley) who arrives with his assertive wife (Patsy Kelly, of whom a little goes a long way). A wise-cracking type, she wears the family pants and calls all the plays. And then there are the usual romantic pairings and misunderstandings that involve engaging student leader Johnny

PIGSKIN PARADE: Betty Grable, Johnny Downs, Patsy Kelly, Jack Haley, Anthony Martin, Dixie Dunbar and the Yacht Club Boys.

Downs, platinum-tressed co-ed Betty Grable, campus vamp Arline Judge, singing Tony (then billed as "Anthony") Martin and tap-dancing Dixie Dunbar. Since the football team needs talent, we get Arkansas melon-tosser Stuart Erwin (if that's what he can do with a melon, imagine how he'll pass that pigskin!), who arrives with his teen-aged sister (Judy Garland) in tow.

Making her feature-film bow at 14, Garland was already under contract to MGM, the studio responsible for the majority of her movie career. And *Pigskin Parade*—in which she's billed ninth—marks the only time Metro ever let her work away from the home lot. Despite her billing, Judy gets three musical numbers, belting out "The Texas Tornado," leading a bevy of collegiate dancers in "The Balboa" and then turning plaintive for "It's Love I'm After." Her talents won notice from the movie's critics.

Highlighting the picture's other musical moments are the catchy "You're Simply Terrific," smoothly delivered by suave Tony Martin and cute Dixie Dunbar. And then there's the sweater-clad Yacht Club Boys (a harmonizing quartet resembling a collegiate version of the Ritz Brothers) whom the movie asks us to believe have spent six years in the University's freshman class! A diminutive blond novice named Alan Ladd may be spotted joining the Boys for the song "Down With Everything." And it's equally interesting to note the pleasant but unimpressive early presence of young Betty Grable, liter-

PIGSKIN PARADE: Jack Haley, Patsy Kelly, Stuart Erwin, Judy Garland, Johnny Downs and Betty Grable.

ally passing through 20th Century-Fox on her way back to RKO and Paramount. Four years later, she'd finally land the contract that would make her one of World War II's top box-office attractions—back at Fox!

Lending *Pigskin Parade* a brief mention in the record books was the Academy Award nomination announced for Best Supporting Actor Stuart Erwin. But in the first year this Oscar was handed out, Walter Brennan received it for *Come and Get It*.

CAMILLE

1936

CREDITS

A Metro-Goldwyn-Mayer Picture. Producers: Irving Thalberg and Bernard Hyman. Director: George Cukor. Screenwriters: Zoë Akins, Frances Marion and James Hilton. Based on the novel *La Dame aux Camelias* by Alexandre Dumas *fils*. Cinematographer: William Daniels. Editor: Margaret Booth. Art Directors: Cedric Gibbons and Frederic Hope. Set Decorator: Edwin B. Willis. Costumes: Adrian. Sound: Douglas Shearer. Music: Herbert Stothart. Choreographer: Val Raset. Running Time: 108 minutes.

PIGSKIN PARADE: Elisha Cook, Jr., Johnny Downs and Betty Grable.

Greta Garbo (*Marguerite Gautier*); Robert Taylor (*Armand Duval*); Lionel Barrymore (*General Duval*); Henry Daniell (*Baron de Varville*); Elizabeth Allan (*Nichette*); Lenore Ulric (*Olympe*); Laura Hope Crews (*Prudence*); Jessie Ralph (*Nanine*); Rex O'Malley (*Gaston*); Russell Hardie (*Gustave*); E.E. Clive (*St. Gadeau*); Douglas Walton (*Henri*); Marion Ballou (*Corinne*); Joan Brodel/Joan Leslie (*Marie Jeanette*); June Wilkins (*Louise*); Elsie Esmond (*Madame Duval*); Fritz Leiber, Jr. (*Valentine*); Edwin Maxwell (*Doctor*); Eily Malyon (*Therese*); Mariska Aldrich (*Friend of Camille*); John Bryan (*DeMasset*); Rex Evans (*Companion*); Eugene King (*Gypsy Leader*); Adrienne Matzenauer (*Singer*); Georgia Caine (*Streetwalker*); Elspeth Dudgeon (*Attendant*); Effie Ellsler (*Grandma Duval*); Olaf Hytten (*Croupier*); Ferdinand Munier (*Priest*); Zeffie Tilbury (*Old Duchess*); Guy Bates Post (*Auctioneer*); Barry Norton (*Emile*); John Picorri (*Orchestra Leader*); Mabel Colcord (*Madame Barjon*); Chappel Dossett (*Priest*); Sibyl Harris (*George Sand*); Maude Hume (*Aunt Henriette*); Gwendolyn Logan (*Governess*).

There seems general agreement that *Camille* is Greta Garbo in her finest screen performance. Despite the passage of years, Garbo's generally subtle, understated acting and extraordinary beauty seem to transcend time and the vogues that date many another of her contemporaries. Always an arresting performer for whom no flesh-and-blood lover could ever have been more faithful and attentive than the motion picture camera, she found in *Camille* the perfect marriage of vehicle, director (George Cukor), script, cast and production; and, of course in the role of the consumptive courtesan Marguerite Gautier, a character with whom she was in complete empathy.

The Alexandre Dumas novel *La Dame aux Camelias* (*The Lady of the Camelias*) had, of course, served as the basis for Verdi's popular opera *La Traviata*, and had long been a stage and screen vehicle popular with leading ladies. Among those who preceded Garbo in portraying the role on the screen were Oda Alstrup (1907), Gertrude Shipman (1912), Sarah Bernhardt (1912), Clara Kimball Young

CAMILLE: Robert Taylor, Greta Garbo, Laura Hope Crews and Rex O'Malley.

(*Opposite page*) CAMILLE: Greta Garbo.

CAMILLE: Lionel Barrymore and Greta Garbo.

CAMILLE: Robert Taylor and Greta Garbo.

(1915), Theda Bara (1917), Alla Nazimova (1921), Norma Talmadge (1927) and Yvonne Printemps in a 1934 French production. Not unexpectedly, Garbo practically erased the memory of all of their performances. Nor has any subsequent Marguerite Gautier surpassed her work in this 1936 movie—even the lavish 1984 television refilming with another Greta—Scacchi.

Following the success of Garbo's 1935 *Anna Karenina*, MGM's production chief Irving Thalberg sought another work of similar classic stature and, assigning George Cukor for the first time to direct her, offered him a choice of either *Camille* or *Marie Walewska*. After Cukor opted for the former, it was a matter of getting a screenplay to suit Thalberg's requirements for a "contemporary feeling" that would allow audiences to immediately forget that they were watching a costume film. And this the work's adapting team of Zoë Akins, Frances Marion and James Hilton managed to accomplish. Thalberg himself chose the supporting cast: as Marguerite's lover Armand, $75-a-week contract player Robert Taylor, cast mainly for his perfect good looks (frequently, Taylor appears prettier than Garbo in the movie); Henry Daniell as Marguerite's cruel protector, the Baron de Varville (Thalberg wanted John

Barrymore, but that once-great actor's alcoholic ill-health ruled him out); Lionel Barrymore for Armand's disapproving father, who persuades Marguerite to give up his son for their family's sake; and, as Marguerite's three uninhibited Bohemian friends, bawdy Laura Hope Crews, sluttish Lenore Ulric and effeminate Rex O'Malley. And only the best of MGM artisans were engaged for behind-the-scenes contributions, including Cedric Gibbons' lavishly detailed sets, Adrian's sumptuous costumes and the painstaking camerawork of Garbo's favorite cinematographer William Daniels. The end result is a tribute to their passionate commitment to the production, made even more eloquent given Thalberg's tragic early death at the age of 37, before the film's completion.

In *Camille*, Garbo's death scene is a classic in itself. Wan and failing, she learns of her lover's return and her mask-like face rallies miraculously. Joy animates her features and for a few minutes, in Armand's loving presence, she once again becomes the Marguerite of old. But she's not self-deluded, and she gently tells him, "Perhaps it's better if I live in your heart, where the world can't see me." As he cries out, "Marguerite, don't leave me!" she falls back, lifeless in his arms. Frank S. Nugent aptly wrote of Garbo in his *New York Times* review of the film, "Through the perfect artistry of her portrayal, a hackneyed theme is made new again, poignantly sad, haunting and lovely."

Camille won Greta Garbo an Academy Award nomination, but the Oscar went to Luise Rainer for another MGM classic, *The Good Earth*. Garbo did walk off with the New York Film Critics award for Best Actress of 1937, the year *Camille* went into general release.

FLASH GORDON

1936

CREDITS

A Universal Serial. Producer: Henry MacRae. Director: Frederick Stephani. Screenwriters: Frederick Stephani, George Plympton, Basil Dickey and Ella O'Neill. Based on the comic strip by Alex Raymond. Cinematographers: Jerry Ash and Richard Fryer. Art Director: Ralph Berger. Special Effects: Norman Drewes. Music: Franz Waxman (from *The Bride of Frankenstein*). Shown in 13 chapters of approximately 20 minutes each.

CAST

Larry "Buster" Crabbe (*Flash Gordon*); Jean Rogers (*Dale Arden*); Charles Middleton (*Ming the Merciless*); Priscilla Lawson (*Princess Aura*); John Lipson (*King Vultan*); Richard Alexander (*Prince Barin*); Frank Shannon (*Dr. Zarkov*); Duke York, Jr. (*King Kala*); Earl Askam (*Officer Torch*); George Cleveland (*Professor Hensley*); Theodore Lorch (*High Priest*); House Peters, Jr. (*Shark Man*); James Pierce (*King Thun*); Muriel Goodspeed (*Zona*); Richard Tucker (*Flash Gordon, Sr.*); Fred Kohler, Jr., Lane Chandler, Al Ferguson and Glenn Strange (*Soldiers*).

With 99 feature films being detailed in this volume, it seems only fair to allot space to the coverage of at least one serial—especially that most popular chapter-play of the Thirties, the original 1936 *Flash Gordon*.

FLASH GORDON: Larry "Buster" Crabbe.

FLASH GORDON: Larry "Buster" Crabbe and Jean Rogers.

The U.S. vogue for cliffhangers, usually offered in 12 to 15 installments of approximately 20 minutes each, started with the early silents of 1912; it wasn't until 1956 that Columbia Pictures would bury the genre with a lacklustre item called *Blazing the Overland Trail*. But Universal's 13-part *Flash Gordon* reflects the heyday of Hollywood serials. Based on the popular King Features comic-strip characters created in 1929 by Alex Ràymond, its space-oriented action provided something relatively fresh and new to mid-Thirties moviegoers: science fiction. In addition, Universal provided a larger-than-average serial budget (although some corners were cut by utilizing both the sets and Franz Waxman's musical score from 1935's *The Bride of Frankenstein*).

Director Frederick Stephani, who collaborated on the appropriately action-oriented screenplay with George Plympton, Basil Dickey and Ella O'Neill, displayed a wonderful flair for this kind of flamboyant adventure fantasy, and the cast was aptly chosen. Larry "Buster" Crabbe wasn't Universal's immediate choice for Flash Gordon, despite his Olympics background, athletic prowess, good looks and several years of filming experience. The studio first tested many actors, including the relatively unknown Jon Hall, before offering the role to Crabbe. But with the offer came a condition: he had to bleach his brown hair blond to better resemble the comic-strip Flash. Crabbe reluctantly agreed. His co-star Jean Rogers had no such problem as Dale Arden. She adequately met the requirements of matching Flash's blond beauty with her own; she also excelled in screaming and fainting. And character actor Charles Middleton was perfection as the serial's chief "heavy," the evil, bald-pated Ming the Merciless.

The planet Mongo is on a collision course with Earth, and the world is in a state of panic. Hopeful of altering the planet's deadly course, Flash and Dale set off for Mongo in his rocketship, with the brilliant scientist Dr. Alexis Zarkov (Frank Shannon). Landing on Mongo, the trio is captured and imprisoned by the soldiers of Ming the Merciless, who plans to be Emperor of the Universe. Providing the nearest thing to what could now be called sexual tension is Ming's voluptuous daughter Princess Aura (Priscilla Lawson), who understandably lusts after Flash, while her father is sufficiently smitten with Dale to want Flash killed.

Twelve additional chapters then allow script and direction to devise as many exciting and disbelief-suspending incidents as possible, as the intrepid Flash battles and defeats incredible adversaries and escapes from Ming's insidious traps. However, as expected, the dangerous megalomaniac is overcome in Chapter 13 in time for Flash, Dale and Zarkov to return to Earth, having saved the world.

Flash Gordon's immense popularity among the Saturday-matinee crowd paved the way for a pair of Buster Crabbe sequels—*Flash Gordon's Trip to Mars* (1938) and *Flash Gordon Conquers the Universe* (1940). The 1936 serial—which many consider the best of the trio—was itself re-edited into feature-length form, and variously shown as *Rocket Ship*, *Spaceship to the Unknown*, *Space Soldiers* and *Atomic Rocketship*.

In 1980, Universal released an updated *Flash Gordon* feature, which impressed everyone more with its eye-filling production design than with the performances of its handsome but colorless stars, Sam Jones and Melody Anderson.

FLASH GORDON: James Pierce, Richard Alexander, Jean Rogers and Larry "Buster" Crabbe.

FLASH GORDON: Richard Alexander, Jean Rogers, Charles Middleton, Larry "Buster" Crabbe, Priscilla Lawson and John Lipson.

LOST HORIZON

1937

CREDITS

A Columbia Picture. Producer-Director: Frank Capra. Screenwriter: Robert Riskin. Based on the novel by James Hilton. Cinematographers: Joseph Walker and Elmer Dyer. Editors: Gene Havlick and Gene Milford. Art Director: Stephen Goosson. Set Decorator: Babs Johnstone. Costumes: Ernst Dryden. Music: Dimitri Tiomkin. Music Director: Max Steiner. Technical Advisor: Harrison Foreman. Assistant Director: C.C. Coleman. Special Effects: E. Roy Davidson and Ganahl Carson. Running Time: 132 minutes.

CAST

Ronald Colman (*Robert Conway*); Jane Wyatt (*Sondra*); Edward Everett Horton (*Alexander P. Lovett*); John Howard (*George Conway*); Thomas Mitchell (*Henry Bar-* *nard*); Margo (*Maria*); Isabel Jewell (*Gloria Stone*); H.B. Warner (*Chang*); Sam Jaffe (*High Lama*); Hugh Buckler (*Lord Gainsford*); John Miltern (*Carstairs*); Lawrence Grant (*First Man*); Max Rabinowitz (*Seiveking*); Willie Fung (*Bandit Leader*); Wyrley Birch (*Missionary*); Richard Loo (*Shanghai Airport Official*); Chief Big Tree, Delmer Ingraham, Ed Thorpe and Harry Lishman (*Porters*); Noble Johnson (*Leader of Porters*); Neil Fitzgerald (*Radio Operator*); Leonard Mudie (*Foreign Secretary*); Boyd Irwin (*Assistant Foreign Secretary*); Dennis D'Auburn (*Aviator*); John Burton (*Wynant*); John T. Murray (*Meeker*); John Tettener (*Montaigne*); David Clyde (*Steward*); Val Durand (*Talu*); Ruth Robinson and Margaret McWade (*Missionaries*); Milton Owen (*Fenner*); Victor Wong (*Bandit Leader*); Carl Stockdale (*Missionary*); Darby Clarke (*Radio Operator*); George Chan (*Chinese Priest*); Eric Wilton (*Englishman*); Beatrice Curtis, Mary Lou Dix, Beatrice Blinn and Arthur Rankin (*Passengers*); The Hall Johnson Choir (*Voices*).

LOST HORIZON: Ronald Colman.

206

Nowadays, the name Frank Capra is immediately associated with his socially conscious comedy-dramas like *Mr. Deeds Goes to Town, Mr. Smith Goes to Washington, Meet John Doe*—and, of course, *It's a Wonderful Life.* But there were also the multi-Academy Award winner *It Happened One Night* and that ultimate escapist fantasy drama, *Lost Horizon.* It's amusing to note that, although novelist James Hilton took only six weeks to write *Lost Horizon*, filmmaker Capra spent two entire years bringing the project to the screen. At a cost of $2.5 million, *Lost Horizon* threatened to ruin little Columbia Pictures, for that sum amounted to half of the studio's customary annual budget!

With Robert Riskin's script as his basis, Capra guided star Ronald Colman and a large cast through the fantastic settings devised by Stephen Goosson, with the lost Himalayan city of Shangri-La—replete with gardens, terraces and reflecting pools—obviously heavily influenced by the architectural style of Frank Lloyd Wright. Snow scenes were shot in a gigantic cold-storage warehouse in below-freezing temperatures that made it possible to create real snow, including the plane crash and avalanche scenes.

Colman plays soldier-turned-diplomat Robert Conway, who manages to escape from a Chinese revolution, only to be mysteriously abducted by plane. Along with four other "foreigners"—his brother George (John Howard), a wanted swindler named Barnard (Thomas Mitchell), the tubercular prostitute Gloria (Isabel Jewell) and Lovett (Edward Everett Horton), a fussy paleontologist—Robert's taken to Shangri-La, a Utopian civilization hidden in the mountains of Tibet. There, everything is peaceful, people are considerate of one another and they live to a remarkably advanced age. Robert falls in love with Sondra (Jane Wyatt), who lives in the escapist enclave. One day, he's summoned to a meet-

LOST HORIZON: Jane Wyatt, Ronald Colman and Margo.

LOST HORIZON: Edward Everett Horton, Isabel Jewell, John Howard, Ronald Colman and Thomas Mitchell.

ing with the ancient, dying High Lama (Sam Jaffe), who informs Robert that he's been designated to succeed him. It's the perfect set-up for a classic

207

adventure tale of romance, tragedy and mysticism, with scenes as unforgettable as that in which Maria (portrayed by Margo), the alleged teen-ager with whom George has fallen in love—and dared to take away from Shangri-La, against all warnings—turns gradually into the old lady she *really* is, dying in the snows outside that idyllic world.

Lost Horizon won Academy Award nominations in seven categories, including Best Picture, Best Supporting Actor (H.B. Warner) and Best Score (Dimitri Tiomkin), while taking home statuettes only for Art Direction, Set Decoration and Film Editing. And, fortunately for Columbia Pictures, it scored a great hit with the public, as well as most of the critics. But, soon after its release, the lengthy 132-minute movie was cut by nine minutes because of pressure from exhibitors, who deplored the fact that overlong movies allowed for fewer showings per day and would, therefore, bring in less money at the box-office. In 1941, the studio re-released *Lost Horizon* in a 110-minute version, and only then did the film begin to break even for Columbia.

In 1973, the studio released a disastrous, 143-minute musical remake in wide-screen and color, starring Peter Finch and Liv Ullmann that added insult to injury by causing the original *Lost Horizon* to be removed from TV syndication. However, in 1986, work was completed on a painstaking restoration of the 1937 movie, with the result that there now exists a 132-minute edition of the Capra original that restores the entire dialogue track. Admittedly, several scenes remain missing, visually, and are represented only by stills projected over *Lost Horizon*'s original soundtrack. It is this version that's now available on videocassette.

MARKED WOMEN

1937

CREDITS

A Warner Bros. Picture. Director: Lloyd Bacon. Executive Producers: Jack L. Warner and Hal B. Wallis. Producer: Lou Edelman. Screenwriters: Robert Rossen, Abem Finkel and Seton I. Miller. Cinematographer: George Barnes. Editor: Jack Killifer. Art Director: Max Parker. Costumes: Orry-Kelly. Music: Bernard Kaum and Heinz Roemheld. Songs by Harry Warren and Al Dubin. Running Time: 96 minutes.

(*Opposite page*) LOST HORIZON: Jane Wyatt, Ronald Colman and Shangri-La.

CAST

Bette Davis (*Mary Dwight [Strauber]*); Humphrey Bogart (*Special Prosecutor David Graham*); Jane Bryan (*Betty Strauber*); Eduardo Ciannelli (*Johnny Vanning*); Isabel Jewell (*Emmy Lou Egan*); Allen Jenkins (*Louis*); Mayo Methot (*Estelle Porter*); Lola Lane (*Gabby Marvin*); Ben Welden (*Charley Delaney*); Henry O'Neill (*District Attorney Arthur Sheldon*); Rosalind Marquis (*Florrie Liggett*); John Litel (*Gordon*); Damian O'Flynn (*Ralph Krawford*); Robert Strange (*George Beler*); James Robbins (*Bell Captain*); William B. Davidson (*Bob Crandall*); John Sheehan (*Vincent, a Sugar Daddy*); Sam Wren (*Mac*); Kenneth Harlan (*Eddie, a Sugar Daddy*); Raymond Hatton (*Lawyer at Jail*); Alan Davis and Allan Matthews (*Henchmen*); John Harron and Frank Faylen (*Taxi Drivers*); Alphonse Martel (*Doorman*); Carlos San Martin (*Headwaiter*); Harlan Briggs (*Man in Phone Booth*); Philip G. Sleeman (*Crap Table Attendant*); Guy Usher (*Ferguson, the Detective*); Ed Stanley (*Casey, the Detective*); Milton Kibbee (*Male Secretary at D.A.'s Office*); Mark Strong (*Bartender*); Emmett Vogan (*Court Clerk*); Jack Mower (*Foreman*); Herman Marks (*Little Joe*); Wendell Niles (*News Commentator*).

MARKED WOMAN: Bette Davis and Jane Bryan.

MARKED WOMAN: Isabel Jewell, Mayo Methot and Bette Davis.

MARKED WOMAN: Rosalind Marquis, Humphrey Bogart, Mayo Methot, Lola Lane and Bette Davis.

In 1936, Bette Davis fought a well publicized legal battle with Warner Bros. over the restrictions of her contract. Having long since proven her talents as an actress, she justifiably wanted good parts in movies better than those she was being offered (*Garden of*

the Moon, God's Country and the Woman), and which she continued to turn down. Davis ultimately lost her court battle with that studio, but, having taken a courageous stand, she appeared to have gained the respect of the industry. She has written, "In a way, my defeat was a victory. At last we were seeing eye to eye on my career."

Consequently, Davis was surprised to get a good role in a worthwhile picture, *Marked Woman*. It was a tough underworld melodrama reflecting the concern that Warners dramas often showed for social injustice during the Thirties. In this instance, a blistering Robert Rossen-Abem Finkel screenplay used the recent trial of Charles "Lucky" Luciano to focus on the career problems of clip-joint girls. Davis played Mary Dwight, a self-sufficient cabaret hostess employed by mobster Johnny Vanning (Eduardo Ciannelli). At a Vanning party, Mary's innocent younger sister (Jane Bryan) is killed for resisting rape, which shocks Mary and her fellow hostesses into open rebellion against their boss. Mary threatens to tell the authorities about Vanning's racket, and he retaliates by having her beaten and disfigured. Through the efforts of a sympathetic attorney (Humphrey Bogart), the girls testify in court and Vanning is convicted.

Lloyd Bacon, a Warners regular who had alternated between Cagney action pictures and musicals like *42nd Street,* directed efficiently, and although the red-light background of the story was restricted by Hays Office censorship, *Marked Woman* came as close to reality as restrictions would permit. The movie belongs mainly to the women in its cast, with Mayo Methot (who married Bogart during the film's production) particularly good as a desperate, aging "hostess." Bette Davis is vivid in the sort of high-strung, neurotic role she had not had since *Dangerous* in 1935, and Ciannelli's chilling portrait of a ruthless gangster is one not easily forgotten.

Variety was impressed with Davis' characterization and had this to say about her talent: "She is among the Hollywood few who can submerge themselves in a role to the point where they become the character they are playing. Her performance here is also rife with subtleties of expression and gesture."

Despite the frankness of contemporary films, much of *Marked Woman* still holds up, although some of Davis' acting does not; in one or two scenes she speaks so rapidly that the ear can barely keep up with her, and she achieves transitions of mood and character with the unbelievable speed of mercury. But in 1937, the critics were more easily pleased: in *The New York Times*, Frank S. Nugent wrote, "Miss Davis has turned in her best performance since she

MARKED WOMAN: Bette Davis and Eduardo Ciannelli.

cut Leslie Howard to the quick in *Of Human Bondage.*" All told, *Marked Woman* was a suitably strong underworld melodrama, and one more indication that Warner Bros. was the most socially conscious of Hollywood studios.

A STAR IS BORN

1937

CREDITS

A United Artists Picture. Producer: David O. Selznick. Director: William A. Wellman. Screenwriters: Dorothy Parker, Alan Campbell, Robert Carson and (uncredited) John Lee Mahin and David O. Selznick. Based on a story by William A. Wellman and Robert Carson. Cinematographer: W. Howard Greene. Photographed in Technicolor. Color Designer: Lansing C. Holden. Technicolor Consultant: Natalie Kalmus. Editors; Hal C. Kern and Ansin Stevenson. Art Directors: Lyle Wheeler and Edward Boyle. Costumes: Omar Kiam. Sound: Oscar Lagerstrom. Special Effects: Jack Gosgrove. Music: Max Steiner. Assistant Director: Eric Stacey. Running Time: 111 minutes.

CAST

Janet Gaynor (*Esther Blodgett/Vicki Lester*); Fredric March (*Norman Maine/Alfred Hinkel*); Adolphe Menjou (*Oliver Niles*); Andy Devine (*Danny McGuire*); May Robson (*Granny*); Lionel Stander (*Libby*); Owen Moore (*Casey Burke*); Elizabeth Jenns (*Anita Regis*); J.C. Nugent (*Theodore Blodgett*); Clara Blandick (*Aunt Mattie*); A.W. Sweatt (*Alex*); Peggy Wood (*Central Casting Receptionist*); Clarence Wilson (*Justice of the Peace*); Franklin Pangborn (*Billy Moon*); Jonathan Hale (*Night Court Judge*); Edgar Kennedy (*Pop Randall*); Pat Flaherty (*Cuddles*); Adrian Rosley (*Harris, the Make-up Man*); Arthur Hoyt (*Ward, the Make-up Man*); Edwin Maxwell (*Voice Coach*); Dr. Leonard Walker (*Orchestra Leader at the Hollywood Bowl*); Jed Prouty (*Artie Carver*); Guinn "Big Boy" Williams (*Posture Coach*); Trixie Friganza (*Waitress*); Paul Stanton (*Academy Award Speaker*); Olin Howland (*Jud Baker, the Rustic*); Francis Ford, Chris-Pin Martin and Kenneth Howell (*Prisoners*); Carole Landis and Lana Turner (*Girls at Santa Anita Bar*); Vince Barnett (*Otto Friedl*); Robert Emmett O'Connor (*Bartender at Santa Anita*); Irving Bacon (*Station Agent*); Marshall Neilan (*Bert*); Charles Williams (*Assistant Cameraman*); Fred "Snowflake" Toones (*Witness*); Claude King, David Newell and Bud Flanagan/Dennis O'Keefe (*Party Guests*).

A Star Is Born won a 1937 Academy Award for Best Original Story, which was credited to its director William A. Wellman and writer Robert Carson. Actually, it wasn't all that original, even in 1937. A 1922 silent called *The World's a Stage* had already introduced several of its plot elements, namely the aspect of a female screen star married to an alcoholic, who accidentally dies by drowning. The 1932 *What Price Hollywood?*—the motion picture most frequently mentioned as the progenitor of *A Star Is Born*—comes even closer, with its theme of a waitress whose friendship with a drink-prone film director leads to her stardom, while he declines and ends a suicide. But the situations in 1937's *A Star Is Born* are reportedly based on real-life Hollywood incidents that happened not only to the movie's accredited writers, but to its producer, as well. With reference to the film's final shooting script, it was widely reported that upon receiving his Oscar for *A Star Is Born*'s story, Wellman immediately presented his statuette to producer David O. Selznick, saying: "Here, you deserve this. You wrote more of it than I did."

The 1937 *A Star Is Born* began its cinematic life with the title *It Happened in Hollywood*. But Selznick felt that the word "Hollywood" had been associated with too many other recent films of lesser merit, and he suggested as a substitute *The Stars Below*. Close, but no cigar. It was Selznick's board

A STAR IS BORN: J.C. Nugent, A.W. Sweatt, Clara Blandick, Janet Gaynor and May Robson.

chairman John Hay "Jock" Whitney who adjusted that to *A Star Is Born*. And so it has remained.

The movie was a particular success for its two stars, Janet Gaynor and Fredric March. Ironically, Gaynor's career had gone into a decline in the mid-Thirties, despite her great popularity in the silents and early talkies of the late Twenties—and her 1928 Academy Award for her cumulative work in *Sunrise*, *Seventh Heaven* and *Street Angel*. At 29, she still looked youthful enough (helped by her childlike vocal quality) to be acceptable as a young woman who comes to Hollywood from a small town seeking a movie career. But at 39, perhaps Fredric March seemed a trifle too young, personable and healthy to be completely accepted as a drunken has-been whose negative personal traits have left him with few friends in the film colony, but who makes a loving husband for starlet Vicki Lester. Fine as March is in the role, perfect casting would, of course, have been John Barrymore. But by then Barrymore was living out *A Star Is Born* on his own; Selznick had no intention either of humiliating him or of putting up with his unpredicatable behavior while the film was being shot.

A STAR IS BORN: Janet Gaynor and Andy Devine.

Interestingly, in this version of *A Star Is Born*, it is the heroine's old grandmother (given a wonderful performance by the reliable May Robson) who not only encourages and finances Esther Blodgett's attempt at a movie career, but who later prevents the widowed and despondent "Vicki Lester" from quitting movieland for good. No such character exists in the 1954 Judy Garland-James Mason remake, although a musician friend (Tommy Noonan) provides the necessary words of encouragement. The film's second remake, 1976's Barbra Streisand rock musical went so far in another direction that one critic was inspired to rename it "A Bore Is Starred."

A Star Is Born was one of the earliest all-Technicolor features to employ that relatively new color process in a story that was neither costume picture, musical nor Western. Indeed, one might wonder why Selznick went to the extra expense for such an intimate drama as *A Star Is Born*. But when the film was released, there was much praise for its color quality, and that undoubtedly helped make it the great critical and box-office success it immediately became.

The Academy of Motion Picture Arts and Sciences gave *A Star Is Born* seven nominations, including Best Picture, Fredric March, Janet Gaynor, director William A. Wellman, screenwriters Alan Campbell, Robert Carson and Dorothy Parker and assistant director Eric Stacey. But aside from the Oscar for Best Original Story there was just a special plaque given to W. Howard Green for the film's color photography.

A STAR IS BORN: Fredric March and Janet Gaynor.

A STAR IS BORN: Janet Gaynor.

214

NIGHT MUST FALL

1937

CREDITS

A Metro-Goldwyn-Mayer Picture. Producer: Hunt Stromberg. Director: Richard Thorpe. Screenwriter: John Van Druten. Based on the play by Emlyn Williams. Cinematographer: Ray June. Editor: Robert J. Kern. Art Director: Cedric Gibbons. Music: Edward Ward. Running Time: 117 minutes.

CAST

Robert Montgomery (*Danny*); Rosalind Russell (*Olivia Grayne*); Dame May Whitty (*Mrs. Bramson*); Alan Marshal (*Justin*); Merle Tottenham (*Dora*); Kathleen Harrison (*Mrs. Terence*); Matthew Boulton (*Inspector Belsize*); Eily Malyon (*Nurse*); E.E. Clive (*Guide*); Beryl Mercer (*Saleslady*); Winifred Harris (*Mrs. Laurie*).

Emlyn Williams' psychological thriller scored a great success in 1935 on the London stage with himself in the leading role and Dame May Whitty co-starred. In 1936, they repeated their triumph on Broadway. On a trip to New York, Robert Montgomery attended a performance, and was so impressed with both the play and its leading role that he badgered the powers at his home studio, MGM, to acquire the movie rights as a vehicle for him. Up to that point, Montgomery's seven years at Metro had mainly been taken up with providing male charm, wit and suave sophistication in support of Joan Crawford, Norma Shearer, Greta Garbo and Madge Evans in a succession of slick films, mostly of the light-comedy variety. In short, there was little thought to casting him in melodrama—until Montgomery waged his campaign to play Danny, the charming but psychopathic killer of *Night Must Fall*. However, Montgomery was never a favorite of Louis B. Mayer, who considered him arrogant—especially since the actor was then president of the activist Screen Actors Guild, and had been making what Mayer considered outrageous salary demands. By buying *Night Must Fall* for him, Mayer (who found the play repugnant) hoped it would be a colossal failure and ruin Montgomery's favor with the fans—and, ultimately, his film career.

Playwright John Van Druten was assigned to adapt *Night Must Fall* for the screen, and Dame May Whitty (making her talking-picture debut at 72) was engaged to repeat her stage role, beginning an association with MGM that would last another decade. Completing the trio of leads was another performer better known for light comedy and domestic drama than anything so strong as *Night Must Fall*—Rosalind Russell, cast as a repressed but imaginative young woman who's the niece and unhappy companion to the elderly, hypochondriac ingrate portrayed by Whitty.

In the movie, Danny (Montgomery) is an Irish charmer who's employed as a bellhop at an English country hotel, from which a wealthy female guest has recently disappeared. Word gets around the area that foul play is suspected, which fires the imagination of young Olivia Grayne (Russell), the attractive but dowdy niece of Mrs. Bramson (Whitty), the wheelchair-bound shrew with whom she lives as companion and whipping-person. At the same time, the Bramson maid Dora (Merle Tottenham) appears to have got herself in romantic "trouble" via Danny, with whom Mrs. Bramson agrees to have a few words, encouraging an imminent wedding. Instead, Danny completely wins over the difficult old woman, while appearing to make an immediate enemy of Olivia. Impulsively, Mrs. Bramson hires him on as a handyman, with the idea of paying him enough salary to enable him to afford a wife. Thus set up, the screenplay then veers in other directions, leaving the Dora situation hanging in limbo as Danny promises to wed her, "but not just now."

The narrative is slow to build—and the movie itself, at nearly two hours in length, could have been briefer—but its characters are so unusual and interesting (all three leading roles offer multi-layered opportunities for the actors) that it's not difficult to remain absorbed throughout. We see Mrs. Bramson get sillier and more careless around Danny—and we learn that she keeps all of her money, not in a bank, but hidden on the premises. And Olivia, who keeps a marriage-minded beau named Justin (Alan Marshal) at arm's length, goes from resenting Danny's self-assured presence in the house to harboring a secret infatuation for him—all the while believing in her heart that it's Danny who killed the wealthy guest from the hotel.

Meantime, Danny maintains his cheerful Irish facade, tending to Mrs. Bramson's comforts, amusing her with his childish sense of humor and totally bewitching the old fool. There are occasional visits from Inspector Belsize (Matthew Boulton) of the local police, but Danny chillingly continues on his

NIGHT MUST FALL: Dame May Whitty, Rosalind Russell and Robert Montgomery.

NIGHT MUST FALL: Robert Montgomery and Dame May Whitty.

self-determined path to wealth by smothering Mrs. Bramson, in Olivia's absence, with a pillow. Later, Olivia finds herself alone in the house with Danny, and her natural fears about him mingle with her attraction to him. But before harm can befall her, Justin enters with the Inspector, and Danny, now seemingly on .the verge of complete madness, is apprehended. All of which leaves unanswered that question about the earlier missing body (subsequently found, in a decapitated state), but may explain why Danny keeps a heavy leather hatbox among his belongings. Thankfully it's never opened in our presence, for this is no *grand guignol* thriller.

Night Must Fall, which shared certain thematic similarities with *Love From a Stranger*, another English stage-and-screen thriller of the same era, proved Louis B. Mayer wrong in that it met with positive and enthusiastic reactions from press and public alike. And, for Robert Montgomery, nothing but praise, for his is truly a brilliant and subtle characterization totally removed from the drawing-room hangabouts he'd so often played over the years at Metro. Equally good, in their offbeat roles, are Rosalind Russell and Dame May Whitty. Montgomery and Whitty both won Oscar nominations, but lost in the final tabulations to, respectively, Spencer

216

Tracy for *Captains Courageous* and Alice Brady for *In Old Chicago*. Understandably, Danny always remained Montgomery's favorite role.

In 1964, Karel Reisz directed a more sexually oriented British remake of *Night Must Fall* with Albert Finney, Mona Washbourne and Susan Hampshire, which was neither popular nor well-received by the critics.

EASY LIVING

1937

CREDITS

A Paramount Picture. Producer: Arthur Hornblow, Jr. Director: Mitchell Leisen. Screenwriter: Preston Sturges. Based on an unpublished story by Vera Caspary. Cinematographer: Ted Tetzlaff. Editor: Doane Harrison. Art Directors: Hans Dreier and Ernst Fegte. Costumes: Travis Banton. Music: Boris Morros. Running Time: 88 minutes.

NIGHT MUST FALL: Rosalind Russell, Robert Montgomery and Matthew Boulton.

EASY LIVING: Ray Milland and Jean Arthur.

CAST

Jean Arthur (*Mary Smith*); Edward Arnold (*J.B. Ball*); Ray Milland (*John Ball, Jr.*); Luis Alberni (*Mr. Louis Louis*); Mary Nash (*Mrs. Ball*); Franklin Pangborn (*Van Buren*); Barlowe Borland (*Mr. Gurney*); William Demarest (*Wallace Whistling*); Andrew Tombes (*E.F. Hulgar*); Esther Dale (*Lillian*); Harlan Briggs (*Office Manager*); William B. Davidson (*Mr. Hyde*); Nora Cecil (*Miss Swerf*); Robert Greig (*Butler*); Vernon Dent (*First Partner*); Edwin Stanley (*Second Partner*); Richard Barbee (*Third Partner*); Bennie Bartlett (*Newsboy*); Jack Raymond (*First Bum*); Adia Kuznetzoff (*Second Bum*); Florence Dudley (*Cashier*); Bob Murphy (*Automat Detective*); Bernard Suss (*Man in Automat*); Rex Moore (*Elevator Boy*); John Marshall (*Osric*); Dora Clement (*Saleslady*); Hayden Stevenson (*Chauffeur*); Arthur Hoyt (*First Jeweler*); Hal K. Dawson (*Second Jeweler*); Hector V. Sarno (*Armenian Rug Salesman*); Gertrude As-

EASY LIVING: Luis Alberni, Jean Arthur, Franklin Pangborn, Barlowe Borland and players.

tor (*Saleswoman*); Hal Greene (*Bellhop*); Lee Phelps (*Hotel Detective*); John Picorri (*Oinest*); Forbes Murray (*Husband*); John Dilson (*Nervous Man*); Virginia Dabney (*Blonde*); Laura Treadwell (*Wife*); Lois Clinton (*Brunette*); Sidney Bracy (*Chauffeur*); Jack Rice (*Clerk*); Frances Morris (*Assistant Secretary*); Jesse Graves (*Porter*); Kathleen Hope Lewis and Helen Huntington (*Stenographers*); Harold Entwistle (*Elevator Man*); Bud Flanagan/Dennis O'Keefe (*Office Manager*); Robert Homans (*Private Guard*); Stanley Andrews (*Captain*); Leonid Snegoff (*Chef*); Wilson Benge (*Butler*); Harry Worth (*Hindu*); George Cowl (*Bank President*); Kate Price (*Laundress*); Amelia Falleur and Lu Miller (*Housemaids*); William Wagner (*Valet*); Francis Sayles and Olaf Hytten (*Housemen*); Florence Wix (*Woman in Hat Shop*)

Easy Living, riding the crest of the "screwball comedy" wave, was a Cinderella fable cooked up by Preston Sturges which he based on a Vera Caspary story. It involved Jean Arthur as a low-salaried employee of the magazine *Boy's Constant Companion*

who's unexpectedly swept into the lap of luxury when, riding atop a double-decker New York City bus, she's suddenly hit by a sable coat that's been tossed from a near-by tall building. It turns out that the tosser of the $58,000 fur is none other than wealthy banker J.B. Ball (Edward Arnold), who is angrily reacting to the collective extravagances of his chef, his son and his wife. On the street, Ball finds Mary Smith (Arthur) attempting to locate the coat's rightful owner, and he urges her to accept it as a gift, escorting the confused young woman home in his chauffeured car. Later, Ball decides to enrich Mary's dull life by giving her the things she cannot afford on her small salary, and he takes her out to shop for clothes. When a shop proprietor (Franklin Pangborn) misunderstands their relationship, he starts spreading rumors that millionaire Ball is setting up a "mistress," and his hotel-owner friend Mr. Louis Louis (Luis Alberni) quickly makes Mary a free guest of his establishment, on which Ball is about to foreclose.

Mary finds herself with a luxurious suite of rooms at her disposal, as well as the owner of assorted pets and a fancy new wardrobe. While all this is happening, she's somehow under the impression that she's in the hotel on a job interview.

At this point in the story, we have the celebrated—and hilarious—Automat scene. Mary goes in search of a cheap dinner; despite her new-found luxury, she still has no cash to spend. At the Automat, she meets Ball's busboy-son John (Ray Milland). Young Ball's there to prove to his father that he's capable of supporting himself. But when he tries to help penniless Mary by slipping her a free meal, he's seen by a cop, who tries to arrest him. In the ensuing fracas, a lever is pulled that immediately opens all the food windows, and chaos ensues as everyone tries to get a free meal.

From there the plot dances madly on, elaborating on its one-joke premise as Arthur and Milland fall in love. But their romance is complicated by her inno-

EASY LIVING: Ray Milland, Edward Arnold, Jean Arthur, Esther Dale and Mary Nash.

cent friendship with Arnold. There's also the sub-plot involving confusion over a stock tip that comes from Milland, while everyone thinks it's from his father; Arnold is suddenly facing possible bankruptcy as well as a furious wife (Mary Nash) who threatens to divorce him. But all is patched up for the fairytale, Depression-era ending in which the elder Balls smooth over their various misunderstandings and Mary ends up with her Prince Charming in the person of Ball the younger.

Director Mitchell Leisen wasn't new to comedy, but *Easy Living*'s slapstick scenes were experimental, in that as filming progressed he was trying out new ideas inspired by the Sturges script. Subtlety obviously has no place in this movie. It begins on a note that immediately sets the tone for the rest of the film: when Edward Arnold falls down his own staircase, crashing to the bottom, he's met by his butler who quips, "I see you're down early, sir." And so it goes . . .

Today, *Easy Living* has become a favorite of film buffs with its beautifully timed performances and hilarious comic inventions throughout. However, in 1937, though well enough received, it was not considered anything out of the ordinary. Interestingly, although Mitchell Leisen and Ray Milland had worked well together before this, the director had not previously been able to persuade the actor to accept a comedy lead. Milland had turned down 1935's classic *Hands Across the Table* with the plea, "Please don't ask me to do it, because I know I can't play comedy." And so that role went to Fred MacMurray, reinforcing that actor's talent for light comedy—a genre in which the initially reluctant Milland would eventually prove MacMurray's equal.

THE LIFE OF EMILE ZOLA

1 9 3 7

CREDITS

A Warner Bros. Picture. Producers: Hal B. Wallis and Henry Blanke. Director: William Dieterle. Screenwriters: Heinz Herald, Geza Herczeg and Norman Reilly Raine. Based on the story by Herald and Herczeg. Cinematographer: Tony Gaudio. Editor: Warren Lowe. Art Director: Anton Grot. Set Decorator: Albert C. Wilson. Costumes: Milo Anderson and Ali Hubert. Music: Max Steiner. Orchestra Direction: Leo Forbstein. Assistant Director: Russ Saunders. Dialogue Director: Irving Rapper. Running Time: 123 minutes.

CAST

Paul Muni (*Emile Zola*); Gale Sondergaard (*Lucie Dreyfus*); Joseph Schildkraut (*Capt. Alfred Dreyfus*); Gloria Holden (*Alexandrine Zola*); Donald Crisp (*Maitre Labori*); Erin O'Brien-Moore (*Nana*); John Litel (*Charpentier*); Henry O'Neill (*Colonel Picquart*); Morris Carnovsky (*Anatole France*); Louis Calhern (*Major Dort*); Ralph Morgan (*Commander of Paris*); Robert Barrat (*Major Walsin-Esterhazy*); Vladimir Sokoloff (*Paul Cezanne*); Harry Davenport (*Chief of Staff*); Robert Warwick (*Major Henry*); Charles Richman (*Monsieur Delagorgue*); Dickie Moore (*Pierre Dreyfus*); Rolla Gourvitch (*Jeanne Dreyfus*); Gilbert Emery (*Minister of War*); Walter Kingsford (*Colonel Sandherr*); Paul Everton (*Assistant Chief of Staff*); Montagu Love (*Cavaignac*); Frank Sheridan (*Van Cassell*); Lumsden Hare (*Mr. Richards*); Marcia Mae Jones (*Helen Richards*); Florence Roberts (*Madame Zola*); Grant Mitchell (*Georges Clemenceau*); Moroni Olsen (*Captain Guignet*); Egon Brecher (*Brucker*); Frank Reicher (*Monsieur Perrenx*); Walter O. Stahl (*Senator Scheurer-Kestner*); Frank Darien (*Albert*); Iphigeni Castiglioni (*Madame Charpentier*); Arthur Aylesworth (*Chief Censor*); Frank Mayo (*Mathieu Dreyfus*); Alexander Leftwich (*Major D'Aboville*); Paul Irving (*La Rue*); Pierre Watkin (*Prefect of Police*); Holmes Herbert (*Commander of Paris*); Robert Cummings, Sr. (*General Gillian*); Harry Worth (*Lieutenant*); William von Brincken (*Schwartzkoppen*).

In the Thirties, elderly George Arliss popularized biographical films with vehicles like *Alexander Hamilton, Voltaire, The House of Rothschild* and *Cardinal Richelieu*. It was a tradition carried on after Arliss by Paul Muni, who won a 1936 Academy Award for his work in *The Story of Louis Pasteur*, which he followed the next year with *The Life of Emile Zola*. The latter brought Warner Bros. its first-ever Oscar for Best Picture, as well as statuettes for Best Supporting Actor Joseph Schildkraut (as the unjustly beleaguered Captain Dreyfus) and to the trio responsible for its excellent screenplay—Heinz Herald, Geza Herczeg and Norman Reilly Raine. The film also won nominations in seven other categories, including Best Actor candidate Paul Muni, who lost out to Spencer Tracy's Portuguese fisherman in *Captains Courageous*. But Muni *was* voted Best Actor of 1937 by the New York Film Critics, who also named his *Zola* Best Picture.

It took Warner Bros. nearly a year to prepare the Zola project. Its screenplay went through a great deal of research and numerous rewrites. One month alone was devoted to experimenting with various make-ups for Muni, who would be seen through four decades, starting from a young man in his twenties to old age. To best accomplish this, the actor grew his own full beard, and the picture was shot in backward sequence, thus allowing his hair and beard to progress from white to dark, being clipped and shortened as the filming progressed.

William Dieterle, who directed the actor in this

220

THE LIFE OF EMILE ZOLA: Paul Muni.

THE LIFE OF EMILE ZOLA: Gale Sondergaard and Joseph Schildkraut.

With the passage of time, Zola's zealous quest to dramatize his country's social ills in the pursuit of freedom and truth makes him celebrated worldwide for his writings. He is visited by a woman named Lucie Dreyfus (Gale Sondergaard), seeking his aid in clearing the name of her husband Capt. Alfred Dreyfus (Joseph Schildkraut), who has been condemned to Devil's Island on a false charge of treason. This was part of a shameful cover-up for which Maj. Walsin-Esterhazy (Robert Barrat) is the guilty party, and for whom Dreyfus was made the scapegoat. Backed by powerful friends, Zola takes

movie, as well as in the earlier *Dr. Socrates* and *The Story of Louis Pasteur*, and the later *Juarez*, has said of him: "There was no harder worker in Hollywood than Paul Muni. Once he started a picture, that was his life. He was a totally unselfish man. I never saw him try to steal a scene. And when the picture was completed, he gave credit to everyone but himself. After the preview of *Zola*, I went home to find a long telegram from him thanking me for making it."

At the film's start, Zola (Muni) is an unknown young Parisian writer sharing with the struggling painter Paul Cezanne (Vladimir Sokoloff) cold quarters where they're visited by Zola's fiancée Alexandrine (Gloria Holden) and his mother (Florence Roberts). Zola's novels about French social causes have only met with indifference from the book-buying public and with disapproval from the government—until an encounter with an attractive young prostitute named Nana (Erin O'Brien-Moore in a small role Bette Davis had wanted, but had been refused because of her star-status). When he develops the girl's unfortunate story into a novel, *Nana* makes Zola the year's best-selling author.

up the Dreyfus case, writing a controversial editorial entitled "I Accuse," which reveals the entire scandalous story. His involvement results in his being tried for libel, accused of being a traitor and ultimately convicted. But before he can be imprisoned, Zola flees to England, where he continues his campaign to exonerate Dreyfus. Eventually, public pressure forces the French government to tackle the case, with the result that the truth is finally revealed and the guilty parties apprehended. The now-elderly, broken Dreyfus is released and his military credentials restored. Zola is finally able to re-

THE LIFE OF EMILE ZOLA: Paul Muni and Gloria Holden.

turn to France. But before he and Dreyfus can meet, Zola is tragically overcome by carbon monoxide and killed. At Zola's funeral, his friend Anatole France (Morris Carnovsky) eulogizes the writer as "a moment in the conscience of man."

The Life of Emile Zola may seem a trifle dry, stodgy and drawn-out nowadays, but it has long been esteemed as one of the greatest historical biographies Hollywood ever put on film. *Variety* called it "a vibrant, tense and emotional story about the man who fought a nation with his pen." *The New York Times* supported the picture wholeheartedly: "It has followed not merely the spirit but, to a rare degree, the very letter of his life and of the historically significant lives around him."

The racial theme involving the Jewish Dreyfus is carefully handled; not once is the word "Jew" mentioned. American motion-picture executives (many of whom were Jewish) were still skittish about explicit confrontation with ethnic controversies. They feared losing the audiences they took such pains to court. With *The Life of Emile Zola*, they had no worries; it brought not only prestige to Warner Bros., but also great financial success. And it solidified Paul Muni's superstardom.

THE LIFE OF EMILE ZOLA: Vladimir Sokoloff, Paul Muni and Erin O'Brien-Moore.

TOPPER

1937

CREDITS

A Metro-Goldwyn-Mayer Picture. A Hal Roach Production. Associate Producer: Milton H. Bren. Director: Norman Z. McLeod. Screenwriters: Jack Jevne, Eric Hatch and Eddie Moran. Based on the novel by Thorne Smith. Cinematographer: Norbert Brodine. Photographic Effects: Roy Seawright. Editor: William Terhune. Art Director: Arthur Rouce. Music: Edward Powell and Hugo Friedhofer. Song "Old Man Moon" by Hoagy Carmichael. Running Time: 97 minutes.

CAST

Constance Bennett (*Marion Kerby*); Cary Grant (*George Kerby*); Roland Young (*Cosmo Topper*); Billie Burke (*Henrietta Topper*); Alan Mowbray (*Wilkins*); Eugene Pallette (*Casey*); Arthur Lake (*Elevator Boy*); Hedda Hopper (*Mrs. Stuyvesant*); Virginia Sale (*Miss Johnson*); Theodore von Eltz (*Hotel Manager*); J. Farrell MacDonald (*Policeman*); Elaine Shepard (*Secretary*); Doodles Weaver and Si Jenks (*Rustics*); Three Hits and a Miss (*Themselves*); Donna Dax (*Hat-Check Girl at Rainbow Nightclub*); Hoagy Carmichael (*Bill, the Piano Player*); Claire Windsor and Betty Blythe (*Ladies*); Ward Bond (*Policeman*).

Made for independent producer Hal Roach, then releasing his pictures through MGM, this adaptation of Thorne Smith's whimsical novel is both a classic "screwball" farce and a masterpiece of trick photography and sound effects. Comedy veteran Norman Z. McLeod, who had directed the Marx Bros. in *Monkey Business* and *Horse Feathers* and W.C. Fields in *It's a Gift*, guided a hand-picked comedy cast that featured Constance Bennett, Roland Young, Billie Burke and Alan Mowbray. And, in the casting of Cary Grant as its male lead, the movie not only offered the actor a delightful change of pace, but also a prophetic look at the upward course of his career as an expert light comedian.

The plot is simple and rife with possibilities well realized by its adaptors Jack Jevne, Eric Hatch and Eddie Moran. George and Marion Kerby (Grant and Bennett), a handsome and wealthy young couple given to a life of partying and pleasure, are killed in an auto crash, but return as spirits devoted to the rehabilitation of their friend Cosmo Topper (Young), an inhibited and henpecked bank president whose dull, routine life they proceed to upset. Blessed with

TOPPER: Roland Young, Alan Mowbray and Billie Burke.

TOPPER: Roland Young and Virginia Sale.

the ability to appear and disappear at will, the Kerbys playfully introduce Topper to the pleasure of champagne and their own hectic former life style.

Aided by skillful camera magic, Grant, Young and Bennett sustained an inspired level of sophisticated whackiness. Undoubtedly, much of *Topper*'s entertainment value derives from the expertise of cameraman Norbert Brodine, editor William Terhune and special-effects expert Roy Seawright, but without the deft performances of its cast, this ectoplasmic soufflé would flatten dismally. Grant and Bennett disport in top form as they participate in street brawls, introduce Young to the pleasures of Bacchus, or confound an incredulous hotel detective (Eugene Pallette) with their materializing act. Their antics are beautifully balanced by Young's gradual emergence from milquetoast to man-about-town, a delineation so charming that it won the actor an Academy Award nomination as Best Supporting Actor.

Despite faintly negative reviews, *Topper*, released at the height of America's craze for "screwball" comedy, became one of 1937's most popular movies. Two years later, its success inspired a sequel, *Topper Takes a Trip*, in which Young and Bennett philandered anew—but without Cary Grant, who was seen only in introductory "recap" footage from the original film, inserted for the benefit of those unfamiliar with the Topper phenomenon. A second sequel, 1941's *Topper Returns* retained Roland Young, but substituted two blondes, Joan Blondell and Carole Landis, for a departed Constance Bennett.

TOPPER: Roland Young, Cary Grant and Constance Bennett.

THE PRISONER OF ZENDA

1937

CREDITS

A United Artists Picture. Producer: David O. Selznick. Directors: John Cromwell and (uncredited) W.S. Van Dyke and George Cukor. Screenwriters: John L. Balderston, Donald Ogden Stewart and Wells Root. Based on the novel by Anthony Hope and the play by Edward Rose. Cinematographer: James Wong Howe. Editors: Hal C. Kern and James E. Newcom. Art Director: Lyle Wheeler. Set Decorator: Casey Roberts. Costumes: Ernest Dryden. Music: Alfred Newman. Sound: Oscar Lagerlof. Special Effects: Jack Cosgrove. Sepia Process: John M. Nicholaus. Assistant Director: Frederick A. Spenser. Technical Advisors: Prince Sigvard Bernadotte and Col. Ivar Enhorning. Time: 101 minutes.

CAST

Ronald Colman (*Rudolph Rassendyl/King Rudolph* V); Madeleine Carroll (*Princess Flavia*); Douglas Fairbanks, Jr. (*Rupert of Hentzau*); Mary Astor (*Antoinette De Mauban*); C. Aubrey Smith (*Colonel Zapt*); Raymond Massey (*Black Michael*); David Niven (*Capt. Fritz von Tarlenheim*); Eleanor Wesselhoeft (*Cook*); Byron Foulger (*Johann*); Montagu Love (*Detchard*); William von Brincken (*Kraftstein*); Phillip Sleeman (*Lauengram*); Ralph Faulkner (*Bersonin*); Alexander D'Arcy (*De Gauiet*); Torben Meyer (*Michael's Butler*); Ian MacLaren (*Cardinal*); Lawrence Grant (*Marshal Strakencz*); Howard Lang (*Josef*); Ben Webster (*British Ambassador*); Evelyn Beresford (*British Ambassador's Wife*); Boyd Irwin (*Master of Ceremonies*); Emmett King (*Von Haugwitz, Lord High Chamberlain*); Charles K. French (*Bishop*); Al Shean (*Orchestra Leader*); Charles Halton (*Passport Officer*); Otto Fries (*Luggage Officer*); Florence Roberts (*Duenna*); Spencer Charters (*Porter*); Russ Powell and D'Arcy Corrigan (*Travelers*); Francis Ford (*Man*); Henry Roquemore (*Station Master*); Lillian Harmer (*Station Attendant*); Pat Somerset and Leslie Sketchley (*Guards at Lodge*).

Anthony Hope's much-filmed 1894 novel first reached the screen in 1912, and was remade successfully as a Metro silent in 1922 with Lewis Stone, Alice Terry and Ramon Novarro in its leading roles. But the version still considered the definitive cinematic treatment was this handsome remake, produced by David O. Selznick in 1937. Selznick was

THE PRISONER OF ZENDA: Ronald Colman.

advised against remaking Hope's hokey old Ruritanian romance, but his persistence proved well-founded, and enthusiastic 1937 audiences showed themselves more than willing to be swept away for nearly two hours of romantic derring-do and escapist melodrama. Selznick's usual dedication to detail (sets, costumes, production values—and especially casting) contributed to his reputation in the Thirties as one of Hollywood's most successful producers. And not even MGM's handsome Technicolored 1952 remake, with Stewart Granger, Deborah Kerr, James Mason and technical-effects wizardry (to

THE PRISONER OF ZENDA: Ronald Colman and Madeleine Carroll.

stand-in at the coronation for a mysteriously vanished Prince Rudolf and, in so doing, falls in love with the princess—who apparently had not seen her intended for some years! And even the suspicious Michael (who, needless to say, is directly responsible for Rudolf's disappearance) is fooled! Additional intrigue, conspiracies and murders occur before a finale which sees the true lovers parted (when Flavia realizes duty over heart) and the rightful heir on his Ruritanian throne.

THE PRISONER OF ZENDA: Raymond Massey, Douglas Fairbanks, Jr. and Mary Astor.

create the illusion that Granger could share scenes with himself) could improve on the 1937 version.

The Prisoner of Zenda's plot is, by now, probably as familiar as it is complicated. A vacationing Englishman, conveniently named Rudolph Rassendyl (Ronald Colman) arrives in the mythical *Mittel-European* city of Strelsau to fish in the countryside. While there, he is recognized by everyone he encounters as bearing an uncanny likeness to their own Prince Rudolf (also played by Colman), who's about to be crowned king. But there's much intrigue behind that coveted throne. The prince's devious brother Black Michael (Raymond Massey), plots to drug and kidnap the future king, hoping to win the throne by default when Rudolf fails to show for his coronation. Michael also covets the Princess Flavia (Madeleine Carroll), Rudolf's beautiful intended, unbeknownst to his faithful mistress Antoinette (Mary Astor), who, in turn, is the lustful object of Michael's roguish henchman, Rupert of Hentzau (Douglas Fairbanks, Jr.).

What follows is as fun to watch as it is predictable: Rudolph the vacationer is pressed into service as a

THE PRISONER OF ZENDA: Madeleine Carroll and Ronald Colman.

227

John Cromwell directed a hand-picked cast in great style, despite problems with Madeleine Carroll, who imagined her face to have a "bad" side (denied by *Zenda*'s cinematographer, James Wong Howe, who told Cromwell, "You couldn't fault her if you stood her on her head."). Despite her feud with Cromwell, Carroll later called this her favorite role. And if Douglas Fairbanks, Jr. nearly stole the picture from his fellow actors, it was because of the good-natured flair with which he invested his villainous Rupert. (In the nearly frame-by-frame 1952 remake, James Mason would eschew Rupert's humor and darken his villainy.)

Selznick's productions were always the subject of his endless quest for perfection, and it's a little-known fact that he enlisted the aid of two other directors (W.S. Van Dyke and George Cukor) to shoot, respectively, *Zenda*'s swashbuckling duel between Colman and Fairbanks, and the farewell scene between Colman and Carroll. Alfred Newman's beautiful Oscar-nominated background score was so effective that MGM recycled it for its 1952 remake.

But *The Prisoner Of Zenda* didn't die out with the Fifties. In 1965, Blake Edwards parodied its storyline in *The Great Race*, and an occasionally amusing 1979 remake turned the Anthony Hope story into a comic *Prisoner Of Zenda* for the talents of Peter Sellers and a largely British cast.

HEIDI

1937

HEIDI: Shirley Temple in the dream sequence.

CREDITS

A 20th Century-Fox Picture. Producer: Darryl F. Zanuck. Associate Producer: Raymond Griffith. Director: Allan Dwan. Screenwriters: Walter Ferris and Julien Josephson. Based on the novel by Johanna Spyri. Cinematographer: Arthur Miller. Editor: Allen McNeil. Art Director: Hans Peters. Set Decorator: Thomas Little. Costumes: Gwen Wakeling. Music: Louis Silvers. Song: "In Our Little Wooden Shoes" by Lew Pollack and Sidney Mitchell. Running Time: 88 minutes.

CAST

Shirley Temple (*Heidi*); Jean Hersholt (*Adolph Kramer*); Arthur Treacher (*Andrews*); Helen Westley (*Blind Anna*); Pauline Moore (*Elsa*); Thomas Beck (*Pastor Schultz*); Mary Nash (*Fraulein Rottenmeier*); Sidney Blackmer (*Herr Sesemann*); Mady Christians (*Aunt Dete*); Sig Rumann (*Police Captain*); Marcia Mae Jones (*Klara Sesemann*); Delmar

Watson (*Peter*); Egon Brecher (*Innkeeper*); Christian Rub (*Baker*); George Humbert (*Organ Grinder*); Greta Meyer (*Villager*).

As a child star, adorable, blonde Shirley Temple was one of a kind. From 1934 to 1939, she was America's Number One box-office attraction—and a financial bonanza for her studio, 20th Century-Fox. Charmingly precocious, as well as talented at acting, dancing and singing, little Shirley also possessed another talent that many an adult actor lacks: the ability to *listen*, in character, to her fellow performers in a scene. For genuine listening often produces the kind of natural, unplanned reactions to another actor that result in the most expressive type of performance. And Shirley Temple was nothing if not expressive.

By 1937, Temple had been starring in an average of four pictures a year for Fox, frequently in titles centering on the word "Little" (*The Little Colonel, Our Little Girl, The Littlest Rebel, Poor Little Rich Girl*), and her studio was kept busy seeking fresh story material for her vehicles. She was also beginning to outgrow the word "little." In response to the suggestions of her many fans, for the second of Shirley's two 1937 movies Fox turned to the familiar childhood classic *Heidi* by Johanna Spyri. The sentimental story of a little mountain girl in 19th century Switzerland, it was considerably lightened for the screen by the teamwork of writers Walter Ferris and Julien Josephson and director Allan Dwan, who devised humorous bits to keep a potentially dark and heavy tale from frightening the younger members of *Heidi*'s potential audience (which would, of course, contain as many adult fans of the Spyri book as the eight-year-old Shirley's contemporary followers). As director Dwan recalled *Heidi* in an interview many years later, "It was a very grim, heavy story, you know: father in prison, beating the kid, practically kidnapping her and selling her into slavery in a rich man's home. Mean old housekeeper and the aunt who sold her down the line. So we had to make it funny." Asked how the diminutive star was to work with, Dwan had no reservations: "Just absolutely marvelous—greatest in the world—you couldn't de-

HEIDI: Jean Hersholt and Shirley Temple.

HEIDI: Marcia Mae Jones, Mary Nash and Shirley Temple.

HEIDI: Shirley Temple and Helen Westley.

scribe her. One in a hundred million. She was fun all the time."

Originally published in German, *Heidi* was transferred to the Hollywood screen with little basic change, except for the diminished presence in Heidi's life of the little goatherd Peter and alterations concerning the injuries which confine the character of Klara—Heidi's city friend—to a wheelchair. The story moves between a charming, snowy mountain village and the city of Frankfurt, where little Heidi is spirited away from her mountain-dwelling grandfather (Jean Hersholt), who is an embittered old man at the film's start when he is reluctantly saddled with his granddaughter. It doesn't take very long for the delightful Heidi to melt the "old heathen" and, to the amazement of his alienated townspeople, bring him back to church, where he and Heidi lead in singing the morning hymn.

Mady Christians effectively plays the mean aunt who coerces the child into leaving her grandfather

THE HURRICANE: Dorothy Lamour.

230

for a "visit" to Frankfurt that has only ulterior motives behind it. Once there, Heidi is virtually sold into servitude in the well-to-do household of a father (Sidney Blackmer) and crippled daughter (Marcia Mae Jones), into whose life the mountain child brings sunshine and laughter, despite their cruel housekeeper (Mary Nash).

Although most of the Temple movies feature song-and-dance numbers, there is only one such in *Heidi*. Introduced in the form of a dream sequence while her grandfather reads to her, Heidi thus is transported to a Dutch setting for "In Our Little Wooden Shoes," sequeing into a brief but lavish scene in which Temple appears as a pint-sized Marie Antoinette.

If, as has been written, Shirley Temple's popularity was beginning to wane in 1936, *Heidi* and her other 1937 feature, *Wee Willie Winkie* put her back on the top of the heap.

Assessing this phenomenal child's great success in her book, *Shirley Temple*, Jeanine Basinger put it astutely: "She was not a child-actress who played it straight, but a child-star personality. Films were adjusted to her talents. She did not tackle a part and become the character—the character was remodeled into Shirley Temple."

THE HURRICANE

1937

CREDITS

A United Artists Picture. A Samuel Goldwyn Production Directors: John Ford and Stuart Heisler. Screenwriters: Dudley Nichols and Oliver H.P. Garrett. Based on the novel by James Nordhoff and James Norman Hall. Cinematographer: Bert Glennon. Editor: Lloyd Nosler. Hurricane sequence directed by James Basevi. Location photographers: Archie Stout and Paul Eagler. Art Directors: Richard Day and Alexander Golitzen. Costumes: Omar Kiam. Music: Alfred Newman. Song: "Moon of Manakoora" by Frank Loesser and Alfred Newman. Associate Producer: Merritt Hulburd. Sound: Thomas Moulton. Running Time: 110 minutes.

CAST

Dorothy Lamour (*Marama*); Jon Hall (*Terangi*); Mary Astor (*Madame de Laage*); C. Aubrey Smith (*Father Paul*); Thomas Mitchell (*Dr. Kersaint*); Raymond Massey (*Governor Eugene de Laage*); John Carradine (*Warden*); Jerome Cowan (*Captain Nagle*); Al Kikume (*Chief Mehevi*); Kuulei

De Clercq (*Tita*); Layne Tom Jr. (*Mako*); Mamo Clark (*Hitia*); Movita Castenada (*Arai*); Reri (*Reri*); Francis Kaai (*Tavi*); Pauline Steele (*Mata*); Flora Hayes (*Mama Rua*); Mary Shaw (*Marunga*); Spencer Charters (*Judge*); Roger Drake (*Guard Captain*); Inez Courtney (*Girl on Ship*).

Many will contend today that "they don't make movies the way they used to," and one thing's for sure: they don't make *disaster* films as they did in the Thirties! One harks back to the earthquake depicted at length in *San Francisco* (and, to a lesser degree, in *Frisco Jenny* and *The Sisters*), the great fire of *In Old Chicago*, the locust plague of *The Good Earth*, the torrent and flood of *The Rains Came* and the desert sandstorm of *Suez*, to name a few of the most readily memorable man-made screen disasters of that era. Instrumental in making some of these sequences so awe-inspiring was special effects master James Basevi, the man responsible for the impressive look of *The Hurricane*'s climactic storm. Constructed entirely within the Goldwyn studio walls, it took four months and $150,000 to build the native village and

THE HURRICANE: Thomas Mitchell, Jon Hall and Mary Astor.

THE HURRICANE: Al Kikume, Dorothy Lamour and Jon Hall.

another $250,000 to destroy it. This was a beautifully detailed miniature set that featured a lagoon bordered by a white beach with swaying palms, native buildings, a wharf, and the Catholic church that figures so importantly in the movie's final portion.

To create the hurricane that literally lays waste to

THE HURRICANE: Raymond Massey, Mary Astor and Jerome Cowan.

the island, Basevi employed a battery of airplane propellers capable of spraying a giant cloud of water over the whole set, while wave machines stirred the lagoon into a sea of angry water, ending in a massive tidal wave consisting of 20,000 gallons coming from a succession of dump tanks all released at the same time. The resulting disaster sequence—running some 20 minutes in the film—has never quite been equalled (and certainly not in the disastrous and costly 1979 Dino De Laurentiis remake that proved a $22-million box-office bomb).

Unfortunately, Hollywood didn't yet reward special effects with Oscars in 1937, although *The Hurricane* did take home a statuette for Best Sound Recording, for Thomas Moulton's work in devising what sounded like an all-too-realistic storm. Among the nominations that year were also Best Supporting Actor Thomas Mitchell (Joseph Schildkraut was the winner for *The Life of Emile Zola*) and Alfred Newman's South Seas-flavored score.

But *The Hurricane* wasn't all one big storm; there was also an exotic plot having to do with a sarong-garbed Polynesian couple (Dorothy Lamour and Jon Hall) and their ill-starred love story (he's always get-

THE HURRICANE: Mary Astor, C. Aubrey Smith and players.

ting in trouble with the law, facing incarceration, then escaping and being returned to prison). This is juxtaposed against the equally bittersweet relationship of a "civilized" couple, the island's martinet governor and his kindly wife (Raymond Massey and Mary Astor). There are also the island's priest (C. Aubrey Smith), its alcoholic doctor (Thomas Mitchell), and the obligatory assorted native types. Lamour was borrowed from Paramount, where she'd introduced her benchmark sarong in *The Jungle Princess*. The relatively unknown Jon Hall (who came with the requisite good looks, rugged physique and athletic prowess) replaced Joel McCrea, Goldwyn's popular contract star. McCrea preferred the loanout that ultimately traded him to Paramount for DeMille's *Union Pacific* in exchange for the Lamour assignment.

The Hurricane proved a tremendous hit in 1937, and nowadays it's still worth an exciting couple of hours' escape for the video viewer.

I MET MY
LOVE AGAIN

1938

I MET MY LOVE AGAIN: Joan Bennett and Alan Marshal.

CREDITS

A United Artists Picture. A Walter Wanger Production. Directors: Arthur Ripley, Joshua Logan and (uncredited) George Cukor. Screenwriter: David Hertz. Based on the novel *Summer Lightning* by Allene Corliss. Cinematographer: Hal Mohr. Editors: Otho Lovering and Edward Mann. Music: Heinz Roemheld. Running Time: 77 minutes.

CAST

Joan Bennett (*Julie*); Henry Fonda (*Ives*); Dame May Whitty (*Aunt William*); Alan Marshal (*Michael*); Louise Platt (*Brenda*); Alan Baxter (*Tony*); Tim Holt (*Budge*); Dorothy Stickney (*Mrs. Towner*); Florence Lake (*Carol*); Genee Hall (*Michael, the Daughter*); Alice Cavenna (*Agatha*).

In the Thirties, the "woman's picture" was an important element at all the big studios, as well as a releasing organization such as United Artists. And a 77-minute feature like *I Met My Love Again* had the added attraction of brevity that easily allows for the co-featuring of another movie that might have more interest for a wider audience, thus assuring attendance at whatever theatre might book them. Reflect-

ing the manners and mores of another era, these films would concentrate on subject matter thought to hold more interest for women than for men—romance and themes like the one expounded in *I Met My Love Again*: a lost love and, eventually, a second chance for the protagonists' happiness. There was the romance novel, the soap opera and radio, but escape was more satisfying at the movies, where the housewife or the working girl could relax

I MET MY LOVE AGAIN: Henry Fonda, Joan Bennett and Tim Holt.

and become vicariously swept away with the onscreen problems of Joan Crawford, Kay Francis, Ruth Chatterton, Barbara Stanwyck and Ann Dvorak, to name a few of the most ubiquitous of the lot. In *I Met My Love Again*, it's the still-natural-blonde Joan Bennett whose romantic problems are at issue. This was an actress more regularly involved in comedy or costume pictures, although her extensive film background had already touched on every genre that then existed.

The story begins in 1927 in a small town in Vermont, where the lively, unconventional Julie (Bennett) and quiet, studious Ives (Henry Fonda) are uneventfully engaged—until their comfortable little world is disrupted by the appearance of a dashing playboy/author named Michael (Alan Marshal), who quite captures Julie's restless heart. Jilting her hometown beau, Julie elopes to Paris with Michael, whom she eventually discovers is more playboy than writer—and an alcoholic, to boot. Ten years later, Julie's a widow with a daughter (also named Michael), and where does she return to but the Vermont family homestead. By this time, Ives, who has never married, is an embittered college professor who refuses to acknowledge his emotions for Julie—until his adoring student Brenda (Louise Platt) threatens suicide if he won't return *her* love. This miraculously makes him understand how Julie must have felt and they reunite to pick up where they left

I MET MY LOVE AGAIN: Dame May Whitty and Henry Fonda.

off a decade earlier, despite wagging local tongues and the opposition of little Michael. We are left to believe that true love will, quite naturally, conquer all.

So much for the movie's hokey plot. It's the performances that succeed in putting it all across, with Joan Bennett particularly impressive as the wild romantic who learns her lessons the hard way. Henry Fonda's role offers less reward, but his solid stage background and down-to-earth Midwestern naturalness go far to make more of Ives than the screenplay gives him. Fonda took the role because he was then under contract to its producer, Walter Wanger (his co-star's husband-to-be). In addition, his old friend Joshua Logan was making his Hollywood debut as *I Met My Love Again*'s co-director (along with Arthur Ripley, whose first feature-picture it was, after some years of directing shorts like W. C. Fields' *The Barber Shop* and *The Pharmacist*). Neither man could have been happy with the knowledge that the veteran George Cukor was later called in to reshoot much of their footage. Logan was then sufficiently disenchanted with movie-making to return to the stage, and did not come back to pictures until *Picnic* 17

I MET MY LOVE AGAIN: Henry Fonda and Joan Bennett.

years later. For all of those reasons, it seems amazing that *I Met My Love Again* is the enjoyable, well-turned-out little sudser that it remains.

A SLIGHT CASE OF MURDER

1938

CREDITS

A Warner Bros. Picture. Producer: Hal B. Wallis. Associate Producer: Sam Bischoff. Director: Lloyd Bacon. Screenwriters: Earl Baldwin and Joseph Schrank. Based on the play by Damon Runyon and Howard Lindsay. Cinematographer: Sid Hickox. Editor: James Gibbons. Art Director: Max Parker. Music Director: Leo F. Forbstein. Songs: M.K. Jerome and Jack Scholl. Running Time: 85 minutes.

CAST

Edward G. Robinson (*Remy Marco*); Jane Bryan (*Mary Marco*); Willard Parker (*Dick Whitewood*); Ruth Donnelly (*Mora Marco*); Allen Jenkins (*Mike*); John Litel (*Post*); Eric Stanley (*Ritter*); Harold Huber (*Giuseppe*); Edward Brophy (*Lefty*); Paul Harvey (*Mr. Whitewood*); Bobby Jordan (*Douglas Fairbanks Rosenbloom*); Joseph Downing (*Innocence*); Margaret Hamilton (*Mrs. Cagle*); George E. Stone (*Ex-Jockey Kirk*); Bert Hamilton (*Sad Sam*); Jean Benedict (*Remy's Secretary*); Harry Seymour (*The Singer*); Betty Compson (*Loretta*); Joe Caits (*No-Nose Cohen*); John Harmon (*Blackhead Gallagher*); George Lloyd (*Little Butch*); Harry Tenbrook (*A Stranger*); Duke York (*The Champ*); Pat Daly (*The Champ's Manager*); Bert Roach (*Speakeasy Proprietor*); Harry Cody (*Pessimistic Patron*); Ben Hendricks, Ralph Dunn and Wade Boteler (*Policemen*); Myrtle Stedman and Loia Cheaney (*Nurses*); Carole Landis (*Party Guest*).

In the Thirties, the top-paid director at Warner Bros. was Lloyd Bacon, who handled more of that studios biggest names than anyone else. Among them: John Barrymore (*Moby Dick*); James Cagney (*Picture Snatcher, Footlight Parade, He Was Her Man, Here Comes the Navy, Devil Dogs of the Air, The Irish in Us, Frisco Kid, Boy Meets Girl, The Oklahoma Kid*); Bette Davis (*Marked Woman*); Dick Powell (*42nd Street, Wonder Bar, Broadway Gondolier, Gold Diggers of 1937, The Cowboy From Brooklyn*); Kay Francis (*Mary Stevens, M.D.*); Joe E. Brown (*You Said a Mouthful, Son of a Sailor, 6-Day Bike Rider*); Clark Gable (*Cain and Mabel*) and Edward G. Robinson (*A Slight Case of Murder*).

Robinson was, of course, not a complete novice at comedy, although he had spent most of the decade in roles of a serious, if not downright intimidating nature, particularly since his public reacted so favorably to the actor's matchless gangster performances. But, in the now little-seen *A Slight Case of Murder*, it's exactly those *Little Caesar*-type of movies that are being kidded so amusingly by Earl Baldwin and Joseph Schrank in this screen version of the 1935 stage play by Damon Runyon and Howard Lindsay. On Broadway, it had closed after a mere 69 performances with no big stars (today, its biggest name belongs to Jose Ferrer, who played "2nd Policeman"). A little-remembered actor named John Harrington portrayed the ex-beer racketeer Marco, the part Robinson plays in the film. But *A Slight Case of Murder* is out-and-out farce, a comedy genre in which the seasoned, 45-year-old Robinson must have felt ill at ease, for it has been recorded that he more than once sought the help of his director. To which a surprised Lloyd Bacon replied, "Don't kid me, Eddie." But Robinson wasn't kidding; he needed Bacon's guidance.

Beer baron Remy Marco has amassed his fortune at the expense of Prohibition. But when the 21st Amendment opens up the market and Remy's business declines, he retires with the intention of breaking into high society. With his wife Mora (Ruth Donnelly) and daughter Mary (Jane Bryan), Remy buys a new country home, which he later finds holds a collection of fresh corpses placed there by rival mobsters to frame him. Compounding Remy's problems is the fact that Mary is engaged to a motorcycle cop named Dick (Willard Parker). Remy has also taken on the rehabilitation of a tough young delinquent who goes by the unlikely monicker of Douglas Fairbanks Rosenbloom (Bobby Jordan, of Dead End Kids fame).

Further details of this hilarious and densely plotted comic misadventure are best left to the potential TV viewers, who might enjoy discovering what happens for themselves. Suffice to say that anyone who sees *A Slight Case of Murder* will find it difficult to take *Little Caesar* seriously again. As *Variety* aptly put it, "The underworld is turned inside out, and scenes which once chilled the spectators with horror are the occasion here for hearty laughter."

Lloyd Bacon directed with an infectious sense of pace and humor, and a skilled cast delivered what he asked of them. Robinson offers a broad parody of his more sinister, earlier criminal studies. Ruth Donnelly is even better as his tough, sarcastic spouse. And there are marvelous performances from so many of what has come to be known as the Warner Bros. stock company—character actors of the irreplaceable ilk of Allen Jenkins, Edward Brophy, Paul Harvey, George E. Stone and a pre-Wicked Witch Margaret Hamilton, as the prim schoolmarm Remy goes back to visit.

Broderick Crawford and Claire Trevor teamed for a mild 1952 remake, which was called *Stop, You're Killing Me*. But it's the original *A Slight Case of Murder* that's worth rediscovering.

A SLIGHT CASE OF MURDER: Ruth Donnelly and Edward G. Robinson.

A SLIGHT CASE OF MURDER: Margaret Hamilton, Bobby Jordan and Edward G. Robinson.

BRINGING UP BABY

1938

CREDITS

An RKO Radio Picture. Producer/Director: Howard Hawks. Associate Producer: Cliff Reid. Screenwriters: Dudley Nichols and Hagar Wilde. Based on a story by Wilde. Cinematographer: Russell Metty. Editor: George Hively.

A SLIGHT CASE OF MURDER: Ruth Donnelly, Jane Bryan and Edward G. Robinson.

Art Directors: Van Nest Polglase and Perry Ferguson. Set Decorator: Darrell Silvera. Sound: John L. Cass. Music: Roy Webb. Special Photographic Effects: Vernon L.

BRINGING UP BABY: Cary Grant, Billy Bevan, Katharine Hepburn and player.

BRINGING UP BABY: Katharine Hepburn.

Walker. Costumes: Howard Greer. Running Time: 102 minutes.

CAST

Katharine Hepburn (*Susan Vance*); Cary Grant (*David Huxley*); Charles Ruggles (*Major Horace Applegate*); May Robson (*Aunt Elizabeth*); Barry Fitzgerald (*Mr. Gogarty*); Walter Catlett (*Constable Slocum*); Fritz Feld (*Dr. Fritz Lehman*); Leona Roberts (*Hannah Gogarty*); George Irving (*Alexander Peabody*); Virginia Walker (*Alice Swallow*); Tala Birell (*Mrs. Lehman*); John Kelly (*Elmer*); Nissa (*Baby, the Leopard*); Asta (*George, the Dog*); Edward Gargan and Buck Mack (*Zoo Officials*); Geraldine Hall (*Maid*); Stanley Blystone (*Doorman*); William Benedict (*David's Caddy*); Buster Slaven (*Caddy*); Frank Marlowe (*Joe*); Pat West (*Mac*); Jack Carson (*Roustabout*); Richard Lane (*Circus Manager*); Frank M. Thomas (*Barker*); Ruth Alder (*Dancer*); Pat O'Malley (*Deputy*); Ward Bond (*Motor Cop*); Adalyn Asbury (*Mrs. Peabody*); Jeanne Martel and Judith Ford (*Cigarette Girls*); George Humbert (*Louis, the Headwaiter*); Billy Bevan (*Bartender*); D'Arcy Corrigan (*Professor La Touche*).

In *Bringing Up Baby*, Cary Grant elected to tackle a role that had already been turned down by no less than Ronald Colman, Robert Montgomery and Ray Milland—the shy, dignified paleontologist who tangles with a madcap heiress in this delightfully daffy farce, opposite Katharine Hepburn. The film's director, Howard Hawks, was an old hand at tough, rugged dramas (*Scarface, Barbary Coast*), but had only one previous 1930s comedy to his credit—the 1934 John Barrymore-Carole Lombard romp, *Twentieth Century*. With *Bringing Up Baby*, Hawks proved himself a versatile director, and Cary Grant obviously responded well to his creative guidance. More fortuitously cast this time than in (their previous) *Sylvia Scarlett*, Grant and Hepburn proved a comedy team of chemical perfection.

Bringing Up Baby's plot has little coherence. Dudley Nichols and Hagar Wilde, working from a short story by Wilde, obviously had great fun concocting this string of amusing comedy clichés and outrageously whacky situations, and the proceedings clearly provided a happy collaboration between cast and director. The movie centers on David Huxley (Grant), a repressed professor whose lifetime project—the reconstruction of a dinosaur skeleton— is totally disrupted by his encounters with Susan Vance (Hepburn), a wealthy young lady who owns a mischievous terrier named George and a pet leopard that answers to "Baby," and who has a contagious penchant for getting into scrapes. When George

BRINGING UP BABY: Cary Grant and Katharine Hepburn.

makes off with the dinosaur's intercostal clavicle (a priceless bone David has just obtained to complete his work), the fun really begins. Dog buries bone;

BRINGING UP BABY: Cary Grant, May Robson and Geraldine Hall.

professor accompanies heiress into the Connecticut countryside; pet leopard gets loose at the same time, coincidentally, that a dangerous cat escapes from the local zoo; David finds himself clad in Susan's negligee, and so on. Hawks and his writers failed to omit any musty sight or sound gag in the proceedings. Yet with the aid of a brilliant cast (including such topnotch character actors as Charles Ruggles, May Robson, Barry Fitzgerald and Walter Catlett), each new turn of the script seems fresh, inspired and infectiously funny.

For Hepburn, *Bringing Up Baby* was a radical departure from the soap operas and costume dramas (A *Woman Rebels*, *Mary of Scotland*, *Quality Street*) that helped get her named "box-office poison." Under Hawks, she displayed a previously untapped knack for comic timing (even slapstick) that gave her career a much needed boost. Grant was on more familiar territory, and one recalls scene after scene in which he excels through the skill of a line reading or a facial nuance. Upon unexpectedly greeting May Robson while he is dressed in a frilly negligee, he glibly explains the situation with a frantic leap and an inspired reading of the line, "I went *gay* all of a sudden!" In a nightclub sequence with Hepburn, he struggles to maintain his dignity while helping the

BRINGING UP BABY: Katharine Hepburn, Cary Grant and Nissa.

dizzy heiress hide the fact that she's torn her dress in back—by walking closely behind her as they shuffle toward an exit. Or when stumbling by night over the New England countryside with Hepburn, as they seek to locate the missing Baby by singing the animal's favorite tune, "I Can't Give You Anything But Love, Baby." The jail sequence, with most of the cast behind bars matching wits with Walter Catlett's excited Constable, is another well-remembered highlight. And the finale is equally mad: Grant mounts a high work platform to complete the dinosaur by attaching the missing clavicle—only to have his life's work collapse when Hepburn clambers up to join him.

Howard Hawks has explained how Grant developed the whinnying device he has occasionally deployed in comedy. "We have a scene in *Bringing Up Baby* where he's angry. I said, 'pretty dull. You get angry like Joe Doakes next door. Can't you think of somebody who gets angry and it's funny?' And then I remembered a man who practically whinnies like a horse when he's angry—so he did it."

If certain elements of this movie ring a familiar bell to Barbra Streisand fans, it might be because her *What's Up, Doc?* was designed as an homage to the screwball comedies of the Thirties, with Ryan O'Neal as a contemporary counterpart to Cary Grant's paleontologist.

ALEXANDER'S RAGTIME BAND

1938

CREDITS

A 20th Century-Fox Picture. Producer: Darryl F. Zanuck. Associate Producer: Harry Joe Brown. Director: Henry King. Screenwriters: Kathryn Scola, Lamar Trotti and Richard Sherman. Cinematographer: Peverell Marley. Editor: Barbara McLean. Art Directors: Bernard Herzbrun and Boris Leven. Set Decorator: Thomas Little. Choreographer: Seymour Felix. Costumes: Gwen Wakeling. Sound: Arthur von Kirbach and Roger Heman. Musical Director: Alfred Newman. Songs by Irving Berlin. New songs written for this film: "Now It Can Be Told," "I'm Marching Along With Time" and "My Walking Stick." Old songs sung in the film: "Alexander's Ragtime Band," "Ragtime Violin," "That International Rag," "Everybody's Doing It Now," "This Is the Life," "When the

ALEXANDER'S RAGTIME BAND: Tyrone Power and Alice Faye.

Midnight Choo-Choo Leaves for Alabam'," "For Your Country and My Country," "I Can Always Find a Little Sunshine at the YMCA," "Oh! How I Hate to Get Up in the Morning," "We're on Our Way to France," "Say It With Music," "A Pretty Girl Is Like a Melody," "Blue Skies," "Pack Up Your Sins and Go to the Devil," "What'll I Do?" "Remember," "Everybody Step," "All Alone," "Gypsy in Me," "Easter Parade" and "Heat Wave." Running Time: 105 minutes.

CAST

Tyrone Power (*Alexander/Roger Grant*); Alice Faye (*Stella Kirby*); Don Ameche (*Charley Dwyer*); Ethel Merman (*Jerry Allen*); Jack Haley (*Davey Lane*); Jean Hersholt (*Professor Heinrich*); Helen Westley (*Aunt Sophie*); John Carradine (*Taxi Driver*); Paul Hurst (*Bill*); Wally Vernon (*Himself*); Ruth Terry (*Ruby*); Douglas Fowley (*Snapper*); Chick Chandler (*Louie*); Eddie Collins (*Corporal Collins*); Joe King (*Charles Dillingham*); Joseph Crehan (*Dillingham's Stage Manager*); Robert Gleckler (*Dirty Eddie*); Dixie Dunbar (*Specialty Performer*); Grady Sutton (*Babe*); Stanley Andrews (*Colonel*); Lon Chaney, Jr. (*Photographer*); Selmer Jackson (*Radio Station Manager*); Paul McVey (*Second Stage Manager*); King's Men (*Quartet*); Tyler Brooke (*Assistant Stage Manager*); Robert Lowery (*Reporter*); Charles Williams (*Agent*); James Flavin (*Captain*); Edward Keane (*Major*); Charles Coleman (*Head Waiter*); Donald Douglas (*Singer*); Jane Jones, Otto Fries and Mel Kalish (*Trio*); Cully Richards (*Member of the Band*); Harold Goodwin (*M.P.*); Jack Pennick (*Drill Sergeant*); Charles Tannen (*Dil-

ALEXANDER'S RAGTIME BAND: Alice Faye, Tyrone Power, Jack Haley (*on drums*) and Don Ameche.

lingham's Secretary); Arthur Rankin (*Third Stage Manager*); Eleanor Wesselhoeft (*Martha*); Ralph Dunn (*Captain*); Cecil Weston (*Woman*); Kay Griffith and Lynne Barkley (*Autograph Seekers*); Sam Ash and Edwin Stanley (*Critics*); Pop Byron (*Conductor*).

Time magazine called it, "easily the best cine-musical of 1938," and in *The New York Times*, Frank Nugent wrote, "Few sentimental gestures have been more expansive, few more lavishly produced than this motion picture tribute to Tin Pan Alley's most famous lodger." The "lodger" in question was, of course, Irving Berlin, whose wonderful popular music provides the whole *raison d'être* for *Alexander's Ragtime Band*. It was a labor of love for Fox producer Darryl F. Zanuck, whose investment included over $2-million, two years of pre-production time and his three most popular stars, Tyrone Power, Alice Faye and Don Ameche. Berlin contributed three new songs to the venture, but it's otherwise a cavalcade of his works spanning the movie's story period from 1911 to 1938. And director Henry King managed to triumph over an episodic and rather shapeless screenplay.

Today, *Alexander's Ragtime Band* looks a bit corny and somewhat phony. There's little believability in the physical look of the years encompassed by the plot. Costumes and hairstyles undergo some slight modification throughout—and World War I figures in the storyline—but otherwise, it could all be taking place over three *years*, instead of the nearly three *decades* it represents. Power, Faye and Ameche—then aged, respectively 25, 26 and 30—look no older at the film's conclusion, because Zanuck refused to permit age make-up for his box-office favorites; screen realism was far less an issue in the Thirties than it is today. But *Alexander's Ragtime Band* was another big hit for 20th Century-Fox and especially for Alice Faye, whose warmth, sincerity and mellow contralto go a long way to put over this sentimental material. Irving Berlin once said of her, "I'd rather have Alice Faye introduce my songs than any other singer I know." Small wonder that *Alexander's Ragtime Band* remains Faye's favorite among her movies.

The story opens in San Francisco, where Roger Grant (Power) disappoints his aristocratic family and teacher (Jean Hersholt) when he elects to abandon classical music to play ragtime with his band on the city's Barbary Coast. The movie's tone is set in the first big musical scene. Just as Roger's band is about to audition for a cabaret owner, floozy-like Stella Kirby (Faye) tries to convince the owner that she could charm his customers with a new song she'd like to introduce called "Alexander's Ragtime Band." Recognizing a friend at a table, she leaves her sheet music on the bar, where Roger picks it up. When, shortly thereafter, Stella hears her music being played, she angrily intrudes herself into the

242

band and sings the lyrics. The owner is so impressed, he wants to hire them all, but Stella won't have any part of the band—until the band's pianist, Charlie Dwyer (Ameche) sweet-talks her into reconsidering.

Stella and Roger fail to hit it off until she introduces "Now It Can Be Told," a new song written by Charlie. Its sentiments suddenly make Roger and Stella realize the depth of their feelings for each other. Everything goes smoothly for the group until they're visited by big-time New York producer Charles Dillingham (Joe King), who wants to engage only Stella. This splits up the group, and Stella leaves for a successful stage career on Broadway, while Roger enlists to go to battle in World War I. On the rebound, Stella marries Charlie, which is a shock to Roger when he visits her upon his return from the war. Even though he still loves Stella, he tries to forget her and he engages a new and vibrant band singer named Jerry Allen (Ethel Merman). Meanwhile, Charlie suggests an amicable divorce to Stella, since he realizes it's Roger she still loves. Upon his return from a European tour with his band, Roger finds that Stella has dropped from Broadway fame, and is now singing one-night stands wherever she can.

ALEXANDER'S RAGTIME BAND: Ethel Merman and Tyrone Power.

ALEXANDER'S RAGTIME BAND: Tyrone Power, Alice Faye and Don Ameche.

The movie's finale is both unbelievable and effective in a hokey way. Roger and his band, rejoined by Charlie, make their big Carnegie Hall bow in a concert being radiocast. Riding in a taxi, Stella hears the broadcast, courtesy of a kindly but quirky cabdriver (John Carradine). The cabbie recognizes her, seems to know all about her relationships with the band, and proceeds to deposit her on the steps of the concert hall. Reluctantly, but impulsively, she goes inside, suddenly appearing in the Carnegie wings, to be noticed first by Charlie and then by Roger. He leaves the podium to bring her on and introduce her to the packed house as they all join in with—what else?—"Alexander's Ragtime Band."

Presumably, Roger and Stella finally get together, both privately as well as professionally, with the selfless Charlie as their Cupid. Of course, by this time, all three principals ought to look a trifle longer in the tooth. But they don't. So no matter; it's only a movie. But what an entertaining movie it is, with all those wonderful Irving Berlin melodies! In this case, unfortunately, the old adage is true: they *don't* make them like this anymore!

The movie won an Academy Award for Alfred Newman's arrangements of the Berlin melodies, as well as five other nominations, including original story, film editing, art direction, the song "Now It Can Be Told"—and Best Picture (which went to *You Can't Take It With You*).

YOU CAN'T TAKE IT WITH YOU: Mary Forbes, James Stewart and Jean Arthur.

YOU CAN'T TAKE IT WITH YOU

1938

CREDITS

A Columbia Picture. Producer/Director: Frank Capra. Screenwriter: Robert Riskin. Based on the play by George S. Kaufman and Moss Hart. Cinematographer: Joseph Walker. Editor: Gene Havlick. Art Directors: Stephen Goosson and Lionel Banks. Sound: John Livadary. Music: Dimitri Tiomkin. Musical Director: Morris Stoloff. Miss Arthur's Gowns: Bernard Newman and Irene. Assistant Director: Arthur Black. Running Time: 127 minutes.

CAST

Jean Arthur (*Alice Sycamore*); Lionel Barrymore (*Martin Vanderhof*); James Stewart (*Tony Kirby*); Edward Arnold (*Anthony P. Kirby*); Mischa Auer (*Kolenkhov*); Ann Miller (*Essie Carmichael*); Spring Byington (*Penny Sycamore*); Samuel S. Hinds (*Paul Sycamore*); Donald Meek (*Poppins*); H.B. Warner (*Ramsey*); Halliwell Hobbes (*De Pinna*); Dub Taylor (*Ed Carmichael*); Mary Forbes (*Mrs. Anthony Kirby*); Lillian Yarbo (*Rheba*); Eddie Anderson (*Donald*); Clarence Wilson (*John Blakely*); Joseph Swickard (*Professor*); Ann Doran (*Maggie O'Neill*); Christian Rub (*Schmidt*); Bodil Rosing (*Mrs. Schmidt*); Charles Lane (*Henderson*); Harry Davenport (*Judge*); Pierre Watkin, Edwin Maxwell and Russell Hicks (*Attorneys*); Byron Foulger (*Kirby's Assistant*); James Flavin (*Jailer*); Ian Wolfe (*Kirby's Secretary*); Irving Bacon (*Henry*); Chester Clute (*Hammond*); Pert Kelton and Kit Guard (*Inmates*); James Burke and Ward Bond (*Detectives*); Edward Hearn (*Court Attendant*); Edward Keane (*Board Member*); John Ince and Edward Peil (*Neighbors*); Dick Curtis (*Strong-Arm Man*); Wallis Clark (*Hughes*); Paul Irving (*Office Manager*); Eddie Kane (*Kirby's Attorney*); Gene Morgan, Lou Davis, Lester Dorr, William Arnold, Jack Gardner, Bill Dill and William Lally (*Reporters*); Stanley Andrews (*Attorney*); Walter Walker (*Mr. Leach*); Robert Greig (*Lord Melville*); Gladys Blake (*Mary*); Eddy Chandler (*G-Man*); Edwin Stanley (*Executive*); Edward Earle (*Bank Manager*); Boyd Irwin (*Attorney*); Pat West (*Expressman*); Frank Shannon (*Mac*); John Hamilton (*Captain Drake*); Laura Treadwell (*Mrs. Drake*); Doris Rankin (*Mrs. Leach*); Hilda Plowright (*Lady Melville*); Blanche Payson (*Matron*); James Farley (*Police Sergeant*).

You Can't Take It With You, the Academy Award-winning Best Picture of 1938, also won a Best Direc-

tor Oscar for Frank Capra—his third—as well as nominations for supporting actress (Spring Byington), screenwriter Robert Riskin, cinematographer Joseph Walker, film editor Gene Havlick and sound technician John Livadary. The Kaufman and Hart comedy hit of the 1936–37 Broadway season had won a Pulitzer Prize, and was considered a sure thing for the movies. But, rather than play it safe by sticking closely to the whacky slapstick play, producer-director Capra encouraged his ace writer Riskin to not only "open it up" for the screen, but also to add warmth and genuine sentiment (as opposed to sentimentality) to the family relationships. Riskin also underscored the play's political threads with side issues like the grandfather's refusal to pay income taxes, and making its inherent humor also thought-provoking.

In the eccentric Vanderhof/Sycamore household, Grandpa (Lionel Barrymore) doesn't pay taxes because he simply doesn't believe in them; his daughter Penny (Spring Byington) writes plays because someone once left a typewriter at their house; her daughter Essie (Ann Miller) practices ballet in her toe-shoes; and her son-in-law Ed (Dub Taylor) plays xylophone and prints money. Among their permanent house guests: Mr. De Pinna (Halliwell Hobbes) who makes fireworks, which he sets off in the basement; Kolenkhov (Mischa Auer), who teaches dance; and Mr. Poppins (Donald Meek), who invents things. The only normal member of the household appears to be Essie's other daughter Alice (Jean Arthur), who holds down a regular office job as secretary to attrac-

tive, young Tony Kirby (James Stewart)—of *the* Kirbys. In fact, Alice and Tony have just decided to get married, much to the chagrin of Tony's snobbish mother (Mary Forbes); Tony's top-businessman father (Edward Arnold) is too busy enjoying his power to show any concern about social positioning.

Things come to a head when, in an effort to pave the way for a peaceful nuptual alliance between the two families, Tony and his parents are invited to the Vanderhof/Sycamore household for dinner—and arrive a day early. Chaos, of course, ensues as the Kirbys take a steadily dimming view of the unusual goings-on about them. But when Alice's father (Samuel S. Hinds) accidentally sets off the basement fireworks—and the entire neighborhood is privy to the subsequent display—the police arrive and haul everybody off to jail.

The plot enjoys more than a few additional whacky twists and turns before a finale in which Tony and Alice, not unexpectedly, wind up in each other's arms and—true to Capra-esque movie sensibilities—everyone ends by mending their ways and liking one another. As Grandpa Vanderhof succinctly sums it all up: "You can't take it with you! The only thing you can take with you is the love of your friends."

YOU CAN'T TAKE IT WITH YOU: Halliwell Hobbes, Lionel Barrymore, Samuel S. Hinds, Donald Meek, Mischa Auer, Jean Arthur, Ann Miller and Spring Byington.

THE YOUNG IN HEART

1938

CREDITS

A United Artists Picture. Producer: David O. Selznick. Director: Richard Wallace. Screenwriters: Paul Osborn and Charles Bennett. Based on the story *The Gay Banditti* by I.A.R. Wylie. Cinematographer: Leon Shamroy. Editor: Hal C. Kern. Art Director: Lyle Wheeler. Costumes: Omar Kiam. Music: Franz Waxman. Special Effects: Jack Cosgrove. Running Time: 90 minutes.

CAST

Janet Gaynor (*George-Ann Carleton*); Douglas Fairbanks, Jr. (*Richard Carleton*); Paulette Goddard (*Leslie Saunders*); Roland Young (*Col. Anthony "Sahib" Carleton*); Billie Burke (*Marmy Carleton*); Richard Carlson (*Duncan Macrae*); Minnie Dupree (*Miss Ellen Fortune*); Henry Stephenson (*Felix Anstruther*); Eily Malyon (*Sarah*); Margaret Early (*Adela Jennings*); Irvin S. Cobb (*Mr. Jennings*); Lucile Watson (*Mrs. Jennings*); Walter Kingsford (*Detective Chief*); Tom Ricketts (*Andrew*); Lawrence Grant (*Mr. Hutchins*); Ian McLaren (*Doctor*); Billy Bevan (*Kennel Man*); Lionel Pape (*Customer*); George Sorrell and Georges Renevant (*Detectives*).

It's unfortunate that one of the best comedies of the Thirties is little known today. *The Young in Heart*, for one reason or another, has been so little seen in recent years that few people seem to be familiar with it. But it's a situation that certain cable-TV networks, with their penchant for dipping further back into the film vaults, have begun to rectify. Commercial stations are now following suit.

In its day, *The Young in Heart* was very highly regarded, and references to it in books on movie history have always been laudatory. Brilliantly mixing the conventions of motion picture social comedy with sentiment, sound moral values and a dash of the "screwball" humor then popular, this is the well-written (Paul Osborn and Charles Bennett) story of the Carletons, a family of Continental con artists and cardsharps, whose charm, wit and resourcefulness have seemingly kept them solvent and far enough ahead of the law to appear very upper middle class, and socially acceptable.

With the delightfully droll and monocle-sporting Roland Young and ditsy, birdlike Billie Burke as the parents, and debonair Douglas Fairbanks, Jr. and girlish-voiced Janet Gaynor as their children, the family—as we first meet them—is operating on the Riviera. While Fairbanks courts the ugly duckling daughter (Margaret Early) of a wealthy American couple (Lucile Watson and Irvin S. Cobb), Gaynor flirts with a handsome young Scot (Richard Carlson, making his movie debut at 26). But the authorities catch up with the Carleton clan and, although unable as to yet pin anything specific on them, strongly suggest that they move on and take their business elsewhere. On the train from France to London, the Carletons encounter, traveling alone, a sweet and delightful old lady named Miss Fortune (Minnie Dupree), who immediately gains their interest by revealing that she's rich and lonely with a big old house all

THE YOUNG IN HEART: Billie Burke, Minnie Dupree, Roland Young and Janet Gaynor.

THE YOUNG IN HEART: Douglas Fairbanks, Jr. and Paulette Goddard.

to herself back home. In short order, she becomes sympathetic to their tall tales of "bad luck," and invites them to come and live with her—which they, of course, do with the intent of taking advantage of her generosity to worm their way into both her affections and her will.

For appearances, father and son make a stab at finding jobs, and are surprisingly successful despite their inexperience at legitimate employment. Young becomes a car salesman demonstrating an ultra-modern, low-slung sports car called The Flying Wombat, and in no time is raised to sales manager. Fairbanks answers a "Boy Wanted" sign at an Anglo-American engineering firm, where skeptical boss Paulette Goddard initially fails to succumb to his suave sophistication—but later becomes his steady lady as he copes, for the first time, with a paying job. Elsewhere, Gaynor (who had dumped Carlson) now finds him pursuing her anew, and she worries that he will give them all away before they can reach first base with dear old Miss Fortune, who sees only the good in everyone. Even after Miss Fortune learns from her lawyer of their shady past, she feels sorry that such nice people have fallen on such hard times that they must cheat people to survive. And she decides to leave everything to them in her will.

When she falls ill, her lawyer reveals to the Carletons that, although he'd kept it from her, her "estate" is nearly bankrupt. By this time, they have learned a lot about the goodness of the human heart, and have mended their ways. Gaynor marries Carlson, who's being sent to India, and Miss Fortune recovers to see the Carletons living in their own

THE YOUNG IN HEART: Billie Burke, Douglas Fairbanks, Jr., Roland Young and Janet Gaynor.

rose-covered cottage, to which she is invited to come and live. Originally, Miss Fortune had died at the end of the movie. But audience reaction at the initial preview showings had been so negative that the cast was recalled, and a new ending shot.

It's a happy-ever-after fairytale that may little resemble real life, even in the waning days of

Depression-era America. But its messages are clear and positive, and the humor with which it is transmitted makes this moral fable a delightful entertainment in any season.

Nearly everyone marveled at the quiet scene-stealing performance of Minnie Dupree, a nearly unknown actress who had come to Hollywood from the legitimate theatre. Originally, producer David O. Selznick had sought 66-year-old retired Broadway star Maude Adams. But after journeying to the movie capital for a test, Adams declined the role in favor of remaining a retired actress-turned-teacher at Missouri's Stephens College. And so Dupree was engaged, and walked away with the picture, returning to films only once more in RKO's 1940 *Anne of Windy Poplars*. Coming on the heels of *A Star Is Born*, and her sensational career-renewal performance, *The Young in Heart* seemed to insure great things to come for Janet Gaynor. But she fooled everyone by marrying MGM designer Gilbert Adrian and altogether retiring from the screen—not to be seen in films again until a one-shot comeback in 1957's forgettable Pat Boone vehicle, *Bernardine*.

Director Richard Wallace (1894–1951) had enjoyed a varied career in the movies since 1925, but *The Young in Heart*, his first picture with Selznick after ending 10 years with Paramount, was his most successful. Its tasteful fine line between madcap humor and heartfelt pathos, so well delineated by a top-notch cast, can be credited to Wallace, who succeeds in making the rehabilitation of the rascally Carleton family not only believable but completely winning. Ironically, *The Young in Heart* won Oscar nominations not for acting or direction, but for Leon Shamroy's cinematography and Franz Waxman's musical score.

THE YOUNG IN HEART: Paulette Goddard, Douglas Fairbanks, Jr., Billie Burke, Minnie Dupree, Roland Young, Janet Gaynor and Richard Carlson.

MARIE ANTOINETTE

1938

CREDITS

A Metro-Goldwyn-Mayer Picture. Producer: Hunt Stromberg. Director: W.S. Van Dyke II. Screenwriters: Claudine West, Donald Ogden Stewart and Ernest Vajda. Based on Stefan Zweig's biography *Marie Antoinette*. Cinematographer: William Daniels. Editor: Robert J. Kern. Art Director: Cedric Gibbons. Musical Score: Herbert Stothart. Montage: Slavko Vorkapich. Dances: Albertina Rasch. Costumes: Adrian and Gile Steele. Song: "Amour Eternal Amour" by Bob Wright, Herbert Stothart and Chet Forrest. Make-Up: Jack Dawn. Running Time: 160 minutes

CAST

Norma Shearer (*Marie Antoinette*); Tyrone Power (*Count Axel de Fersen*); John Barrymore (*King Louis XV*); Gladys George (*Mme. DuBarry*); Robert Morley (*King Louis XVI*); Anita Louise (*Princess DeLamballe*); Joseph Schildkraut (*Duke of Orleans*); Henry Stephenson (*Count de Mercey*); Reginald Gardiner (*Comte D'Artois*); Peter Bull (*Gamin*); Albert Van Dekker (*Provence*); Barnett Parker (*Prince De Rohan*); Cora Witherspoon (*Mme. De Noailles*); Joseph Calleia (*Drouet*); Ivan F. Simpson (*Sauce*); George Meeker (*Robespierre*); Marilyn Knowlden (*Princess Theresa*); Scotty Beckett (*Dauphin*); Henry Daniell (*LaMotte*); Alma Kruger (*Empress Marie Theresa*); Leonard Penn (*Toulan*); George Zucco (*Governor of Conciergerie*); Ian Wolfe (*Herbert*); John Burton (*LaFayette*), Mae Busch (*Mme. La Motte*); Cecil Cunningham (*Mme. De Lerchenfeld*); Brent Sargent (*St. Pre*); Tom Rutherford (*St. Clair*); Ruth Hussey (*Mme. DePolignac*); Victor Killian (*Guard in Louis's Cell*); Charles Waldron (*Swedish Ambassador*); Walter Walker (*Benjamin Franklin*); Zeffie Tilbury (*Dowager at birth of Dauphin*); Claude King (*Choisell*); Frank Elliott (*King's Chamberlain*); Herbert Rawlinson (*Goguelot*); Wade Crosby (*Lanton*); George Houston (*Marquis De St. Priest*); Moroni Olsen (*Bearded Man*); Barry Fitzgerald (*Peddler*); Kathryn Sheldon (*Mrs. Tilson*); Lionel Royce (*Guillaume*); Lyons Wickland (*Laclos*); Anthony Warde (*Marat*); Olaf Hytten (*Boehmer*); Rafaela Ottiano (*Louise, Marie's Maid*); Guy Bates Post (*Convention President*); Gustav von Seyffertitz (*King's Confessor*); Nigel DeBrulier (*Archbishop*); Howard Lang (*Franz*); Mary Howard (*Olivia*); Ramsay Hill (*Major Domo*); Jack George (*Orchestra Leader*); Thomas Braidon (*Lackey*); Denis d'Auburn (*Beauregard*); Frank Campeau (*Lemonade Vendor*); Harts Lind (*Nurse*); Theodore von

Eltz (*Officer in Entrance Hall*); Frank Jaquet (*Keeper of the Seal*); Harry Davenport (*Monsieur de Cosse*); Jacques Lory (*French Peasant*); Bea Nigro (*Woman at the Opera*); Hugh Huntley (*Man in Opera Gallery*); Harold Entwistle (*Old Aristocrat at Opera*); Guy D'Ennery (*Minister at King's Council*); Edward Keane (*General*); Frank McGlynn, Jr. (*Soldier with Rude Laugh*); Esther Howard (*Streetwalker*)

Hollywood no longer turns out movies like this one. *Marie Antoinette*, a big money-maker in 1938, has always been surprisingly underrated as a motion picture, and the present-day TV viewer who encoun-

ters it on one of the film's relatively rare airings (undoubtedly due to its two-hour-40 minute length . . . without commercials!) may well revel in the sensation of discovering an unheralded treasure from the great heyday of Metro-Goldwyn-Mayer.

Marie Antoinette's consistently high level of quality is astonishing, from its sumptuous sets and costumes to the expertise with which Hunt Stromberg produced this spectacular film biography and the smoothness of W.S. Van Dyke's direction. It's especially impressive in light of Van Dyke's reputa-

MARIE ANTOINETTE: Joseph Schildkraut, Robert Morley and Norma Shearer.

MARIE ANTOINETTE: Joseph Schildkraut, Norma Shearer, Albert Van
Dekker and Reginald Gardiner.

MARIE ANTOINETTE: Robert Morley, John Barrymore and Norma
Shearer.

tion for fast, economical one-take filmmaking—and
the fact he was brought in as a cost-saving replacement for the movie's original director, Sidney Franklin. *Marie Antoinette* had been long in the planning
as a vehicle for MGM's classy queen of the lot,
Norma Shearer. In fact, William Randolph Hearst
and his favorite star Marion Davies had (following a
lengthy affiliation) left Metro for Warner Bros. due
to Hearst's inability to persuade Louis B. Mayer that
this historical epic should be a *Davies* vehicle.

Filmed at a then-impressive cost of $1.8 million,
Marie Antoinette displays every penny of that sum in
the opulence of its ballrooms, royal chambers, court-
rooms, palace halls, and lavish crowd sequences.
Two hundred of its proverbial "cast of thousands,"
were choreographed by the once-celebrated Albertina Rasch for the sweeping ball scenes, and 152
actors were given speaking roles. The diligent viewer
can identify, in one-scene parts, many a still-familiar
face under the powdered wigs and period headgear.

Marie Antoinette's grandiose size alone tends to
dwarf the contributions of all but its major players,
among the most memorable of whom are Robert
Morley (eloquent as the ineffectual, dim-witted
Louis XVI), John Barrymore (personally declining,
but still a powerful actor as the dying old Louis XV),
Joseph Schildkraut (at his hammy best as the du-
plicitous Duke of Orleans) and Gladys George (appropriately sharp-tongued as the king's notorious
mistress, Madame DuBarry).

250

Tyrone Power (on loan-out from 20th Century-Fox, in exchange for Metro's Spencer Tracy in *Stanley and Livingstone*) is the film's nominal leading man. But his part, though well enough played, allows Power (whose role just as well could have been done by MGM's own Robert Taylor) to be little more than a handsome presence who shares an occasional scene with Norma Shearer. This sufficiently angered Fox production chief Darryl Zanuck to put an embargo on all future exchanges for his top male box-office attraction.

As for Shearer, *Marie Antoinette* simply records the finest performance of her career. From naïve young Austrian princess to the gaunt, gray-haired figure who resignedly ascends to the guillotine, she offers a star performance of as many changing facets as there are scenes. Hers is a marathon role that keeps her before William Daniels' masterful cameras nearly throughout the movie's 160 long minutes. In her day, Norma Shearer was an audience favorite, especially among women. But her popularity lessened considerably following her 1942 retirement from the screen, and her name has been absent from the kind of retrospective tributes accorded some of her contemporaries.

Among *Marie Antoinette*'s Oscar nominations were to Art Director Cedric Gibbons, to Best Supporting Actor Robert Morley, and to Shearer, whose Best Actress nod was conceded to Bette Davis for *Jezebel*.

MARIE ANTOINETTE: Tyrone Power and Norma Shearer.

ANGELS WITH DIRTY FACES

1938

CREDITS

A Warner Bros. Picture. Producer: Sam Bischoff. Director: Michael Curtiz. Screenwriters: John Wexley and Warren Duff. Based on a story by Rowland Brown. Cinematographer: Sol Polito. Editor: Owen Marks. Art Director: Robert Haas. Sound: Everett A. Brown. Costumes: Orry-Kelly. Music: Max Steiner. Song: "Angels With Dirty Faces" by Fred Fisher and Maurice Spitalny. Orchestrator: Hugo Friedhofer. Assistant Director: Sherry Shourds. Running Time: 97 minutes.

CAST

James Cagney (*Rocky Sullivan*); Pat O'Brien (*Jerry Connelly*); Humphrey Bogart (*James Frazier*); Ann Sheridan (*Laury Martin*); George Bancroft (*Mac Keefer*); Billy Halop (*Soapy*); Bobby Jordan (*Swing*); Leo Gorcey (*Bim*); Bernard Punsley (*Hunky*); Gabriel Dell (*Pasty*); Huntz Hall (*Crab*); Frankie Burke (*Rocky as a Boy*); William Tracy (*Jerry as a Boy*); Marilyn Knowlden (*Laury as a Girl*); Joe Downing (*Steve*); Adrian Morris (*Blackie*); Oscar O'Shea (*Guard Kennedy*); William Pawley (*Bugs the Gunman*); Edward Pawley (*Guard Edwards*); Earl Dwire (*Priest*); John Hamilton (*Police Captain*); Theodore Rand and Charles Sullivan (*Gunmen*); The St. Brendan's Church Choir (*Themselves*); William Worthington (*Warden*); James Farley (*Railroad Yard Watchman*); Pat O'Malley (*Railroad Guard*); Harry Hayden (*Pharmacist*); Dick Rich, Stevan Darrell and Joe A. Devlin (*Gangsters*); Charles Wilson (*Buckley, the Police Chief*); Frank Coghlan, Jr. and David Durand (*Boys in Poolroom*); Charles Trowbridge (*Norton J. White*); Lane Chandler (*Guard*); Jack Perrin (*Death Row Guard*); Poppy Wilde (*Girl at Gaming Table*); Eddie Brian (*Newsboy*); Vera Lewis (*Soapy's Mother*); Roger McGee, Vince Lombardi, Sonny Bupp and A.W. Sweatt (*Boys*); Chuck Stubb (*Red*); Eddie Syracuse (*Maggione Boy*); George Sorel (*Headwaiter*); Robert Homans (*Policeman*); Harris Berger (*Basketball Captain*); Lottie Williams (*Woman*); Donald Kerr, Jack Goodrich, Al Lloyd, Jeffrey Sayre, Charles Marsh, Alexander Lockwood, Earl Gunn and Carlyle Moore (*Reporters*); Lee Phelps and Jack Mower (*Detectives*); Belle Mitchell (*Mrs. Maggione*); William Edmunds (*Italian Storekeeper*).

ANGELS WITH DIRTY FACES: Ann Sheridan and James Cagney.

ANGELS WITH DIRTY FACES: poster art.

ANGELS WITH DIRTY FACES: James Cagney and Humphrey Bogart.

There are those who call James Cagney's performance in this gangster classic his finest on film, surpassing even his memorable Tom Powers in *The Public Enemy*. Whatever the case, Cagney and Pat O'Brien head a top-notch cast, with Ann Sheridan, Humphrey Bogart, George Bancroft and the Dead End Kids offering solid support in an outstanding production, directed to the hilt by Michael Curtiz, aided and abetted by one of Max Steiner's most effective background scores.

It can be argued that Cagney, as Rocky Sullivan in *Angels With Dirty Faces*, used just about the entire trick-bag of mannerisms employed by his impersonators. In his book *Cagney by Cagney*, the actor revealed: "Rocky was in part modeled on a fella I used to see when I was a kid. He was a hophead and a pimp, with four girls on his string. He worked out of a Hungarian rathskeller on First Avenue and 78th Street—a tall dude with an expensive straw hat and an electric-blue suit. All day long he would stand on that corner, hitch up his trousers, twist his neck and move his necktie, lift his shoulders, snap his fingers, then bring his hands together in a soft smack. His invariable greeting was 'Whadda ya hear? Whadda ya say?' The capacity for observation is something every actor must have to some degree, so I recalled

this fella and his mannerisms, and gave them to Rocky Sullivan just to bring some modicum of difference to this roughneck."

Cagney was, with his annual earnings of $234,000, Warners' highest-paid male star (Kay Francis was his female counterpart), and consequently was provided with better showcases for his energetic talents. *Angels With Dirty Faces* had the actor at his swaggering best.

Warner Bros. had already used the New York street kids from *Dead End* in the Humphrey Bogart programmer *Crime School*. In a few more years, they would star in their own popular Forties film series. Because of their pugnacious personalities, the title of this movie was changed from *Battle of City Hall* to *Angels With Dirty Faces*.

Vaguely recalling the beginnings of both *The Public Enemy* and *Manhattan Melodrama*, this film opens with its leading characters as boyhood pals who get into trouble. One escapes the law and grows up to become Father Jerry Connelly (Pat O'Brien); the other is apprehended and sent to reform school, where he emerges years later as a full-fledged criminal named Rocky Sullivan (Cagney). Back in his old neighborhood, Rocky resumes a friendship with his childhood girlfriend Laury Martin (Ann Sheridan), at the same time he's the idolized role model for the local tough boys (the Dead End Kids: Billy Halop, Bobby Jordan, Leo Gorcey, Bernard Punsley, Gabriel Dell and Huntz Hall). Rocky also threatens to undo all the rehabilitative good Father Jerry has thus far accomplished with the neighborhood youths.

Rocky tries to get an old debt of $10,000 due him from his corrupt lawyer-turned-nightclub-owner Frazier (Humphrey Bogart). But Frazier and his partner, political boss Keefer (George Bancroft), give him a hard time—until Rocky's strong-arm tactics force the three of them into an uneasy criminal partnership. The childhood chums now find themselves on actively opposite sides of the law as the priest campaigns to rid his city of its criminal element. But Irish sentiment prevails and Rocky wipes out Frazier and Keefer before the duo can activate their plan to kill Father Jerry. Arrested and convicted of those murders, Rocky is sentenced to the chair. When the priest visits him in his death cell, he asks Rocky to help stamp out the kids' idolatry of him by feigning cowardice as he's led to the chair. And, although Rocky scorns that request, as he walks the last mile, the condemned man's fearful cries and bodily contortions indicate otherwise. When the kids ask Father Jerry for confirmation that Rocky "turned yellow" at the end, they're told that he did.

However, the movie's ending has continued to stir controversy. In his book, Cagney reports: "Through the years, I have actually had little kids come up to me on the street and ask, 'Didya do it for the father, huh?'" And he adds: "I think in looking at the film it is virtually impossible to say which course Rocky took—which is just the way I wanted it. I played it with deliberate ambiguity so that the spectator can make his choice."

The critics praised *Angels With Dirty Faces*, while commenting on the "bloody, brutal and savage" aspects of its melodramatic action scenes. And the public ate it up, filling the Warner Bros. coffers and eventuating a less ambitious 1939 sequel, *Angels Wash Their Faces*.

Angels With Dirty Faces won no Oscars, but it garnered nominations for Best Actor Cagney, Best Director Michael Curtiz and Rowland Brown's Best Original Story. However, the New York Film Critics helped compensate by naming Cagney 1938's Best Actor for this movie.

ANGELS WITH DIRTY FACES: James Cagney, Pat O'Brien and players.

SUEZ

1938

CREDITS

A 20th-Century Fox Picture. Producer: Darryl F. Zanuck. Associate Producer: Gene Markey. Director: Allan Dwan. Screenwriters: Philip Dunne and Julien Josephson. Based on a story by Sam Duncan. Cinematographer: J. Peverell Marley. Editor: Barbara McLean. Music Director: Louis Silvers. Art Directors: Bernard Herzbrun and Rudolph Sternad. Set Decorator: Thomas Little. Costumes: Royer. Special Effects: Fred Sersen and Louis J. Witte. Second Unit Director: Otto Brower. Sound: Arthur Von Kirback and Roger Heman. Running Time: 104 minutes.

CAST

Tyrone Power (*Ferdinand de Lesseps*); Loretta Young (*Empress Eugenie*); Annabella (*Toni*); J. Edward Bromberg (*Said*); Joseph Schildkraut (*La Tour*); Henry Stephenson (*Count de Lesseps*); Sidney Blackmer (*Du Brey*); Maurice Moscovich (*Mohammed Ali*); Miles Mander (*Benjamin Disraeli*); George Zucco (*Prime Minister*); Leon Ames (*Louis Napoleon*); Rafaela Ottiano (*Maria De Teba*); Victor Varconi (*Victor Hugo*); Jacques Lory (*Millet*); Odette Myrtil (*Duchess*); Frank Reicher (*Gen. Chargarnier*); Carlos J. de Valdez (*Count Hatzfeld*); Albert Conti (*Fevier*); Brandon Hurst (*Liszt*); Marcelle Corday (*Mme. Paquineau*); Egon Brecher (*Doctor*); Alphonse Martel (*Gen. St. Arnaud*); C. Montague Shaw (*Elderly Man*); Leonard Mudie (*Campaign Manager*); Jean Perry (*Umpire*); Robert Graves (*Official*); Christina Mantt (*Maid*); Anita Pike (*Julia*); Louis LaBey (*Servant*); Frank Lackteen (*Swami*); Alberto Morin (*Achmed*); Michael Visaroff, Louis Vincenot and Fred Malatesta (*Jewel Merchants*); Denis d'Auburn, Jerome De Nuccio and Tony Urchal (*Wrestlers*); Jean De Briac (*Engineer*); George Sorel (*Assistant*); Jacques Vanaire (*Old Engineer*).

Hollywood has never had any particular regard for truth over fiction when it comes to effective drama, and this was especially true in the Thirties, when filmmakers were so frequently preoccupied with movie biographies and costumed melodramatics. A prime example of this cavalier approach was the massive 1938 epic that Darryl F. Zanuck and Gene Markey produced under the title *Suez*. It purported to tell the story of Ferdinand de Lesseps (portrayed by Fox's Number One male glamour figure and box-office draw, 24-year-old Tyrone Power), the Parisian engineer who was 64 when he completed building the Panama Canal. But not in this account! Instead, we have the nobly-born young de Lesseps falling in love with a beàuteous young lady named Eugenie de Montijo (Loretta Young, teamed opposite Power for the fifth and final time). But Young is destined for greater things, as Empress Eugenie, the wife of France's Louis Napoleon (Leon Ames).

In Egypt, de Lesseps finds happiness anew, both with the country and the half-French, half-Egyptian daughter of a French soldier, Toni Pellerin (Annabella, the vivacious French actress who would become Mrs. Tyrone Power the following year). But, of course, he still loves Eugenie, who, by this time, has only become Napoleon's *mistress*. De Lesseps sees her again when he returns to Paris to seek financial support for his dream to build a canal linking the Mediterranean with the Red Sea as a shorter trade route to the East. Eugenie intercedes with

256

SUEZ: Tyrone Power, Loretta Young and players.

Napoleon on his behalf, but there's a lot more plot to this expensive motion picture before the climactic desert hurricane that kills Toni and wounds de Lesseps. In the aftermath of the storm, as our hero seems particularly despondent, word comes that Disraeli has been re-elected, and with it the assurance that British aid will soon be forthcoming.

Interviewed for Peter Bogdanovich's 1971 volume about his long directorial career, Allan Dwan recalled details of the famed cyclone sequence: "The special effects were unusually good. In one instance, I had to have a windstorm come up, blow away some buildings and actually blow the people through the air. So I got about a hundred of those huge airplane prop fans we use to make wind and lined them up. At first they were blowing sand, but I had to discard that because it would cut the skin off people, so instead we used ground up cereal that we threw in front of the blades. The people had to move through that all day long, and I'm telling you, that was an ordeal. Everybody got beaten up good—particularly Ty Power and Annabella. In one scene, he was supposed to be knocked unconscious, and she ties him to a post, and then the wind whips her away. We had to put her on a wire and fling her through the air. It was drastic."

Suez garnered Oscar nominations for J. Peverell

SUEZ: Annabella, Loretta Young and Tyrone Power.

257

Marley's fine photography and for the musical score by Louis Silvers, but the handsomeness of its $2-million production failed to sway the critics, whose contempt ranged from *The New York Times* ("a ponderously implausible description of how the Suez Canal came to be built by a dark-haired juvenile") to *Variety* ("misses out on its epic aims"). When *Suez* was released in France, the descendants of the real de Lesseps were so outraged that they sued Fox because of the extent that the film distorted historical facts (de Lesseps was 54 and a widower with five children when he first left France for Egypt, and never had an affair with the Empress Eugenie). Ruling that *Suez* had brought more honor to their country than dishonor to the de Lesseps family, a French court threw out the case altogether. And, to the relief of 20th Century-Fox, the international public lined up to see it.

SUEZ: Annabella and Tyrone Power.

IDIOT'S DELIGHT

1939

CREDITS

A Metro-Goldwyn-Mayer Picture. Producer: Hunt Stromberg. Director: Clarence Brown. Screenwriter: Robert E. Sherwood, based on his stage play. Cinematographer: William Daniels. Editor: Robert J. Kern. Art Directors: Cedric Gibbons and Wade Rubottom. Set Decorator: Edwin B. Willis. Gowns: Adrian. Music Director: Herbert Stothart. Song: Gus Kahn and Herbert Stothart. Choreographer: George King. Sound: Douglas Shearer. Montage: Slavko Vorkapich. Running Time: 105 minutes.

CAST

Norma Shearer (*Irene Fellara*); Clark Gable (*Harry Van*); Edward Arnold (*Achille Weber*); Charles Coburn (*Dr. Waldersee*); Joseph Schildkraut (*Captain Kirvline*); Burgess Meredith (*Quillery*); Pat Paterson (*Mrs. Cherry*); Skeets Gallagher (*Donald Navadel*); William Edmunds (*Dumptsey*); Laura Hope Crews (*Mme. Zuleika*); Virginia Grey (*Shirley Laughlin*); Fritz Feld (*Pittatek*); Edward Raquello (*Chiari*); Paula Stone (*Beulah Tremoyne*); Virginia Dale (*Francine Merle*); Joan Marsh (*Elaine Messiger*); Bernadene Hayes (*Edna Creesh*); Lorraine Krueger (*Bebe Gould*); Frank Orth (*Benny Zinssar*); Peter Willes (*Mr. Cherry*); George Sorel (*Majore*); Hobart Cavanaugh (*Frueheim, Theatre Manager*); Adolph Milar (*Fellara*); Clem Bevans (*Jimmy Barzek*); Claire McDowell (*Mother*); Emory Parnell (*Fifth Avenue Cop*); Robert Middlemass (*Hospital Commandant*); Evalyn Knapp (*Nurse*); Joe Yule (*Comic*); Mitchell Lewis (*Indian*); Eddie Gribbon (*Cop*); Jimmy Conlin (*Stagehand*); Buddy Messinger (*Usher*); Charles Judels (*Greek Restaurant Owner*); Paul Panzer (*Greek Chef*); E. Alyn Warren (*Clerk, Grand Hotel*); Frank Faylen (*Ed*); Frank M. Thomas (*Bert*); Gary Owen (*Newsstand Man*); Lee Phelps (*Train Announcer*); Francis McDonald (*Flight Captain*); Bernard Suss (*Auguste*); William Irving (*Sandro*); Harry Strang (*Sergeant*); Bud Geary (*Ambulance Driver*); Gertrude Bennett (*Woman with Powders*); Bonita Weber (*Woman with Catsup*); Rudolf Myzet (*Czech Announcer*).

Just before tackling the biggest film of his career, *Gone With the Wind*, Clark Gable helped usher in that banner year of 1939 by reuniting with Norma Shearer, his co-star of *A Free Soul* and *Strange Interlude*. Originally a one-set stage play, Robert E. Sherwood's *Idiot's Delight* opened on Broadway in March of 1936 as a flamboyant vehicle for the incomparable husband-and-wife team of Alfred Lunt and Lynn Fontanne. Described by critic Burns Man-

IDIOT'S DELIGHT: Clark Gable and Norma Shearer.

tle as "essentially a comedy with a definite overlay of philosophic conviction covering the war theme," the play ran a total of 299 performances and won a Pulitzer Prize as "the most distinguished play of the year by an American author, preferably dealing with an American theme."

(The Alan Jay Lerner-Charles Strouse musicalizing of it in 1983 as *Dance a Little Closer*, on the other hand, might go down as the least distinguished show of the century!)

Sherwood was engaged by MGM to adapt his play to the screen, and was called upon to make substantial alterations, devising a lengthy prologue, in which it's shown how the Gable and Shearer characters first meet, in the post-World War I period: she's a high-flying acrobat, and he's an enterprising vaudevillian who appears to alternate between hoofing and assisting an alcoholic old clairvoyant (Laura Hope Crews). Fate brings them together on the same variety bill in an Omaha theatre, and they spend a night together before going their separate show business ways.

IDIOT'S DELIGHT: Clark Gable and Norma Shearer.

When they meet again, it's in the European Alps in the late Thirties, where he's the leader of a six-girl song-and-dance act called Les Blondes, and she's the flamboyant, Russian-accented companion of a munitions tycoon (Edward Arnold). With Europe teetering on the brink of war, they're confined to the same mountaintop luxury hotel, because the Swiss border is temporarily closed to travelers. Issues of war, fascism and pacifism are exchanged among the guests and, in some cases, hotly debated, while occasional sirens remind everyone that just below them in the valley lies a giant military airport whose bombers await the signal to gear up for battle.

Our protagonists, of course, are romantically reunited before the fadeout, but not before unsettling issues of life and death are thoroughly aired, the munitions king walks out on his lady-friend, and Shearer finally abandons her somewhat Garboesque accent to admit to knowing Gable in that Omaha theatre. And, as strafing planes and falling bombs miraculously miss them, they sit down at the hotel piano to join their voices in the hymn "Abide with

IDIOT'S DELIGHT: Clark Gable and Laura Hope Crews.

260

IDIOT'S DELIGHT: Joseph Schildkraut, Norma Shearer and Edward Arnold.

Me." In the play, Lunt and Fontanne were obviously doomed. But such could hardly be the case in a 1939 MGM movie where, it was decided, audiences would never accept a downbeat ending. All of which leaves Gable and Shearer smiling through one of the strangest romantic comedy-dramas of either of their lengthy careers.

Yet, somehow, *Idiot's Delight*, with all its haranguing, moralizing and ruminations of war and peace, still entertains us some 50 years later, thanks largely to the collective charm of its stars. Gable gives a surprisingly lively, tongue-in-cheek performance, and even gets away with some lightweight hoofing, both in a male chorus and, with cane and boater, at the head of his all-girl troupe. Shearer has sometimes been criticized for the artificiality of her acting, but here it's perfectly appropriate, and she manages the Russian accent and its accompanying comportment with an abandon that suggests Greta Garbo, Gloria Swanson and (although they had yet to make themselves noticed on the international scene) the Gabor sisters. Despite the occasional knocking of this performance as a mere carbon of the Fontanne stage original, Shearer must be applauded for the sheer variety, cleverness and *chutzpah* of her performance. A generally underrated actress, especially nowadays, Shearer appears to her best advantage in *Idiot's Delight*. And director Clarence Brown, who had guided her and Gable through career milestones eight years earlier in *A Free Soul*, somehow brings it all off. Faced with the basic seriousness of Sherwood's play, Louis B. Mayer must have suffered some sleepless nights, wondering if it would all "work." But, of course, it does.

STAGECOACH: Claire Trevor and John Wayne.

STAGECOACH

1939

CREDITS

A United Artists Picture. A Walter Wanger Production. Director: John Ford. Screenwriter: Dudley Nichols. Based on the story *Stage to Lordsburg* by Ernest Haycox. Cinematographer: Bert Glennon. Editors: Otho Lovering, Dorothy Spencer and Walter Reynolds. Art Director: Alexander Toluboff. Set Decorator: Wiard B. Ihnen. Costumes: Walter Plunkett. Music Director: Boris Morros. Music Adaptors: Richard Hageman, Franke Harling, John Leipold and Leo Shuken. Special Effects: Ray Binger. Second Unit Director: Yakima Canutt. Assistant Director: Wingate Smith. Running Time: 96 minutes.

CAST

Claire Trevor (*Dallas*); John Wayne (*The Ringo Kid*); John Carradine (*Hatfield*); Thomas Mitchell (*Dr. Josiah Boone*); Andy Devine (*Buck*); Donald Meek (*Samuel Peacock*); Louise Platt (*Lucy Mallory*); Tim Holt (*Lieutenant Blanchard*); George Bancroft (*Sheriff Curly Wilcox*); Berton Churchill (*Henry Gatewood*); Tom Tyler (*Hank Plummer*); Chris-Pin Martin (*Chris*); Elvira Rios (*Yakima, his Wife*); Francis Ford (*Billy Pickett*); Marga Daighton (*Mrs. Pickett*); Kent Odell (*Billy Pickett, Jr.*); Yakima Canutt (*Cavalry Scout*); Chief Big Tree (*Indian Scout*); Harry Tenbrook (*Telegraph Operator*); Cornelius Keefe (*Captain Whitney*); Walter McGrail (*Captain Sickels*); Brenda Fowler (*Mrs. Gatewood*); Louis Mason (*Sheriff*); Florence Lake (*Mrs. Nancy Whitney*); Joseph Rickson (*Ike Plummer*); Vestor Pegg (*Hank Plummer*); Paul McVey (*Express Agent*); Jack Pennick (*Jerry the Bartender*); William Hoffer (*Sergeant*); Bryant Washburn (*Captain Simmons*); Nora Cecil (*Dr. Boone's Housekeeper*); Helen Gibson and Dorothy Appleby (*Dance Hall Girls*); Buddy Roosevelt and Bill Cody (*Cowboys*); Chief White Horse (*Geronimo*); Duke Lee (*Sheriff of Lordsburg*); Mary Kathleen Walker (*Lucy's Baby*); Ed Brady (*Saloon Keeper*); Robert E. Homans (*Editor in Lordsburg*); Franklyn Farnum (*Deputy*); Jim Mason (*Jim the Expressman*); Merrill McCormick (*Ogler*); Artie Ortega (*Barfly in Lordsburg*).

John Ford's *Stagecoach* has achieved the status of greatness in the 50 years since its release, as well as its rightful designation as a landmark Western. It also set the pattern for Westerns to come, not only establishing John Ford as a great director of the genre (he hadn't done a Western since the silent *Three Bad*

STAGECOACH: Andy Devine, George Bancroft, John Carradine, Donald Meek, Louise Platt, Claire Trevor and John Wayne.

Men in 1926), but also making a star out of John Wayne, who had spent the decade performing mostly in B-Westerns, following bit parts in several of Ford's early talkies. Wayne's only previous A-Western was 1930's expensive fiasco *The Big Trail*. When Ford started casting *Stagecoach*, he fought to get Wayne for the leading role, despite producer Walter Wanger's pushing for Gary Cooper. But Ford's faith in Wayne won out, and the pair would team again on no less than 13 subsequent occasions—mostly Westerns.

Stagecoach's storyline is simple and by now quite familiar. For various reasons, nine strangers (seven within and two atop) are thrown together on a perilous coach trip over the dusty desert trails from Tonto, New Mexico through Monument Valley to Lordsburg, Arizona. Before their departure, they are warned that the dreaded Apache chief Geronimo is on the warpath again, and that they're taking their lives into their own hands if they board the stagecoach.

Yet each has a reason to proceed on the journey: Dallas (Claire Trevor), the fancy lady being booted out of town by the self-righteous female citizens; Dr. Josiah Boone (Thomas Mitchell), the alcoholic physician no one wants to entrust with his life; Samuel Peacock (Donald Meek), the timid little traveling liquor salesman; Hatfield (John Carradine), the slightly sinister gambler with the Southern-gentleman manners; Lucy Mallory (Louise Platt), the pregnant wife willing to cross the rugged country to be with her Army officer husband; Mr. Gatewood (Berton Churchill), the banker absconding with a suspicious-looking satchel; Buck (Andy Devine), the cheerful stagecoach driver; Sheriff Wilcox (George Bancroft), who's riding shotgun with Buck; and the Ringo Kid (John Wayne), a cowboy recently escaped from prison. The stage comes upon Ringo in the desert wilderness where a lame horse abandoned him during his getaway; Sheriff Wilcox makes him a prisoner and seats him among the coach passengers.

263

There's nothing new about the dramatic device of throwing disparate souls together in a dangerous situation to see what will happen. But Ford invests the stagecoach journey with such interesting turns of character and event that even the Western-weary critics of 1939 sat up and took notice. Not only was United Artists successful in booking *Stagecoach* into New York's prestigious show palace, Radio City Music Hall, but reviewers gave it long and thoughtful coverage. In *The New York Times*, Frank S. Nugent wrote, "In one superbly expansive gesture . . . John Ford has swept aside 10 years of artifice and talkie compromise and has made a motion picture that sings a song of the camera." *Variety*'s critic said, "In maintaining a tensely dramatic pace all the way, Ford still injects numerous comedy situations, and throughout sketches his characters with sincerity and humaneness. It's absorbing drama without the general theatrics usual to picturizations of the early West." Nearly four decades later, the hard-to-please Pauline Kael called *Stagecoach*, "Perhaps the most likable of all Westerns, and a *Grand Hotel*-on-wheels movie that has just about everything—adventure, romance, chivalry—and all of it very simple and traditional."

Released in a year of great competition from every quarter, the movie only copped two Oscars—for Best Supporting Actor (Thomas Mitchell, whose performance as Scarlett's father in the same year's *Gone With the Wind* must also have influenced the voters) and Best Score. But *Stagecoach* was also nominated for Best Picture, Best Director, and for Art Direction, Film Editing and Bert Glennon's Black-and-White Cinematography of the awe-inspiring Southwestern locations.

In 1966, 20th Century-Fox produced a brightly colored but forgettable CinemaScope remake of *Stagecoach* with Ann-Margret, Alex Cord and Bing Crosby in the Trevor, Wayne and Mitchell roles. And, never a town to stop trying to improve on a classic, Hollywood tried again in 1986, and came up with a third *Stagecoach*, this time made for TV, with country singers Willie Nelson and Johnny Cash and, in the reformed-sinner romantic leads, Kris Kristofferson and Elizabeth Ashley. But it only left one anxious to go back and revisit the 1939 original.

STAGECOACH: Thomas Mitchell, Claire Trevor and Louise Platt.

MIDNIGHT

1939

CREDITS

A Paramount Picture. Producer: Arthur Hornblow, Jr. Director: Mitchell Leisen. Screenwriters: Charles Brackett and Billy Wilder. Based on an original screen story by Edwin Justus Mayer and Franz Schulz. Cinematographer: Charles Lang, Jr. Editor: Doane Harrison. Art Directors: Hans Dreier and Robert Usher. Special Effects: Farciot Edouart. Claudette Colbert's Costumes: Irene. Music and Lyrics: Ralph Freed and Frederick Hollander. Running Time: 92 minutes.

CAST

Claudette Colbert (*Eve Peabody*/"*Baroness Czerny*"); Don Ameche (*Tibor Czerny*); John Barrymore (*Georges Flammarion*); Francis Lederer (*Jacques Picot*); Mary Astor (*Helene Flammarion*); Elaine Barrie (*Simone*); Hedda Hopper (*Stephanie*); Rex O'Malley (*Marcel*); Monty Woolley (*Judge*); Armand Kaliz (*Lebon*); Lionel Pape (*Edouart*); Ferdinand Munier and Gennaro Curci (*Major Domos*); Leander deCordova, William Eddritt, Michael Visaroff and Joseph Romantini (*Footmen*); Carlos De Valdez (*Butler*); Joseph De Stefani (*Head Porter*); Arno Frey (*Room Clerk*); Eugene Borden (*First Porter*); Paul Bryar (*Second Porter*); Leonard Sues (*Bellboy*); Robert Graves (*Doorman*); Eddy Conrad (*Prince Potopienko*); Elspeth Dudgeon (*Dowager*); Helen St. Rayner (*Coloratura*); Billy Daniels (*Roger*); Bryant Washburn (*Guest*); Max Luckey (*Lawyer*); Alexander Leftwich (*Court Clerk*); Donald Reed (*Ferdinand*); Louis Mercier (*Leon*); Nestor Paiva (*Woman's Escort*); Harry Semels (*Policeman*); Harry Vejar (*Garageman*); Judith King and Joyce Mathews (*Girls*).

If it had been released during any year but 1939—Hollywood's all-time vintage year for fine motion pictures—*Midnight* would surely have won some awards. As it was, this movie that in retrospect has been called director Mitchell Leisen's "masterpiece" and "one of the authentic delights of the Thirties," failed to win a single Oscar nomination. It nevertheless remains the favorite film of its brilliant star Claudette Colbert.

Working from the original story by Edwin Justus Mayer and Franz Schulz, screenwriters Charles Brackett and Billy Wilder devised the wonderful role of Eve Peabody. Barbara Stanwyck was originally slated for the part until a conflict in schedules (Paramount's loaning her to Columbia for *Golden Boy*)

MIDNIGHT: John Barrymore and Claudette Colbert.

MIDNIGHT: Francis Lederer, Mary Astor, Rex O'Malley, Claudette Colbert and John Barrymore.

265

MIDNIGHT: Francis Lederer, Claudette Colbert, Mary Astor, Rex O'Malley and Don Ameche.

necessitated her replacement with Colbert. Undoubtedly, the switch was fortuitous. Colbert and Leisen were already a proven star-director success and, as Paramount's then biggest box-office attraction, her casting enabled the studio the luxury of a $1 million-plus budget and the benefit of a splendid supporting cast that included Don Ameche, John Barrymore, Mary Astor and Francis Lederer.

Midnight's plot is delightfully amusing. Eve Peabody (Colbert) is a showgirl somehow stranded in Paris, bereft of everything save her wits, her guile and a gold lamé evening gown. Early on, fate throws her together with Tibor Czerny (Ameche), a worldly Hungarian taxi driver who treats her to dinner. In the hope of bettering her lot, Eve crashes what turns out to be a boring musicale held by a socialite (Hedda Hopper). There she is befriended by wealthy George Flammarion (Barrymore), whose wife Helene (Mary Astor) is present, along with *her* lover Jacques Picot (Lederer). Noticing the latter's interest in Eve, Flammarion engages her to lure Jacques away from Helene. Eventually all turn up at the Flammarion country estate near Versailles where Eve poses as "Countess Czerny," and the taxi driver joins them in the guise of Eve's husband, "Count Czerny." Additional whacky complications follow at a dressy evening affair, with the principals dancing from an hilarious conga line into a Parisian courtroom, where relationships are properly sorted out. The Flammarions reconfirm their marriage vows,

266

and Czerny, who really is a count but drives taxis for his own enjoyment, appears headed for a wedding with Eve.

In David Chierichetti's fine biography of Mitchell Leisen, Claudette Colbert later described her *Midnight* director: "He was not a 'Svengali' director, ever. He never imposed his will on any player that I can recall. He left the acting to the actors, who presumably knew their job. He would suggest perhaps 'a little more of that' or 'a little less,' and he knew exactly when it was right." Not that Leisen always had an easy time of it with *Midnight*. The declining John Barrymore's inability (refusal?) to learn his lines necessitated his reading them from "idiot cards" held just off camera; Mary Astor's increasingly apparent pregnancy made masking her body imperative; and Claudette Colbert's famed left-profile-only obsession meant that Leisen had his hands full in the construction of sets and the devising of camera movement. But apparently Leisen never objected: "I didn't fight with her about it. I always said that if an actress is satisfied with the way she looks in a picture, she can give her full attention to her acting." It was an attitude that obviously paid off. Likening Leisen's directorial touch to that of famed sophisticated-comedy master Ernst Lubitsch, *The New York Times* called *Midnight* "one of the liveliest, gayest, wittiest and naughtiest comedies of a long hard season."

Unfortunately, the same couldn't be said for Leisen's 1946 remake, *Masquerade In Mexico*, which is at best remembered for Ann Dvorak's expert performance in the Mary Astor role and Dorothy Lamour's stylish wardrobe.

MIDNIGHT: Claudette Colbert, Francis Lederer, Mary Astor, Rex O'Malley, Elaine Barrie, Lionel Pape, Billy Daniels and John Barrymore.

267

GOLDEN BOY

1939

CREDITS

A Columbia Picture. Producer: William Perlberg. Director: Rouben Mamoulian. Screenwriters: Lewis Meltzer, Daniel Taradash, Sarah Y. Mason and Victor Heerman. Based on the play by Clifford Odets. Cinematographers: Nick Musuraca and Karl Freund. Editor: Otto Meyer. Sound: George Cooper. Music: Victor Young. Costumes: Kalloch. Art Director: Lionel Banks. Montage: Donald W. Starling. Running Time: 99 minutes.

CAST

Barbara Stanwyck (*Lorna Moon*); Adolphe Menjou (*Tom Moody*); William Holden (*Joe Bonaparte*); Lee J. Cobb (*Mr. Bonaparte*); Joseph Calleia (*Eddie Fuseli*); Sam Levene (*Siggie*); Edward S. Brophy (*Roxy Lewis*); Beatrice Blinn (*Anna*); William H. Strauss (*Mr. Carp*); Don Beddoe (*Borneo*); Frank Jenks (*Pepper White*); Charles Halton (*Newspaperman*); John Wray (*Manager-Barker*); Clinton Rosemond (*Father*); James "Cannonball" Green (*Chocolate Drop*); Robert Sterling (*Elevator Boy*); Bob Ryan and Charles Sullivan (*Referees*); John Harmon and George Lloyd (*Gamblers*); Thomas Garland (*Fighter*); Charles Lane (*Drake*); Harry Tyler (*Mickey*); Stanley Andrews (*Driscoll*); Alex Melesh (*Stranger*); Minerva Urecal (*Costumer*); Eddie Fetherston (*Wilson*); Lee Phelps (*Announcer*); Larry McGrath (*Referee*); Sam Hayes (*Broadcaster*); Alfred Grant (*Daniel*); Mickey Golden, Gordon Armitage and Joe Gray (*Fighters*); Bruce Mitchell (*Guard*); Earl Askam (*Cop*); Irving Cohen (*Ex-Pug*).

Clifford Odets' play *Golden Boy* had scored a Broadway run of 250 performances during the 1937–38 season. A Group Theatre effort, it featured Luther Adler as the prizefighter-musician hero; Frances Farmer (on sabbatical from moviemaking) as the fight-manager's girl friend; Roman Bohnen as the boxing entrepreneur, and such up-and-coming "method" actors (and future directors) as Lee J. Cobb, Elia Kazan, Martin Ritt and Jules (soon to become famous as "John") Garfield.

Columbia Pictures bought the screen rights and assigned its direction to Rouben Mamoulian, whose films had ranged from the harshly realistic (*Applause* and *City Streets*) to the romantic (*Queen Christina*) and the tuneful (*High, Wide and Handsome*). Barbara Stanwyck and Adolphe Menjou were set for the respective roles of mistress and fight-manager, but

GOLDEN BOY: Barbara Stanwyck and William Holden.

the difficult title role of Joe Bonaparte remained to be filled. Many actors, both established and unknown, were tested for this character that required an amalgam of sensitivity and toughness. Where to find an actor who could convince audiences that he was both a skilled violinist and a formidable contender in the boxing ring? Broadway's Richard Carlson nearly had the role when, against the objections of Columbia chief Harry Cohn, Mamoulian picked William Holden, a Paramount bit player who had appeared briefly in *Prison Farm* and *Million Dollar Legs*. Holden was very green as an actor and had a tough uphill battle to succeed in the role. But he spent his offscreen hours working hard: on his acting, his boxing and his musicianship. He always gave credit to Stanwyck, not only for giving freely of her time and acting knowledge, but also for interceding on his behalf when it seemed Columbia would replace him. Ultimately he came through with an amazing performance for such a novice. Years later

GOLDEN BOY: William Holden, Don Beddoe, Adolphe Menjou and Barbara Stanwyck.

GOLDEN BOY: Barbara Stanwyck, William Holden, Adolphe Menjou and Joseph Calleia.

the actor said, "I don't think there's anyone who has done more for me in my career than Barbara Stanwyck."

Since Odets was unavailable to adapt his play to the screen, Columbia engaged no less than *four* writers to do the job. In the transition, some of the drama's political harangues were either softened or eliminated, and the original tragic ending was altered, allowing Joe Bonaparte to survive and get the girl. Naturally, the boxing scenes were, by the very nature of the medium, rendered more convincing on film. It is here that Mamoulian turns out some of the movie's most authentic moments.

As Lorna Moon, the tough "dame from Newark," who's more than just a "girl Friday" to fight-boss Menjou (he can't marry her until his wife grants him a divorce), Stanwyck is in excellent form. Blunt and without illusions, she is clearly a woman who knows the score. When Menjou takes on the young boxer Joe Bonaparte, she agrees to use her allure to help persuade him to stay in the fight game, and not return to the violin his father wants Joe to master. And when Joe falls in love with Lorna, and she with him, the lady softens, and her surface toughness gives way to a tenderness that Stanwyck's art makes wholly convincing.

269

In the story's climax, Joe wins the big fight, but accidentally kills his opponent. This convinces him to leave the ring. "I wanted to conquer myself," he tells Lorna, "but instead I smashed myself." Her response is a typical Stanwyck line, delivered with all the earthy sincerity the actress can muster: "Nothing can stop you when you do what's in your heart."

Much of *Golden Boy* now seems oversimplified and unnecessarily sentimental, particularly in Lee J. Cobb's overwrought performance as Joe's "you-a good-a boy" Italian father. But it retains solid virtues in the authentic fight scenes and in the performances of the pros: Stanwyck, Menjou and Joseph

Calleia. With its downbeat Depression-era backgrounds, the film didn't go over with 1939's audiences as well as expected. But it made a star of 21-year-old William Holden, thanks to the intervention of Stanwyck, who coached the young actor patiently every night on the next day's scenes. According to reports, Holden continued to remember Stanwyck's kindness annually for the rest of his life by sending her roses on the anniversary of *Golden Boy*'s starting date.

In a year too rich with vintage motion pictures to allow accolades to more than a few, *Golden Boy* won no awards; but it did garner one nomination—for Victor Young's original score.

GOLDEN BOY: Lee J. Cobb, William Holden, Beatrice Blinn, Sam Levene, Barbara Stanwyck and William H. Strauss.

THE OLD MAID

1939

CREDITS

A Warner Bros. Picture. Producers: Hal B. Wallis and Henry Blanke. Director: Edmund Goulding. Screenwriter: Casey Robinson. Based on the play by Zoë Akins and the novel by Edith Wharton. Cinematographer: Tony Gaudio. Editor: George Amy. Music: Max Steiner. Art Director: Robert Haas. Costumes: Orry-Kelly. Running Time: 95 minutes.

CAST

Bette Davis (*Charlotte Lovell*); Miriam Hopkins (*Delia Lovell*); George Brent (*Clem Spender*); Jane Bryan (*Tina*); Donald Crisp (*Dr. Lanskell*); Louise Fazenda (*Dora*); James Stephenson (*Jim Ralston*); Jerome Cowan (*Joe Ralston*); William Lundigan (*Lanning Halsey*); Cecilia Loftus (*Grandmother*); Rand Brooks (*Jim*); Janet Shaw (*Dee*); William Hopper (*John*); Marlene Burnett (*Tina as a Child*); Rod Cameron (*Man*); Doris Lloyd (*Aristocratic Maid*); Frederick Burton (*Mr. Halsey*).

Based on a novelette by Edith Wharton, Zoë Akins' 1935 Broadway play was awarded the Pulitzer Prize for drama and, in so doing, raised controversy among the New York critics, who thought the play unworthy of that honor—especially in a year that also produced Lillian Hellman's powerful *The Children's Hour*. As a result, the Drama Critics Circle was formed in order to make its own annual awards.

As a stage play, *The Old Maid* isn't very good. But, with seasoned Broadway professionals Helen Mencken and Judith Anderson as the leading antagonists, it achieved considerable popularity in its day, especially among women—which was reason enough for Warner Bros. purchasing the vehicle for their leading dramatic actress Bette Davis. Apparently, it was decided that Davis was well suited to costume pictures, for three out of her four 1939 films were period pieces. After winning an Oscar for her Southern vixen in 1938's *Jezebel*, there was only the contemporary *Dark Victory* to offer her modern dress, before the long-skirted sequence of *Juarez*, *The Old Maid* and *The Private Lives of Elizabeth and Essex*.

Although it's unfathomable how Akins' Wharton adaptation could have copped any awards, Casey Robinson's screenplay was a definite improvement.

THE OLD MAID: Miriam Hopkins and Bette Davis.

Guided by Edmund Goulding's firm, assured direction, and with a controlled Bette Davis suffering superbly through an unfulfilled love affair (with George Brent), unwed motherhood and aging spinsterhood (Davis's first screen delineation of an "older" woman), the result was a four-handkerchief picture. Warners had bought the property from Paramount, obviously realizing its strong potential for Davis and, cast as cousin and romantic rival, Miriam Hopkins. Although this was the first time they had co-starred in a movie, the two ladies had shared their theatrical early days in Rochester, New York, where Hopkins had been the star and Davis the ingenue of the George Cukor-George Kondolf Stock Company in 1928.

THE OLD MAID: Marlene Burnett, Donald Crisp and Bette Davis.

As originally written, Delia Lovell was a selfish and conniving woman. However, as played by Hopkins, the character now seems gentler and more charming. Davis says Hopkins loathed the idea of playing such an unsympathetic character, and made the picture living hell for Davis by continually trying to upstage her, spoiling take after take of Davis'

major scenes with trivial interruptions, and by her generally unprofessional behavior. "Miriam is a perfectly charming woman, socially," Davis has said. But she adds, "Working with her is another story." Paul Muni and Edward G. Robinson are among the other Hopkins co-stars who shared those sentiments.

But, of course, such rivalry tends to produce results on a motion picture screen, and *The Old Maid* scarcely suffers from its behind-the-scenes problems. In fact, Warner Bros. had the inspiration to re-team Davis and Hopkins as on-screen rivals four years later in *Old Acquaintance*. Davis attributes their working problems to misplaced envy on her co-star's part, generously recalling, "She was more than capable of holding her own. She finally ruined her career because of this. No one would work with her. It was too exhausting."

As expected, Bette Davis disappointed no one. Her Charlotte Lovell is a richly detailed portrait of an essentially loving woman who is hardened by circumstances into a sour, disapproving spinster. Young actresses learning their craft would be wise to study Davis in this film: swaying to an inaudible waltz after she hears her illegitimate daughter Tina (Jane Bryan)—who believes Charlotte to be her maiden *aunt*—exclaim angrily that "*she's* never danced!"; in a staircase confrontation with her cousin Delia on Tina's wedding day ("Tonight she belongs to me! Tonight I want her to call me

THE OLD MAID: Bette Davis and Miriam Hopkins.

Freedman and Anita Loos. Based on the musical play by Richard Rodgers and Lorenz Hart. Cinematographer: Ray June. Editor: Frank Sullivan. Art Director: Merrill Pye. Set Decorator: Edwin B. Willis. Costumes: Dolly Tree. Songs: "Babes in Arms," "Where or When" and "The Lady Is a Tramp" by Rodgers and Hart; "You Are My Lucky Star" and "Good Morning" by Arthur Freed and Nacio Herb Brown; "I Cried for You" by Arthur Freed, Gus Arnheim and Abe Lyman; "God's Country" by E.Y. Harburg and Harold Arlen. Music Director: George Stoll. Music Adapter: Roger Edens. Orchestrators: Conrad Salinger and Leo Arnaud. Running Time: 96 minutes.

CAST

Mickey Rooney (*Mickey Moran*); Judy Garland (*Patsy Barton*); Charles Winninger (*Joe Moran*); Guy Kibbee (*Judge Black*); June Preisser (*Rosalie Essex*); Grace Hayes (*Florrie Moran*); Betty Jaynes (*Molly Moran*); Douglas McPhail (*Don Brice*); Rand Brooks (*Jeff Steele*); Leni Lynn (*Dody Martini*); John Sheffield (*Bobs*); Henry Hull (*Madox*); Barnett Parker (*William*); Ann Shoemaker (*Mrs. Barton*); Margaret Hamilton (*Martha Steele*); Joseph Crehan (*Mr. Essex*); George McKay (*Brice*); Henry Roquemore (*Shaw*); Lelah Tyler (*Mrs. Brice*); Lon McCallister (*Boy*); Sidney Miller (*Sid*).

mother!"); and finally exchanging good-byes with the girl who will never know the truth about the "old maid."

The Old Maid was brought to the screen by director Edmund Goulding and screenwriter Casey Robinson, the team responsible for Bette Davis's earlier 1939 triumph in *Dark Victory*. And it's a credit to Goulding's tactful guidance that, despite their differences, both Hopkins and Davis deliver performances of skill and contrast, though neither won an Academy Award nomination for work here. As for the picture, it proved another solid hit for Warner Bros.

BABES IN ARMS

1939

CREDITS

A Metro-Goldwyn-Mayer Picture. Producer: Arthur Freed. Director: Busby Berkeley. Screenwriters: Jack McGowan, Kay Van Riper and (uncredited) Florence Ryerson, Edgar Allan Woolf, Noel Langley, Joe Laurie, John Meehan, Sid Silvers, Walter DeLeon, Irving Brecher, Ben

BABES IN ARMS: Judy Garland and Mickey Rooney.

273

BABES IN ARMS: Mickey Rooney, Douglas McPhail and Judy Garland.

Babes in Arms is the quintessential "let's put on a show" Thirties film-musical. It marked the producing debut of lyricist Arthur Freed, whose unit at Metro would be responsible for the best musicals that studio would turn out up through 1960's Bells Are Ringing. And it also marked the MGM debut of Busby Berkeley, the director-choreographer responsible for the revolutionary look of all those great (and some not-so-great) Warner Bros. musicals for which 42nd Street set the style in 1933.

Babes in Arms featured a young and talented cast of "song-and-dancers," with more than a few seasoned veterans bringing up the rear. But it's 19-year-old Mickey Rooney, with his varied musical talents, finely tuned ability to switch between comedy and drama, and even perform expert impersonations of Clark Gable and Lionel Barrymore, who runs away with the movie. It has been reported that Mickey's tremendous energy so far outdistanced that of his co-star Judy Garland that Berkeley had to badger her considerably to get the performance now preserved on film. Judy, it seems, relied more on her natural talents. She disliked rehearsing and didn't respond well to a disciplined taskmaster like Berkeley. She and Mickey had teamed before, but never in a big musical; and the huge success of this one paved the way for their delightful vehicles to come: Strike Up the Band, Babes on Broadway and Girl Crazy.

Although based on a Broadway hit, Babes in Arms adhered only loosely to the premise of the stage

vehicle, retaining but three of the great Rodgers and Hart songs. Inexplicably, the film omitted such memorable melodies as "Johnny One Note," "My Funny Valentine" and "I Wish I Were in Love Again." MGM had decided to structure Babes in Arms to showcase the incredible versatility and talent of Mickey Rooney. While Judy Garland did not go unappreciated, this film is more Mickey's than hers. Some 50 years after its premiere, it remains a landmark musical of refreshing entertainment.

The storyline is simple. In a brief prologue, it is 1921 and vaudevillians Joe and Florrie Morgan (Charles Winninger and Grace Hayes) become parents to a son born backstage during a variety engagement. The film smoothly integrates childhood footage of Rooney himself performing in vaudeville to depict the growing-up years of the cinematic Mickey. The viewer easily makes the transition to the late-Thirties, when most of the film's action takes place. With the entertainment inroads of talking pictures, sources of employment have almost completely dried up for Mickey's parents. Mickey and his sister Molly (Betty Jaynes, a talented young soprano) and a group of their friends, one of whom is Patsy (Judy Garland), but all of whom are also the offspring of former showfolk, band together to stage a show of their own.

There are setbacks: a local busybody (Margaret Hamilton), knowing that the youngsters' parents are away on a musical tour, tries to have the local judge (Guy Kibbee) place them in a trade school, "for their own good." But the sympathetic judge gives the kids a month to show what they can do, and Mickey sets about writing and devising a vehicle to showcase their collective talents. A former child star, Rosalie Essex (blonde and totally obnoxious June Preisser) sweet-talks Mickey into giving her Patsy's part in his show if she (Rosalie) will provide the backing they need. Patsy is put into the humiliating position of understudy. At the eleventh hour, Rosalie pulls out of the show and Patsy gets her chance, only to have their opening ruined by a violent thunderstorm.

The movie's close is as charming as it is unreal: a New York producer, who's an old friend of Mickey's father, offers Mickey the opportunity to mount his show on Broadway, with his dad as consultant. So, of course, Babes in Arms closes in a burst of Berkeley-inspired production numbers. The big "God's Country" finale alone cost MGM a reported $32,970, with the addition of 61 dancers, 10 added extras and 20 musicians.

A hit with both the press and the public, Babes in Arms pulled in a box-office gross of $3,335,000 on its first release. Its production costs: $748,000. And it

BABES IN ARMS: Mickey Rooney, Judy Garland and female chorus.

garnered Oscar nominations for Rooney as Best Actor and for the scoring of Roger Edens and George E. Stoll. However, the one *winner* was Garland, who (like Mickey in 1938) received a special statuette "for her outstanding performance as a screen juvenile during the past year."

UNION PACIFIC

1939

CREDITS

A Paramount Picture. Executive Producer: William LeBaron. Producer/Director: Cecil B. DeMille. Associate Producer: William H. Pine; Screenwriters: Walter De-Leon, C. Gardner Sullivan, Jesse Lasky, Jr. and Jack Cunningham. Based on the novel *Trouble Shooter* by Ernest Haycox. Cinematographers: Victor Milner and Dewey Wrigley. Editor: Anne Bauchens. Sound: Harry Lindgren and John Cope. Musical Score: George Antheil, Sigmund Krumgold and John Leipold. Art Direction: Hans Dreier and Roland Anderson. Set Decoration: A.E. Freudeman. Costumes: Natalie Visart. Special Effects: Farciot Edouart, Gordon Jennings and Loren L. Ryder. Second-Unit Photography: Harry Hallenberger. Second-Unit Director: Arthur Rosson. Running Time: 135 minutes.

CAST

Barbara Stanwyck (*Mollie Monahan*); Joel McCrea (*Jeff Butler*); Akim Tamiroff (*Fiesta*); Robert Preston (*Dick Allen*); Lynne Overman (*Leach Overmile*); Brian Donlevy (*Sid Campeau*); Robert Barrat (*Duke Ring*); Anthony Quinn (*Cordray*); Stanley Ridges (*Casement*); Henry Kolker (*Asa M. Barrows*); Francis McDonald (*Grenville M. Dodge*); Willard Robertson (*Oakes Ames*); Harold Goodwin (*Calvin*); Evelyn Keyes (*Mrs. Calvin*); Richard Lane (*Sam Reed*); William Haade (*Dusky Clayton*); Regis Toomey (*Paddy O'Rourke*); Fuzzy Knight (*Cookie*); Lon Chaney, Jr. (*Dollarhide*); Joseph Crehan (*General U.S. Grant*); Sheila Darcy (*Rose*); Julia Faye (*Mame*); Joseph Sawyer (*Shamus*);

UNION PACIFIC: Joining the railroads.

UNION PACIFIC: Joel McCrea,
Barbara Stanwyck and Robert
Preston.

UNION PACIFIC: Robert Preston, Joel McCrea and Brian Donlevy.

UNION PACIFIC: Barbara Stanwyck.

278

John Marston (*Dr. Durant*); Morgan Wallace (*Senator Smith*); Byron Foulger (*Whipple*); Selmer Jackson (*Jerome*); May Beatty (*Mrs. Hogan*); Ernie Adams (*General Sheridan*); Stanley Andrews (*Dr. Harkness*); Jack Pennick (*Harmonica Player*); J.M. Kerrigan (*Monahan*); Harry Woods (*Al Brett*); Dick Alexander, Max Davidson, Oscar G. Hendrian and Jim Pierce (*Card Players*); Walter Long (*Irishman*); Monte Blue (*Indian*); John Merton (*Laborer*); Jim Farley (*Paddy*); Buddy Roosevelt (*Fireman*); Richard Denning and David Newell (*Reporters*); Chief Thundercloud, Ray Mala, Iron Eyes Cody, Sonny Chorre, Gregg Whitespear, Richard Robles and Tony Urchel (*Indian Braves*); Earl Askam (*Bluett*); Russell Hicks (*Sergeant*); William J. Worthington (*Oliver Ames*); Guy Usher (*Leland Stanford*); James McNamara (*Mr. Mills*); Gus Glassmire (*Governor Stafford*); Paul Everton (*Rev. Dr. Tadd*); Frank Yaconelli (*Accordion Player*); Elmo Lincoln (*Card Player*); Syd Saylor (*Barker*); Lane Chandler (*Conductor*); Nestor Paiva (*C.P. Conductor*).

Cecil B. DeMille's considerable reputation as producer-director of epic spectacles owed everything to his painstaking flair for the Big Effect, be it via Biblical stories, Westerns or such lesser, oddly diverse offerings as *Dynamite* (1929), *Four Frightened People* (1934) and *The Greatest Show on Earth* (1952). In the latter half of the Thirties, C.B. turned from ancient history to Americana, with *The Plainsman* (1937), *The Buccaneer* (1938) and *Union Pacific*, his large-scale 1939 saga of the first transcontinental railroad and how it came to be.

The story a battery of writers reworked from the prolific Western novelist Ernest Haycox's *Trouble Shooter* is set in 1868 on a train moving west from St. Louis, with Barbara Stanwyck (who replaced Jean Arthur) as Mollie Monahan, the spunky Irish daughter of Union Pacific Railroad engineer (J.M. Kerrigan) and the tracklayers' postmistress. Mollie finds adventure and romance with both rugged troubleshooter Jeff Butler (Joel McCrea) and quick-triggered gambler Dick Allen (Robert Preston)—and much danger from marauding Indians en-route to California.

Characteristic of DeMille, whose last black-and-white film this was, Technicolor was the only expense spared in making his Western "big" in every possible sense. Its action sequences, including spectacular train wrecks and Indian sieges, and its colorful characters were what audiences had been led to expect of a DeMille picture, and in 1939, *Union Pacific* was immensely popular.

As Mollie, Stanwyck delivers a performance that is honest, engaging and full of energy. With her voice pitched higher than usual, she employs an Irish brogue a good bit thicker than the one drawn from her by John Ford three years earlier for Sean

O'Casey's *The Plough and the Stars*. She gives it a good try here, but the accent occasionally gets in the way of her line-readings.

In his *Autobiography*, DeMille, understandably reluctant to name his favorite among the actresses he had directed, nevertheless paid Stanwyck high tribute: "I would have to say that I have never worked with an actress who was more cooperative, less temperamental, and a better workman, to use my term of highest compliment, than Barbara Stanwyck." Despite that praise, DeMille never used her again.

Union Pacific's second-unit director Arthur Rosson shot the picture's outdoor action segments in Iron Springs, Utah, including the tracklaying and derailment scenes, as well as the Indian raids. The effectiveness of these sequences won the film an Academy Award nomination for special effects, but the Oscar went, deservedly, to *The Rains Came*.

Union Pacific was accorded a star-studded premiere in Omaha, Nebraska—where that railway line started. The movie not only played well in Omaha, but it became so big a money-maker that Paramount accorded DeMille complete freedom on all of his future productions.

NINOTCHKA

1939

CREDITS

A Metro-Goldwyn-Mayer Picture. Producer/Director: Ernst Lubitsch. Screenwriters: Charles Brackett, Billy Wilder and Walter Reisch. Based on a story by Melchior Lengyel. Cinematographer: William Daniels. Editor: Gene Ruggiero. Art Directors: Cedric Gibbons and Randall Duell. Set Decorator: Edwin B. Willis. Costumes: Adrian. Sound: Douglas Shearer. Music: Werner Heymann. Assistant Director: Horace Hough. Running Time: 110 minutes.

CAST

Greta Garbo (*Lena "Ninotchka" Yakushova*); Melvyn Douglas (*Count Leon Dolga*); Ina Claire (*Grand Duchess Swana*); Sig Rumann (*Michael Iranoff*); Felix Bressart (*Buljanoff*); Alexander Granach (*Kopalski*); Bela Lugosi (*Commissar Razinin*); Gregory Gaye (*Count Alexis Rakonin*); Richard Carle (*Vaston*); Edwin Maxwell (*Mercier*); Rolfe Sedan (*Hotel Manager*); George Tobias (*Russian Visa Official*); Dorothy Adams (*Jacqueline, Swana's Maid*); Charles Judels (*Pere Mathieu, the Cafe Owner*); Lawrence Grant (*General Savitsky*); Frank Reicher and Edwin Stanley (*Lawyers*); Peggy Moran (*French Maid*); Mary Forbes (*Lady*

NINOTCHKA: Greta Garbo and Bela Lugosi.

NINOTCHKA: Felix Bressart, Greta Garbo, Sig Rumann and Alexander Granach.

Lavenham); Armand Kaliz (*Louis, the Headwaiter*); Tamara Shayne (*Anna*); William Irving (*Bartender*); Bess Flowers (*Gossip*); Jody Gilbert (*Streetcar Conductress*); Kay Stewart and Jenifer Gray (*Cigarette Girls*); Marek Windheim (*Manager*); Alexander Schonberg (*Bearded Man*); George Davis (*Porter*); Wolfgang Zilzer (*Taxi Driver*); Elizabeth Williams

(*Indignant Woman*); Paul Weigel (*Vladimir*); Harry Semels (*Neighbor-Spy*); Florence Shirley (*Marianne*); Elinor Vandivere, Sandra Morgan, Emily Cabanne, Symona Boniface and Monya Andre (*Gossips*); Lucille Pinson (*German Woman at Railroad Station*).

"Garbo laughs!" was the slogan that headlined the advertising copy for this Ernst Lubitsch comedy classic, followed by the admonition, "Don't pronounce it . . . See it!" Of course, Greta Garbo, the cool Swedish goddess of MGM, had laughed on the screen before—but never enough to qualify her as a comedy actress. Indeed, Louis B. Mayer was very much against his top tragedienne turning to outright comedy, though Garbo herself welcomed the opportunity to make a movie with an upbeat ending in which neither she nor her on-screen lover would die.

With a script by the clever team of Charles Brackett, Billy Wilder and Walter Reisch (working from a Melchior Lengyel story), *Ninotchka* exemplified producer-director Ernst Lubitsch as a skilled purveyor of sly comedy. In the film's first half, Garbo appears as a solemn, humorless Russian, dispatched to Paris by her commissar boss (Bela Lugosi) to untangle the red tape that appears to be delaying the business dealings of three Soviet comrades (Sig Rumann, Felix Bressart and Alexander Granach). They are in France to peddle imperial jewels to finance the purchase of farm equipment for the motherland. This comic trio has, in no time, fallen under the enticing spell of capitalism. Lena Yakushova (Garbo) arrives to find that the Grand Duchess Swana (Ina Claire), a White Russian exile, has claimed, as rightfully hers, the jewels confiscated in the Bolshevik takeover. She has had her lover Count Leon Dolga (Melvyn Douglas) obtain an injunction to prevent their sale.

Unaware of Lena's identity, Leon encounters her on a Paris street, and is immediately taken by the challenge of her severe manner, drab clothing and no-nonsense Communist line. His amorous advances meet with a chilly, analytical reception, which only whets his appetite for conquering her forbidding Russian austerity with his urbane charm. And gradually, "Ninotchka" (as he names her) begins to melt a bit. An amusing Parisian chapeau he insists on buying for her helps—and so does the restaurant scene in which he tries to break her stern demeanor by telling jokes: "A man comes into a restaurant. He sits down at the table and he says: 'Waiter, bring me a cup of coffee without cream.' Five minutes later, the waiter comes back and says: 'I'm sorry, sir, we have no cream. Can it be without *milk?*' "

But Ninotchka stares glumly back at him, while Leon becomes so agitated by her lack of humor that he tumbles over backwards in his chair, thereby setting her off into gales of deep-throated laughter—in which he soon joins her.

Ninotchka has its occasionally slow moments and sometimes bogs down a bit in sociological rhetoric. But it's basically a delightful Cinderella story that also managed to spoof the Soviets and Stalin's Russia—facts that made Louis B. Mayer uneasy in 1939.

In a year dominated by great motion pictures—and in which many of the Oscars were awarded to *Gone With the Wind*—four nominations went to *Ninotchka*, including Best Picture, Best Original Story and Best Screenplay—and, for Garbo, her fourth as Best Actress (in 1954, the actress would be awarded an Honorary Oscar, "for her unforgettable screen performances").

The comedy drew accolades for all concerned, from Garbo to her smooth co-star Douglas and the wonderful supporting cast, those delightful comic character actors Rumann, Bressart and Granach, as well as (in a very small part) the usually horror-associated Lugosi, the movie's sole villain. And, in one of her several "comeback" performances, there's the stylish sophistication of the incompar-

NINOTCHKA: Greta Garbo and Melvyn Douglas.

281

able Ina Claire, still very much in command of her comedic artistry at 46.

Greta Garbo would appear in only one more picture—1941's failed attempt to make her a mad-cap American comedienne in *Two-Faced Woman*—before calling it a career. And *Ninotchka* would surface again under other titles, in an attempt to repeat the Lubitsch magic. But neither *Comrade* X, nor *The Iron Petticoat*, nor *Ninotchka*'s officially credited musical remake, *Silk Stockings*, has ever recaptured the elusive essence of the 1939 original.

THE LIGHT THAT FAILED: Ida Lupino and Ronald Colman.

THE LIGHT THAT FAILED

1939

CREDITS

A Paramount Picture. A William A. Wellman Production. Producer/Director: William A. Wellman. Screenwriter: Robert Carson. Based on the novel by Rudyard Kipling. Cinematographer: Theodor Sparkhul. Editor: Thomas Scott. Art Directors: Hans Dreier and Robert Odell. Music: Victor Young. Second-Unit Director: Joseph Youngerman. Stunt Coordinator: Yakima Canutt. Running Time: 97 minutes.

CAST

Ronald Colman (*Richard Heldar*); Walter Huston (*Torpenhow*); Muriel Angelus (*Maisie*); Ida Lupino (*Bessie Broke*); Dudley Digges (*The Nilghai*); Ernest Cossart (*Beeton*); Ferike Boros (*Madame Binat*); Pedro De Cordoba (*M. Binat*); Colin Tapley (*Gardner*); Ronald Sinclair (*Dick as Boy*); Sarita Wooten (*Maisie as Girl*); Halliwell Hobbes (*Doctor*); Francis McDonald (*George*); George Regas (*Gassavetti*); Wilfred Roberts (*Barton*); George Chandler (*Correspondent*); Harry Cording, Clyde Cook, James Aubrey, Charles Bennett and David Phursby (*Soldiers*); Colin Kenny (*Doctor*); Charles Irwin (*Soldier Model*); Maj. Sam Harris (*Wells*); Connie Leon (*Flower Woman*); Cyril Ring (*War Correspondent*); Barbara Denny (*Waitress*); Pat O'Malley (*Bullock*); Clara M. Blore (*Mother*); Leslie Francis (*Man with Bandaged Eyes*); Barry Downing (*Little Boy*); Harold Entwistle (*Old Man with Dark Glasses*); Joe Collings (*Thackery*); Carl Voss (*Chopps, the Officer*); Hayden Stevenson (*War Correspondent*); Gerald Rogers (*Sick Man*).

It's ironic that *The Light That Failed* contains one of Ronald Colman's finest performances, because behind the scenes there was little but strife between the star and his temperamentally opposite director William Wellman. Wellman's "Wild Bill" reputation stemmed from a rugged, ungentlemanly, no-nonsense approach to filmmaking that often resulted in the printing of a "first take." Colman strived for perfection, but was always the English gentleman. Wellman had intended the picture, of which he was also the producer, for Ray Milland, an actor he had already worked with in great harmony on *Men With Wings* and *Beau Geste*. But he was forced to accept Colman. As Wellman later wrote,

THE LIGHT THAT FAILED: Ronald Colman and Muriel Angelus.

"He didn't like me; I didn't like him—the only two things we fully agreed upon."

The Light That Failed was a first novel for 26-year-old short-story writer Rudyard Kipling. Its English artist-protagonist Richard Heldar (Colman) loves Maisie (Muriel Angelus), his childhood sweetheart, but her own artistic ambitions drive her to study in Paris. Heldar goes to the Sudan, during the Gordon relief expedition, to serve as an illustrator for a British newspaper, and there finds a friend for life in the war correspondent Torpenhow (Walter Huston). Wounded by a saber, Heldar returns to London, where he shares quarters with Torpenhow, and becomes a successful painter. But their well ordered bachelor life is disrupted by Bessie Broke (Ida Lupino), a flashy tart who becomes Heldar's model and his friend's mistress. Learning that his war wound is about to blind him permanently, Heldar drives the selfish, restive Bessie to pose for long, exhausting sessions and, contemptuous of her low-class background and influence over Torpenhow, he breaks up their relationship. In spite, Bessie returns after Heldar goes blind, and angrily destroys his

masterpiece—a portrait of her—with smears of turpentine. Maisie comes back into Heldar's life, but he bitterly refuses what he takes for her pity, and sends her away. When he discovers what the now-contrite Bessie has done to his painting, he returns to the Sudan and dies in enemy gunfire.

Of *The Light That Failed*'s three film adaptations, Wellman's 1939 version was the first to retain Kipling's downbeat ending (the previous, silent editions had both seen fit to reunite Heldar with Maisie). The film won praise for this refusal to conform to a romanticized ending, although perhaps this very lack of concession to then-popular moviegoing tastes is partially accountable for its only moderate box-office success.

The on-screen credits list Ida Lupino fourth in billing, her name following those of Colman, Huston and even the rather obscure Muriel Angelus, an unimportant British actress herein making her U.S. film bow after appearing on Broadway in *The Boys From Syracuse*. Yet Lupino's performance, along with Huston's, is the one the critics singled out with adjectives like "splendid" and "superb." Good as

THE LIGHT THAT FAILED: Ida Lupino and Ronald Colman.

Colman is as the film's tragic hero, critic Graham Greene thought he was "sometimes acted right off the set" by Lupino and Huston.

Ida Lupino had taken an aggressive approach to landing the role of Bessie Broke. Stealing an advance copy of the script, she learned it by heart and stormed Wellman's office, insisting that he give her a chance at it. While Wellman read Colman's part, Lupino then proceeded to give such a vivid performance as Bessie that Wellman insisted she be engaged—even over the protestations of Colman, who wanted his friend Vivien Leigh instead. When Wellman threatened to walk out on the movie, Paramount production chief B. P. Schulberg ruled in his favor. But if Colman doubted the ability of his young English colleague, Lupino refused to allow the actor's on-the-set insecurities to intimidate her. Faced with the challenge of a peer, she more than made up in confidence, intensity and application what she might have lacked in experience as a serious dramatic actress.

Today, some five decades after its release, *The Light That Failed* continues to stand up as an excellent movie graced with fine acting, and moving in its uncompromised ending.

THE LIGHT THAT FAILED: Ronald Colman and Walter Huston.

THE HUNCHBACK OF NOTRE DAME

1939

CREDITS

An RKO Radio Picture. Producer: Pandro S. Berman. Director: William Dieterle. Screenwriters: Sonya Levien and Bruno Frank. Based on the novel *Notre-Dame de Paris* by Victor Hugo. Cinematographer: Joseph H. August. Editors: William Hamilton and Robert Wise. Music: Alfred Newman. Art Director: Van Nest Polglase. Special Effects: Vernon L. Walker. Dance Director: Ernst Matray. Running Time: 115 minutes.

CAST

Charles Laughton (*Quasimodo*); Sir Cedric Hardwicke (*Frollo*); Thomas Mitchell (*Clopin*); Maureen O'Hara (*Esmeralda*); Edmond O'Brien (*Gringoire*); Alan Marshal (*Phoebus*); Walter Hampden (*Archbishop*); Harry Davenport (*King Louis XI*); Katharine Alexander (*Fleur's Mother*); George Zucco (*Procurator*); Helene Whitney (*Fleur*); Minna Gombell (*Queen of Beggars*); Fritz Leiber (*Old Nobleman*); Etienne Girardot (*Doctor*); Arthur Hohl (*Olivier*); George Tobias (*Beggar*); Rod La Rocque (*Phillipo*); Spencer Charters (*Court Clerk*).

Victor Hugo's classic 1831 novel has, of course, been much filmed over the years. Beginning in 1906 with the French adaptation called *Esmeralda* (after the story's gypsy heroine)—and most recently in a pair of made-for-TV versions—this timeless beauty-and-the-beast melodrama has fired the imaginations of countless audiences. But of all the various motion picture *Hunchback*s, the two best have been Universal's 1923 silent with Lon Chaney, and the first sound version in 1939 that provided Charles Laughton with one of his greatest characterizations.

Pandro S. Berman's handsome (and obviously costly) RKO production unfolds on a scale that Universal could hardly have managed with its Chaney edition. From the astute casting to its minute details of sets and costumes, the adaptation by Sonya Levien and Bruno Frank lacks for nothing, save perhaps the employment of Technicolor (then a costly process and whose use was partially restricted due to the dearth of necessary equipment). But, even though a better-than-usual "colorized" print of

1939's *The Hunchback of Notre Dame* recently surfaced on cable television, it is nevertheless recommended that this great movie be seen in its original black and white.

In contrast to 1939's most honored motion picture, the $3.7-million *Gone With the Wind*, a then-astounding near-$2-million was spent on *Hunchback*. Producer Berman and his German-born director, William Dieterle, opted for authenticity in their depiction of some of the grimmer aspects of medieval Paris, from scenes of torture and public floggings to the exciting climactic sequence in which molten lead is poured down upon the unruly crowd from the parapets of the Cathedral itself. And, always dominating the proceedings, is that most grotesque of creatures, the deformed bellringer Quasimodo, portrayed so amazingly by Charles Laughton (almost unrecognizable behind heavy costuming and make-up—a mountain of prosthetic ugliness that completely obliterated one of his eyes, while reproducing it further down his face). All told, it was a deformity both physical and artistic that Laughton was forced to wear, and it remains a considerable tribute to his talent as an actor that he was able not only to move about with alacrity, but also to convey the requisite pathos of Quasimodo's tortured soul. RKO reflected its uneasy feelings about Laughton's appearance by putting an embargo on any still photographs that

THE HUNCHBACK OF NOTRE DAME: Sir Cedric Hardwicke and Charles Laughton.

THE HUNCHBACK OF NOTRE DAME: Minna Gombell, Maureen O'Hara, Thomas Mitchell and Edmond O'Brien.

THE HUNCHBACK OF NOTRE DAME: Maureen O'Hara and Sir Cedric Hardwicke.

would reveal details of the actor's face—which will explain why the pictures accompanying this text are shot from shadowy and oblique angles.

Of much pleasanter appearance is, of course, the glowing young Maureen O'Hara, who portrays Esmeralda, the "beauty" of this nightmarish fairy tale. The Irish-born O'Hara was, at that time, a Laughton discovery who had already played opposite him in Alfred Hitchcock's British-made *Jamaica Inn*, and would go on to enjoy a major Hollywood career, albeit one in which she was never more enchanting than in *The Hunchback of Notre Dame*. Nor was any villain more hissable than Sir Cedric Hardwicke's evil and lecherous Frollo, Quasimodo's brooding nemesis.

In this age of extensive location work, one can especially admire the collaborative efforts of the Hollywood studio craftsmen in the Thirties and Forties, when nearly everything was accomplished within studio walls, where weather conditions would not delay production on an expensive picture and where lighting could be carefully controlled. To this extent, watching *The Hunchback of Notre Dame* again, one can only stand in awe of this outstanding example of the RKO artisans. It is difficult to understand how a production of this excellence could lack for prizes. But, even in a year as movie-rich as 1939, the picture only garnered a single Academy Award nomination—for Alfred Newman's background music (the Best Score Oscar went to *Stagecoach*). Lest RKO be disappointed, an enthusiastic public made it one of the top-earning movies of the 1939–40 season.

THE HUNCHBACK OF NOTRE DAME: Charles Laughton.

FREE!

Citadel Film Series Catalog

From James Stewart to Moe Howard and The Three Stooges, Woody Allen to John Wayne, The Citadel Film Series is America's largest film book library.

Now with more than 125 titles in print, books in the series make perfect gifts—for a loved one, a friend, or yourself!

We'd like to send you, free of charge, our latest full-color catalog describing the Citadel Film Series in depth. To receive the catalog, please send your name and address to:

Citadel Film Series/Carol Publishing Group
Distribution Center B
120 Enterprise Avenue
Secaucus, New Jersey 07094

The titles you'll find in the catalog include:
The Films Of...

Alan Ladd
Alfred Hitchcock
All Talking! All Singing!
    All Dancing!
Anthony Quinn
The Bad Guys
Barbara Stanwyck
Barbra Streisand:
    The First Decade
Barbra Streisand:
    The Second Decade
Bela Lugosi
Bette Davis
Bing Crosby
Black Hollywood
Boris Karloff
Bowery Boys
Brigitte Bardot
Burt Reynolds
Carole Lombard
Cary Grant
Cecil B. DeMille
Character People
Charles Bronson
Charlie Chaplin
Charlton Heston
Chevalier
Clark Gable
Classics of the Gangster
    Film
Classics of the Horror Film
Classics of the Silent Screen
Cliffhanger
Clint Eastwood
Curly: Biography of a
    Superstooge
Detective in Film
Dick Tracy
Dustin Hoffman
Early Classics of the
    Foreign Film

Elizabeth Taylor
Elvis Presley
Errol Flynn
Federico Fellini
The Fifties
The Forties
Forgotten Films
    to Remember
Frank Sinatra
Fredric March
Gary Cooper
Gene Kelly
Gina Lollobrigida
Ginger Rogers
Gloria Swanson
Great Adventure Films
Great British Films
Great French Films
Great German Films
Great Romantic Films
Great Science Fiction Films
Great Spy Films
Gregory Peck
Greta Garbo
Harry Warren and the
    Hollywood Musical
Hedy Lamarr
Hello! My Real Name Is
Henry Fonda
Hollywood Cheesecake:
    60 Years of Leg Art
Hollywood's Hollywood
Howard Hughes in Hollywood
Humphrey Bogart
Ingrid Bergman
Jack Lemmon
Jack Nicholson
James Cagney
James Stewart
Jane Fonda
Jayne Mansfield

Jeanette MacDonald and
    Nelson Eddy
Jewish Image in American
    Films
Joan Crawford
John Garfield
John Huston
John Wayne
John Wayne Reference
    Book
John Wayne Scrapbook
Judy Garland
Katharine Hepburn
Kirk Douglas
Lana Turner
Laurel and Hardy
Lauren Bacall
Laurence Olivier
Lost Films of the
    Fifties
Love in the Film
Mae West
Marilyn Monroe
Marlon Brando
Moe Howard and The
    Three Stooges
Montgomery Clift
More Character People
More Classics of the
    Horror Film
More Films of the '30s
Myrna Loy
Non-Western Films of
    John Ford
Norma Shearer
Olivia de Havilland
Paul Newman
Paul Robeson
Peter Lorre
Pictorial History of Science
    Fiction Films

Pictorial History of Sex
    in Films
Pictorial History of War
    Films
Pictorial History of the
    Western Film
Rebels: The Rebel Hero
    in Films
Rita Hayworth
Robert Redford
Robert Taylor
Ronald Reagan
The Seventies
Sex in the Movies
Sci-Fi 2
Sherlock Holmes
Shirley MacLaine
Shirley Temple
The Sixties
Sophia Loren
Spencer Tracy
Steve McQueen
Susan Hayward
Tarzan of the Movies
They Had Faces Then
The Thirties
Those Glorious Glamour Years
Three Stooges Book of Scripts
Three Stooges Book of Scripts,
    Vol. 2
The Twenties
20th Century Fox
Warren Beatty
W. C. Fields
Western Films of John Ford
West That Never Was
William Holden
William Powell
Woody Allen
World War II